Recurring Dream Symbols

Recurring Dream Symbols

Maps to Healing Your Past

Kathleen Sullivan

Paulist Press
New York/Mahwah, N.J.

Cover design by Trudi Gershenov
Book design by Lynn Else

Library of Congress Cataloging-in-Publication Data

Sullivan, Kathleen, 1941–
    Recurring dream symbols : maps to healing your past / Kathleen Sullivan.
        p.   cm.
    Includes bibliographical references (p.   ).
    ISBN 0-8091-4184-1
    1. Dream interpretation. 2. Self-realization. I. Title.
BF1091.S813 2004
154.6'32—dc22

                                                            2003022852

Published by Paulist Press
997 Macarthur Boulevard
Mahwah, New Jersey 07430

www.paulistpress.com

Printed and bound in the
United States of America

CONTENTS

For the Faithful Fourteen:
Your willingness and devotion lead the way.

FOREWORD

Recurring Dreams
Connect Us All to Deeper Mysteries

Kathleen Sullivan has been exploring the dream world and helping others to understand the deeper meanings of their dreams for many years. She does this regularly on her radio program, through one-to-one and group dream work sessions, and through her wonderfully clear and flowing writing. Her abiding interest in recurring dreams and dream motifs was given shape in her earlier book, *Recurring Dreams: A Journey to Wholeness*, which was, and still is in my view, the best book on the subject to date. Now, with this new book that you hold in your hand, she extends her research and sensitive exploration of the world of repeating/recurring dream experiences into even broader realms.

This book documents and explores the ways in which the recurring dream comes to serve a greater evolutionary imperative. All dreams help to move the individual dreamer toward a greater understanding of confusing emotions, greater expressive strength and clarity, and a greater integration and conscious focus of scattered personal energies. The recurrent dream is particularly helpful in healing deep personal psycho-spiritual injuries and resolving individual emotional dramas. Kathleen demonstrates the tremendous tenacity with which the dreams, particularly recurring dreams, continue to serve our individual and collective health and wholeness, helping us to evolve more and more into who and what we are capable of becoming.

Anything worthy of the noble names *dream* and *symbol*, is, by definition, a carrier of multiple meanings and multiple layers of significance. Some of those layers will necessarily be intimately personal and some move beyond the personal into the collective patterns of universal human striving and experience. What Kathleen so elegantly writes in the pages that follow is a manifestation of the deep, shared evolutionary imperative that wells up spontaneously out of the unconscious depths of our being. This deep developmental urge and the energy that fuels it is shared by all humans and all dreams. The recurrent dream is a particularly important manifestation of this collective drive to grow and evolve, not only as individuals, but also as a species. In the wealth of specific examples and anecdotes that Kathleen provides, the reader will undoubtedly find stories that echo and resonate with his or her own interior experience, and the deeper longing to evolve into more conscious and expressive beings which we all share.

As a long-time dream worker myself, I always begin with the assumption that whatever dream the dreamer has is, in some important sense, the best possible dream that person could have had at that moment. There is always a kind of "best fit" quality to dreams; they give symbolic shape to the deeper truths of the dreamer's life in a way that is uniquely reflective of the dreamer's true circumstances, above, below, and beyond his or her conscious convictions about life.

The dream can do anything it wants. It doesn't have to come in under budget. It doesn't have to follow the laws of physics. It doesn't have to respect the opinions of society, or even conform to the dreamer's own waking conscious beliefs and opinions. All the dream has to do is tell the truth about the deeper reality of the dreamer's life in a symbolically compelling way.

The recurrent dream experience also points out that some important element of the dreamer's life is exactly the same as it was the last time the dream occurred. The longer the period of time over which the dream experiences repeat themselves, the fewer things remain on the list of things that are exactly the same as all the other times this dream recurred. I have had the opportunity to work recurrent dreams on people in their late eighties, dreams that have recurred since the dreamer's early childhood. In those instances, I have been particularly impressed with the implication that there is in fact only one thing remaining on that list of unchanging things in the dreamer's life, and that is the dreamer's deepest authentic self, your true self, or as the Zen Buddhists are fond of saying, "your face before you were born." As Kathleen demonstrates, the recurrent dream is particularly reflective of the dreamer's deepest genuine character.

Read on—your waking and dreaming worlds will be enriched and extended by Kathleen's gentle and compelling insights.

Reverend Dr. Jeremy Taylor
San Rafael, 2003

PREFACE

I charged along the Pacific Grove walking path on a bright December morning, alerting all I passed that whales could be seen off the coast. For the first time this season, I had spotted six spouts as I approached the Pacific Ocean from my home.

Catching sight of the California gray and killer whales as they brush the coast on their migration south is one of the many benefits of living on California's Monterey Peninsula. Because the tip of Pacific Grove extends into the Pacific Ocean, these awe-inspiring creatures are easily seen from the shore during the early winter months. It is thrilling to see the whales blow, often in clusters of five or more, creating small rainbows above the mist as it reflects the low winter sun. Every now and then, a fluke breaks the surface as the whales cavort and plunge into the depths of the Monterey Canyon, a deep underwater abyss that adjoins the coast.

"The whales are running!" I sang to passersby. It struck me that this is what I do professionally: I alert others to the grandeur that breaks into consciousness from the depths of the psyche, if one is vigilant enough to watch. This geographic area is definitely an appropriate environment for a dream fanatic such as I.

As I hailed others on the path, shouting the news that the whales have begun their annual display, people of all ages light up, energized by the hope of catching a glimpse of the magnificent, gigantic life that passes so close to us. A similar type of energy travels around the circle of a dream group when a dreamer recognizes another kind of majesty from the unconscious, brought by his or her dream.

Increase that charge tenfold and you will begin to fathom the excitement experienced by the participants in this book. Each one of the dreamers reached a point in their studies when they began to realize their own recurring symbol's significance and the intent expressed in their dream series. I hope that you will be as profoundly impacted by their dream stories as were they. Writing this book is my way of sharing with you my morning walk, of pointing out the whales that surface from depths within each of us when we are willing to pay attention to recurring dream symbols.

This book follows my first, which tracked one recurring symbol, a dream character who has inhabited my dreams for four decades. Writing about this persistent figure, Victor Biento, in *Recurring Dreams: A Journey to Wholeness* so benefited me that I was certain that studying repeating symbols would serve other dreamers. My expectations were surpassed. With wonder and delight, I have watched the growth and transformation of fourteen dreamers, all willing to engage fully with a repeating dream symbol.

By *engage*, I mean that each dreamer worked first with each series dream separately, using an interpretive process in which the dream was, when possible, viewed against the background of the dreamer's life at the time of the dream. Next, a critical weaving process identified connections between the series dreams. This usually showed what aspects or images were changing or remaining the same, both within the dreams and within the waking life of the dreamer. At this point, most of the dreamers experienced a sense of awe, which led to even deeper engagement with and excitement about the series dreams: The dreamers real-ized that chronic awake-life patterns were being illustrated and that new patterns were being created from or by the dreams. In most cases, these realizations led to a willing commitment to the transformation of waking-reality beliefs, attitudes, and behaviors being called for by the dreams.

And finally, about midway through most studies, the dreamer had a profound shift of perception. Suddenly his or her focus moved from individual dreams to an eagle's-eye view, see-ing the dreams as one whole piece, rather than separate and unrelated sections. At this point, most of the dreamers could see that the intent stated in the first dream of the series ran through the others, like an unbroken strand of seaweed meandering over all the rocks on the shore. Most students of the dream would call this the *workings of the Self*. To me, this force feels like a *dream over-soul*, guiding the movement of the dreams with a sense of history, purpose, and expectation. More than one dreamer tear-fully expressed this understanding. Most participants felt great peace and safety when they recognized the healing intent of their series dreams. My personal experience is great relief that some part of me—the dream maker—can see the big picture of my life, needs, and potential, even though my awake self is some-times oblivious.

Individual dreams are sometimes like snapshots, reflecting feelings and situations in the awake world. But this limited view of the dream is expanded by examining a lengthy series. Perceiving our series dreams as reflections of daily life cannot lead to the profound sense of overall guidance experienced by the dreamers in this book. Tom (the dreamer featured in chapter 11) wrote about this feeling beautifully: "By weaving each dream together, uninterrupted in series form, I can more deeply feel the presence of an inner force determined to get me free to feel all the joy that life affords. I am nearly overwhelmed with the love that I feel from and for this unknown masculine dream character (the recurring symbol) and for the dream process itself. Even at my age (seventy-three), it is clear that this dreaming force holds me tenderly, ever moving me home."

Fourteen dreamers participated in the series studies presented in this book. They had recorded dreams containing recurring symbols for periods varying from nine months to more than thirty-five years. Five of the case studies covered twenty-five years of recorded dreams. All the dreamers became aware of the repeating symbols as the dreams were occurring. Several had worked with the series dreams by themselves, with a professional, or in a dream group. Only two people had simply recorded the dreams without attempting to understand the material. Despite these differences, all of the participants had a similar experience of growth and transformation because of working the individual dreams as a series.

In undertaking these studies, my hypothesis was that it is working with the dreams as a series that so profoundly promotes healing and furthers development. Thus, by implication, simply having the dreams, recording them, and even working with each one individually, does not provide a similarly deep level of growth.

And so, this book has four distinct purposes:

1. To share the transformational stories of dreamers who have engaged with their recurring symbols;
2. To motivate readers to search for and work with their own recurring symbols;
3. To help readers develop procedures for working with recurring symbols; and

4. To encourage dreamers to commit their waking consciousness to what is called for by their recurring symbols.

Studying the recurring dreams of the participants in this study convinces me that we all contain an inner healing force that shows itself, ardently, in serial dreams. This force has an intention that is always leading conscious dreamers toward wholeness. And it is determined to be recognized and to be received. To guarantee its reception, it will send us messages, over and over again, for decades, until it is not only noticed, but also valued. How encouraging to realize that, despite our lack of awareness, despite our resistance, this force for healing never abandons us. It migrates up and down our coasts of consciousness until we see it spouting.

ACKNOWLEDGMENTS

I am grateful to Kelly Bulkeley, whose support provided the focus and courage to begin; to Jeremy Taylor for reassurance and clarification; to Laura Ramsay for her listening, wisdom, and joyful enthusiasm for the work; to Lenore Dunn for cheerful, timely, and quality editing; to Hannah Dalbey, Lee Marchitelli, and Barbara Nelson, who were always willing to listen and advise; to KAZU radio for supplying the airwaves to gather and learn from the dreams of callers; and to Mary Thiele Fobian, whose unstinting presence and editorial skills made this book a reality.

INTRODUCTION

A voice calls gently in the night, hoping to waken the sleeping one to notice, to wonder, and to learn. A feeling or slight awareness may penetrate, but not enough to rouse into wakefulness. The voice sounds again, sending the message repeatedly, for years and even decades, eventually creating a feeling of urgency in even the most unconscious. If unheeded still, the determined voice becomes a shrill scream, forcing an awakening. Too often, the unconscious one dismisses the experience, relieved that it was only a dream. With that rejection, the dream returns to the underworld, awaiting another chance to surface, to break through. When at last, by luck or by design, the sleeper hears and responds, the futile cycle is broken, making way for new possibilities, for healing wounds from the past, and for the development of wholeness.

In one form or another, this was the experience of the fourteen dream-study participants in this book. Finally roused by the call from the depths, each was then moved to record what had broken into consciousness. On an envelope, a stenographer's notebook, a recipe card, a journal, even a paper bag, the awakened ones struggled to capture the images that had surfaced. Something in each of the dreamers sensed the importance of what had happened, and knew it could not be discarded as "only a dream."

If a recurring symbol has caught your attention, this book may provide the necessary motivation for you to work with your series. Whether your recurring dream has blasted you awake or just left a feeling of intrigue, foreboding, confusion, or irritation, it is as valuable as flashing warning lights ripping the darkness on a night highway. If you stop and pay attention to these flashing dreams, they may be just as lifesaving as applying the brakes at the first sign of danger.

Perhaps your recurring dreams bring a feeling of hope, inspiration, simple fun, or extreme joy. These are equally important to your health and growth. The messages in such dreams may provide valuable maps that show the way to a destination (destiny) you might otherwise overlook. The rewards of following a recurring dream map are definitely worth the journey, though the trip is rarely easy or simple. The purpose of this book is to provide you with what is needed for the excursion. As you read the transformational stories of fourteen dream travelers who accepted the challenge of finding and following their recurring symbols, you will discover the maps created by their dream series. Some of the stories are more dramatic than others, but all show the profound reasons that a dream symbol recurs, for years and even decades.

Part 1 of this book provides the foundation by presenting, in chapter 1, examples of the many types of dreams generally referred to as recurring dreams. Chapter 2 describes a common type of recurring dream motif, that of searching for something; this chapter contains my personal searching series and examines this question: Is there an intention, an intrinsic purpose, to recurring symbols and the dream series they create? Chapter 3 presents the important theory of life scripts and their relationship to serial dreams, while chapter 4 examines the mythic level of recurring symbols.

Part 2 presents fourteen case studies. These will allow you to look inside the heads and hearts of the dream-study pilgrims as they discover the destination of their recurring dreams. Each chapter is introduced by a synopsis of data about the study, including internal messages revealed by the series that the dreamer needed to overcome. These script messages appear within quotation marks because these beliefs are experienced as dominating inner voices.

The methodologies used were as valuable as they were varied and complex. At the beginning, each participant received a preliminary packet describing the process we two were beginning, as a team. The goal was to see what value studying a recurring symbol would have on the dreamer; therefore, each study participant was the primary researcher, following suggestions for structure and process, but developing his or her own approach to the dream material.

I met with each participant, in person or via e-mail, throughout the entire study. (The longest study spanned four years and focused on fifty-nine dreams. The shortest study was completed with only five sessions and examined nine dreams.) The majority of dreamers worked their dreams with me, as we would have in a private counseling session. Some dreamers also attended ongoing dream groups and presented their serial dreams in that format, as well. As each dreamer developed an understanding of his or her material, I began the writing process, sculpting the dreamer's experiences into a form that would fit the structure of a book. After every writing session, the written material was reviewed and edited by the dreamer, clarifying his or her own knowing and my understanding. Many realizations, personal memories, and reflections experienced by the study participants are not included in the chapters because of the need for brevity; nonetheless, all had a profound effect on the dreamers.

I wanted to see how a variety of individuals would approach the study of a recurring symbol. The amount and type of responsibility taken by each dreamer varied dramatically. Two women, both experienced dreamers, possessed natural organizational aptitudes that helped them to unwind their series dreams with few complications. Neither of them needed much assistance from me to work with and interpret their dreams. They were the exceptions, as the remaining twelve dreamers needed a great deal of guidance to find a structure that would satisfy their own particular learning/working styles. (These various processes are described in chapter 19.)

Though I recognized and respected the intuition and intellectual process of each dreamer, I naturally brought my own particular dream skills and interpretive biases to these sessions. Eventually I began to notice that one particular theory provided a valuable system for understanding important dreams from ten of the fourteen studies. This theory, espoused by psychiatrist Carl Jung, suggests that all people are energized by a dynamic of ever-vacillating archetypes referred to, in the West, as the masculine (*animus*) and feminine (*anima*) principles. (Some Eastern cultures express a similar belief as *yin/yang*.) If you have difficulty understanding your dreams featuring unidentified characters of either gender, the masculine and feminine principles are discussed frequently in the chapters in part 2. The Significant Other study (chapter 8) offers Carla's struggle with her personal inner masculine in the guise of a former lover. The Big Cats Moving In, Unknown Blonde Woman, and Internal Strangers series address Francesca's, Lynda's, and Jessica's needs, respectively, to alter a negative masculine and activate a more healthy drive. Dennis's need to recognize and accept his feelings and spiritual life (feminine) were addressed by his "homosexual" dreams (chapter 16). William (chapter 13) and Janice (chapter 9) had dream series describing the disequilibrium of the masculine and feminine dynamic. At the archetypal level, several dreams in chapter 7, Bodies and Bones, unearth the roots of Griffin Rose's masculine/feminine dynamic. Tom (chapter 11) discovered a healthier, more feminine approach to life through the character of the young man in his study. Both Jessica (chapter 10) and Barbara (chapter 18) discovered the need to consciously welcome, develop, and support their inner masculine energy.

In part 3, chapter 19 offers a detailed map for studying a recurring symbol series; the ideas in this chapter are a compilation of techniques used in all the studies in this book. Chapter 20 presents recurring symbol dreams that the dreamers recalled but did not journal, and explores methods for working with this kind of material. The chapter illustrates the value of contemplating recurring symbol dreams even if they are not recorded and therefore cannot be thoroughly researched. Ways to work with this type of material are explored. Chapter 21 presents fourteen recurring dream themes, so common they are considered universal dreams. These dreams themes—Teeth Falling Out, Naked in Public, Car Out of Control, and Tidal Waves—are the best known recurring dreams.

Even if you have no recall of a recurring symbol, others' dreams and experiences will be valuable to your healing, growth, and evolution. If you are nagged, tickled, or irritated by a vague recollection of a recurring symbol, this book should motivate you to dance with it. And if you have already recorded a recurring symbol series, the journeys of the fourteen intrepid dream pioneers will lay a trail for you follow. Bon voyage!

PART ONE
Foundation

CHAPTER ONE

Recurring Dream Themes

While asleep, Joseph becomes aware that he has entered that frightening place again. He struggles to break free of the agony he knows is coming, but the Nazi storm troopers are fast on his heels. He must run with all his might to escape annihilation. He flees through dark cobblestone streets, hoping that this time someone will come to help him before it is too late. As usual, he wakes up groaning and shaking.

Jeney reports to her dream group that she has had another in the series of her "father" dreams. "This time he is very different from the man I knew. He is gentle and concerned about me," she says.

Harold wakens his wife, Sally. "You were whimpering, honey. Was it the baby dream again?" he asks quietly. Sally responds by crying as Harold holds her. He, too, feels tears fall from his eyes.

"I had that weird dream about wandering into my college biology class to take the final exam," Max reports to his girlfriend over coffee. "Just like the last dream, I had forgotten to attend the class all semester and know I haven't a prayer of passing the test. Damn! I hate that dream. I always feel so dragged out after it."

Talking on the phone to her mother, Lucinda tells of another boat dream:

Two men fight, the boat turns over and we all spill
into the ocean. I'm sure we will drown but the Coast
Guard picks us up. Some men in uniforms come to
send us back and I wake up crying.

Lucinda's voice is still filled with the dream fear she has felt
for over twenty-five years. "We've got to do something about
these nightmares, Doctor Abbot. I'm afraid to sleep. I can't bear
to have that arm grasping for me anymore. Can't you prescribe
some medication to stop the dreams?"

Joan writes in her journal: "Another dream about Joe. I
can't understand why that character appears in my dreams over
and over. What does this guy want from me?"

Jerry excitedly reports another of his "house" dreams to his
new dream group. "In the dream I enter my studio apartment to
find a door leading to an unknown stairway. It leads to the second and third floor. I'm expectant as I begin to explore the rooms
I didn't know were there."

It is likely that people in your community experienced
some of these dream scenarios within the past twenty-four hours.
These and dozens of other common recurring dream motifs
intrigue or upset dreamers all over the world. Some dreamers
feel victimized by an inner process they do not understand and
seem unable to change. Others learn about their physical, psychological, or spiritual progress by carefully observing repeating
symbols to discern what has changed since the image last
appeared. And still others methodically study repeating dreams,
believing that they expose the next step in actualizing their life's
purpose.

Many aspects of a dream experience can repeat. Again and
again we may find ourselves in the same dream environment. A

certain emotion accompanies a specific place. An animal (common or extraordinary), a person (known or unfamiliar), or a type of behavior (chasing trains or searching for someone) may revisit us until we pay attention and begin to work with whatever is persistently prodding us. As we gather all the dreams with the same symbol or motif, we may well wonder why psyche has organized a special syllabus of inner material for us to study. We find that we have a curriculum called a dream series.

The word *series* connotes both a sense of continuity and a significant cluster of common elements, together characterizing one subset within a larger totality. When we classify a particular grouping as a series, we "bracket" time and events, distinguishing the series from the mundane. The World Series is both a chronology and a grouping of games that are special and unusual. A TV miniseries consists of individual programs strung out over several nights to tell a single story. A series of accidents at a certain juncture on a highway indicates that many drivers have difficulty at the same place. A serial killer is one who repeatedly murders with the same *modus operandi*. Historians identify a series of events that inevitably lead to war. In each of these uses, the word has both a linear quality and a sense of quantity— of things accumulated until a certain level of awareness is reached. That mass can be called a series.

We often are unaware of a problem until repeated events gather enough significance to require our attention. The Public Works Department will do nothing about poor visibility on a road until a string of mishaps occurs. Parents overlook their child's sullen, surly behavior until a crisis gets their attention. A man may have to be fired from many jobs before he can identify himself as the problem. Finally, after her fifth asthma attack, a woman realizes that she becomes ill only after arguing with her husband.

So it is with dreamwork. A dream series is a grouping of material that, for a variety of reasons, the dreamer considers related and significant. All the dreams from one night can create a series because they usually present the same awake-life issue or developmental task from differing perspectives. In addition, it is common for an element of one dream to link into other dreams, suggesting a *continuity*, an unfolding, a moving through the fog until forms can be distinguished. Because of this, most serious dreamers have difficulty working one dream without referring to the dream that preceded or followed it. When the dreamer senses a unifying thread, some element shared by several dreams, a series has been identified.

Historians reviewing world events, road crews identifying blind spots, parents comparing feelings about children, and detectives uncovering crime patterns are working with a process similar to that used by a dreamer researching, for example, a series of five dreams about cats. All parties ask the same questions: What's repeating? What patterns are formed? What significance can we assign to the data? What does this repetition suggest about the future?

Each of the repeating dream "snippets" presented at the beginning of this chapter speaks in the personal symbolic language of the dreamer. Every recurrence is another knock on the door of consciousness. What wants to enter the dreamer, in all cases, is a form of healing. Some of the forms, often experienced as nightmares, come to warn us of danger. Repeating dreams that fit this category can occur when the awake world is too much for us. At such times, we may dream of a previously traumatic period during which we felt helpless. For example, since Joseph's precarious childhood in pre-WWII Germany, he has dreamed of being pursued by Nazis whenever he feels emotionally or professionally threatened in his waking life. Alerted that danger exists, Joseph can take action to alleviate it. Thus, this kind of dream, using traumatic events from the past to warn of present vulnerability, is a particularly helpful form of dream warning.

As we focus on the development of an inadequate, dormant, or absent part of ourselves, a repeating dream symbol may highlight our progress. Jeney had been working many years to feel professionally adequate and successful. For this she needed a supportive and instructive inner father energy or force to guide her. Over the course of her father series, Jeney's dream father's critical and sarcastic voice underwent a dramatic alteration and an equivalent change manifested in her career advancement, as well.

Sometimes a dream series leads to recall of memories or a specific period of time that has been hidden away until the dreamer is strong enough to consciously remember. For Harold and Sally, dreams are an important part of the grief process, allowing (or inviting) the dreamer to experience emotions the awake self has been unable to process or comprehend completely. After the sudden death of their sixteen-month-old daughter, Sally's dreams provided both her and her husband with the stimulation needed to grieve and process this horrific loss.

Repeating symbols often direct our attention to a forgotten or discarded talent or developmental state that we have bypassed. This was the case with Joan and her repeating dream character Allen, a friend from college. A brilliant mathematician, Allen represented the innate intellectual talent and teaching career that Joan had abandoned when she married. The dream series featuring Allen began after Joan's last child had left the nest. Working with the series caused Joan to remember and relive the excitement of discovery and thrill of teaching. Eventually, the Allen dreams lured Joan back to graduate school to complete her doctoral work in mathematics.

Recurring dream motifs may help to process a trauma from the past and show the dreamer's healing, or lack thereof. This type of dream is often referred to as a posttraumatic stress disorder (PTSD) dream because the actual scene of trauma is relived. However, healing is evident even in PTSD dreams, when the dream action changes significantly from the original waking life experience, or when the dreamer feels empowered instead of victimized. In Lucinda's dream, the scene was exactly the same as it had always been since her family's attempted escape from Cuba in 1977. Fifteen years after her sponsorship by a Cuban-American family, the despairing dreams took Lucinda to a PTSD group. With support from other victims of similar circumstances, her dreams began to change, often showing the arrival of unexpected help. In one dream, suggesting the progress she was making in taking more control of her life, Lucinda predicted that one of the men would begin a fight that would capsize the boat. "This is a dream and I can change it," she said to herself. Lucinda pushed the troublemaker into the ocean, where he was promptly eaten by a shark! The others in the boat unpacked some food and began to eat. This was a turning-point dream for Lucinda and the beginning of the end of her terrifying boat series dreams.

Most of the recurring dreams presented in this chapter are more dramatic in content and feeling tone than the usual serial dreams. Much more common are dreams that show the dreamer's steady growth and development. Jerry's house series fits this developmental type of recurring symbol dream. Before

Jerry joined a dream group, and years after he bought a rambling, California-style home in a farming community in the San Joaquin Valley, he dreamed that he again lived in the tiny studio apartment of his college years. He always felt "cramped and cranky" in these dreams, which he recorded but did not understand. Within two weeks of joining his first dream group, his series took an unexpected turn by showing additional levels and rooms attached to his little studio apartment. The cranky feeling was replaced with excitement that was obvious when Jerry presented his dream. It heralded a great deal of inner growth and many outer life changes. This man in his middle years was ready to trade in a limited image of himself that no longer fit. Jerry was developing a larger sense of himself (the expanding apartment) that would accommodate the changes he yearned to experience.

These and other types of recurring dreams are powerfully precise tools for perceiving the health of a dreamer and providing the direction needed on the journey to psycho-spiritual wholeness.

CHAPTER TWO

Searching Themes in Recurring Dreams

Years ago I bought a beautiful, handcrafted belt for a friend. Since it was several months before her birthday, I carefully stowed the belt in a safe place. I have not found it since. A logical explanation alludes me, so I revert to the superstitions of my Irish heritage. Obviously, mischievous Leprechauns hid the belt and I will find it only when I move from this house.

Searching for what has been lost is a common dream motif. I have heard dreams from the bereaved in search of their lost loved one; aging people hunting for lost youth and productivity; victims of crime pursuing the objects or innocence stolen from them; and individuals, deeply wounded by a former relationship, desperately searching for the emotions and love they no longer enjoy. Dreamers often feel frantic during the dream search, but are unable to name what they are pursuing until they consciously work with the dream.

All of these examples reflect losses in the outer world, but there is another kind of searching theme that expresses an inner yearning—the symbolic search for a lost part of the self. An example of this type of dream came from a successful artist who gave up her career to raise three stepchildren. Two years into her new life she was plagued by dreams about a shabbily dressed, barefoot woman who was often crying. Connecting to the significance of the barefoot woman clarified the series. Prior to her marriage, the dreamer's most creative and joyful years had been spent barefoot and dressed in crummy clothes, painting large canvases or sidewalk murals. Although she had chosen to exchange her art career for the role of wife and mother, the artist within her demanded attention.

Another interesting searching series came from a successful businessman who prided himself on his ability to manipulate people. He considered his ability to control the emotions of others as his greatest business asset. However, he could not control recurring dreams about an idealistic young man who wandered from town to town, searching for something very important. Over and over again, the dream character stopped strangers to ask if they knew where it was. After examining four similar dreams, the *it* turned out to be values and beliefs the man had exchanged for a philosophy of "success at any cost." This man's midlife crisis was greatly alleviated by reconnecting to the young man he had once been and to the values he had once held.

A profound searching series first caught my attention in 1961, two years after my high school graduation. For the next twenty-four years, I repeatedly dreamed of attending high school reunions, hoping to connect with someone who seemed to be very important to me. In each dream, I asked others if he was here, had anyone seen him yet, did anyone know where he was, without knowing for whom I was searching. During the first years of the series, I felt mildly interested in finding this person. With each passing year, the need to see him intensified. The search always proved futile, leaving me increasingly frustrated and depressed, both in the dream and during the following day.

We see the need for reunion in many searching dream themes. The examples of the stepmother and the businessman show a reuniting with forgotten or abandoned ways of being, feeling, and thinking. Reunion with those separated parts brought each dreamer a greater sense of personal wholeness. By embracing the messages from the dreams and reuniting with lost parts of themselves, the dreamers expanded and balanced their lives.

After twenty-four years of dream searching, that theme came to an end when I finally "saw" the person I had so desperately sought. In the dream, I was thrilled. Awake, however, I was deeply perplexed. I barely remembered the boy/man I had finally found. I was able to connect him with a name and even find his picture in high school annuals, but beyond that he meant very little to me. I could not imagine why I had spent so many dream nights looking for him, for more than two decades. It would take many years for me to understand my personal need for reunion with this character, finally identified as Victor Biento (pseudonym).

Seven years after meeting Vic in the dream, the series produced a sufficient mass of awareness to get my full involvement. I finally realized that this recurring symbol had been important to my dream world for thirty years, and committed to doing whatever it might take to understand this determined element of my psyche. For a year and a half, I devoted one week every month to organize, study, and write about all of the dreams containing this dream character. Several friends and dreamwork associates became involved in the project. We were all determined to know what this character represented within me and what he wanted from or for me.

As I studied more than one hundred dreams spanning more than thirty years, a variety of intriguing patterns emerged that brought the significance of Victor Biento into focus. Unlike the previous dream searches discussed in this chapter, my series was not about searching for something I had lost, but about desperately trying to find and activate an entirely new way of being in the world and within myself. I began to see that each Victor dream connected me to a vital, yet unlived, aspect of my self. In addition, it seemed that all of these dreams highlighted aspects of my life and my inner process that needed to be changed. It was as if Victor were a profound psychic tailor, pinching in here, letting out there, adding decoration and style to an old garment, and creating several costumes that had never been worn before. Each new costume created another role for me to play, providing options that expanded my life script immensely.

One of the greatest benefits of the Victor series was its ultimate healing effect on a plethora of chronic physical symptoms that had forced me to withdraw from life. For seventeen years I had struggled with body/mind *dis-ease*. Many of my dreams reflected the various facets of these debilitating problems, but none were more instructive than the Victor dreams.

A repeating symbol focuses our attention. For the eighteen months during which I actively researched this series, I was extremely alert for a new Victor dream. Thus, very few dreams disappeared into that fuzzy place that contains New Year's resolutions, potentially great inventions, profound realizations, and forgotten dreams. Other dreams referred to the same issues as the Victor series, but I was always more impressed by the messages from Vic. It was easier to see the unfolding of one particular part of my personality or the crumbling of an old, useless belief, when the dream was packaged in the Victor container.

I worked and played with the dreams as long as it took to understand them, or at least to be moved by them. I learned to trust that the messages I received needed to be activated, not just understood. This active engagement created many changes in my life, leading to new ways of feeling and being in the world. Each of these changes were imperative to heal the myriad of chronic ailments that robbed my life of joy and possibility. Eventually, this prolonged study was published as my first book, *Recurring Dreams: A Journey to Wholeness.*

Most dreamers are intrigued by recurring symbols that alert them to the presence of a dream series. Working actively with the series connects them to a feeling of vital psychic activity. Series dreams bring a realization of inner movement, or lack thereof, beyond random dreams. An ongoing series inspires seriousness and attention that the homeostatic ego self cannot deflect. In part, this is because of the sense of intention the dreamer experiences as the series is studied. This was certainly true for all of the dreamers whose series are presented in this book.

I can best describe this experience from my Victor study. As I saw the patterns created by the Victor dreams, I felt a great sense of intention from an inner force determined to lead me carefully through the minefields of my life. After every intense period of study, I felt awe and gratitude for this force that was determined to reach me. As I studied the Victor series, I recognized that a beneficent and loving inner force had always been directing my life, even when I was unaware of it. This realization created a great sense of security that cannot be found in the material world.

The most delightful dream of the Victor series illustrates the element of intentionality: I am conversing with Vic by phone while walking several miles on a dirt road. The conversation is possible because the phone is attached to a bulky, yellow power cable of unending length. When I comment about this marvelous phone, Victor says that he has provided the power cable! Thus, the long connection between me and Vic was created, or made possible, by Vic. The energy I had been searching for my entire adult life intended for me to reach it and provided the means to do so!

As you read the recurring symbol studies that follow, you will learn how this feeling of intentionality affected other dreamers, all searching in one way or another for healing and wholeness.

CHAPTER THREE

Life Scripts and Dreams

In the middle of the last century, psychiatrist Eric Berne popularized a way of understanding human experience through a theory called *life scripts*. This theory contends that humans are given roles to play within their families and cultures. The hypothesis asserts that each of us is assigned a very specific role to play within that script. Berne, the originator of transactional analysis, taught that, to be true to one's authentic self, these scripts must be made conscious. With some inner adjustment and a great deal of courageous development, one can then be free to choose one's own life rather than live a life that had been assigned.

A major benefit of doing consistent dreamwork is becoming conscious of the old scripts. Dreams also provide glimpses of alternate scripts that offer possibilities for new ways of feeling, thinking, doing, and being. Many dreams cast us in roles we have never before played, allowing us to experience the feelings of this new, and perhaps far more healthy, character or personality. The dream experience provides a visceral reality that can actually motivate the dreamer to choose options outside of the script. This demands a great commitment to personal integrity, and often requires the support of professionals familiar with the process of transformation. Support groups can help people move into identities different from those imposed by the family script. The self-help sections of bookstores, as well as many radio and television programs, are designed to help with this process of transformation. The information age brings personal development benefits unimagined even fifty years ago.

Exchanging a limiting personal script for one that is more fulfilling is an ongoing process. Happily, every night we are presented with dreams that remind us of the need for such changes. About ninety minutes after we fall asleep, our first dream message is transmitted. Once understood, the images in these dreams can lead us toward healthier lives lived in more complete and fulfilling ways. This inner drive toward wholeness is experienced most clearly when the self that co-created the original script is snoozing and relatively powerless. When that old "This is who I have always been and must always be" part of the self is not writing the play, another author can sneak its scenes into the awareness of those lucky enough to recall their dreams. This guiding force is so patient that it will repeatedly present us with "alteration" dreams, in case we miss the first two or two hundred proposed scenarios.

Our dreams need ways to catch us, to entice us to reel them in from the deep waters of our psyche. Short of nightmares, one of the best ways dreams have of grabbing our attention is to repeatedly present an intriguing symbol. The dream may hook us even within the dream state, when we recognize that we are having a dream experience that we've had many times before. We then awaken to the mystery of the repetition rolling around our consciousness and find it as hard to ignore as a marble clattering inside a revolving glass jar. Whether we feel intrigued or irritated by this inner repetitive rumbling, we have become aware.

If we dive deeply enough into our psychic waters to retrieve the beckoning symbol, we may find ourselves entangled in a dream series. Engaging with the series allows us to be towed by an inner current determined to lead us to new and different views of ourselves and the world. Thus begins the unfolding of a counter-script, a fresh way of perceiving ourselves and of creating healthier roles to play in our own lives.

When we consciously establish a relationship with this inner scriptwriter, the dream material will change. As the symbol repeats we may begin, within the dream, to relate to it differently. This process of wrangling with a repeating dream experience strengthens our psychological "muscles," altering our sense of self in the awake world, and expanding our life options.

Working with the repeating dream images often shows us that the way we operate in waking life is no longer effective. This awareness encourages transformation in a wide variety of ways. Changes both subtle and dramatic help the dreamer to create and live a more valuable life script. Being at home in one's skin, better organized, and more authentic are the benefits of living this consciously chosen script. After decades of doing this work, I feel as if I have exchanged an uncomfortable suit of armor for silk pajamas. I have traded in old beliefs and patterns of behavior that led me down dead-end streets for a personal helicopter capable of taking me where I really want to go.

By rewriting their life scripts, all of the people who studied their recurring symbols for this book discovered more meaningful and joyful ways to connect with themselves, their intimate relationships, and the world at large. After working deeply with a recurring symbol, the dreamers all felt that their recurring image was offered by a deeply loving intention to heal, to fill in their holes, to create a whole circle from the separated wedges of themselves. They felt protected as they recognized aspects of their being that had previously escaped notice. Feeling safe with this dream guidance is extremely important because what we are encouraged to see is not always beautiful, and what we are expected to do is not always easy. However, developing a trusting relationship with this profound inner force emboldens us to perform the tasks set before us. Each step we take, regardless of our hesitation, takes us ever closer to feeling at home and at peace within ourselves. This is illustrated by the following example of a short dream series. As you read the dreams, look for what is changing and developing.

Dream One

Many people are ahead of me. We are all following Harvey. All the others crawl through a cave and out the other side. I refuse to do so for fear I will get stuck. Harv assures me that I can easily get through, but I refuse to try.

Dream Two

Harvey has been promoted to supervisor of the airline. He says he has a job for me. I'm thrilled and say I'll take it. But first I must become a pilot.

Dream Three

I'm meeting the old gang at the tavern. When it's time to leave, I say goodbye and am surprised by the sadness this creates. However, I leave by dropping to the floor and crawling through three tiny holes. I'm afraid as I go through the holes, but I do so anyway. When outside, I'm surprised to find myself sitting beside Harvey on a limb in a tall tree.

Dream Four
I'm in the middle of a gang of people mountain climbing. I cannot believe I have put myself in such a perilous position but I'm actually exhilarated. I want to tell Harvey about this.

Dwayne identified these dreams as a series because in each he feels challenged by threatening tasks and because all of the dreams included or mentioned Harvey. The dreams show movement from fear and immobilization to exhilaration in a perilous position. Examined from the perspective of a life script, there is movement from saying no to saying yes. Examining the dreams as a series allowed Dwayne not only to see the transformation in his dream self, but also to feel an unfamiliar and delightful sense of courage.

We can add flesh to the skeleton presented above by knowing a few of the dreamer's personal associations. Dwayne is small in stature. This discouraged him from playing sports in both high school and college. Harvey, on the other hand, is the consummate jock, excelling at any sport he tries. Harvey is Dwayne's opposite—physically strong, extroverted, socially adept, and financially successful. Harvey has been Dwayne's hero for many years, and is often a character in Dwayne's dreams.

At the time of these dreams, Dwayne was being encouraged by his co-workers to take a civil service test for a promotion. Dwayne feared he would fail, though he had previously excelled with similar tasks. He was concerned that taking and failing the test would diminish his standing at work. In dream language, he was afraid he would get stuck if he followed his hero, Harvey, through the threatening space and took the test (Dream One).

Working with this conflict in dream group, Dwayne remembered his mother's favorite saying: "Better to be safe than sorry." This was clearly a part of his limiting life script. This message was linked to Dwayne's sense of inferiority, preventing him from freeing himself from a stagnating and boring job.

Dwayne's "Harvey" series reflects one particular life experience, but it has much broader implications. The "better-safe-than-sorry" motto was deeply imbedded in Dwayne's script. Every possibility was seen through this filter. As a result, taking risks at any level was forbidden to him. Dwayne always stopped at yellow lights, never had more than one drink, could not go outside without a hat and sunscreen, considered asking a woman for a date as threatening as jumping off a bridge, and always arrived at work and events a half hour early. Not only was Dwayne afraid to eat in unknown restaurants, but he literally feared any food that he had not eaten in childhood. Dwayne's sense of self and of the world allowed him few choices in a very controlled life.

Yet each of his "Harvey" dreams moved Dwayne farther into new ways of being, into playing the role of hero. He experienced these dreams with great delight and loved role-playing them in dream group. Dwayne was able to literally feel the conflict between his old script and the one that wanted to evolve. He loved the feelings that developed with his short series.

Whether Dwayne's dream growth will manifest in his awake life depends on many factors. Overcoming the tremendous power and habituation of the original script demands commitment, mindfulness, courage, and opportunities. His dream series allowed him to embrace new possibilities, squeeze through tight places, go out on a limb, and learn to fly. For an individual who feels incapable of professional and personal expansion, these dreams suggest a crack in the container of his limited script and offer great hope for birth, growth, and transformation.

In addition to family scripts, larger cultural and ancestral scripts also may dictate our roles. Until we become conscious of these scripts, they can drive us with beliefs that are outdated, perhaps by hundreds of years. This was brought home to me by an experience with a charming Irish gardener who was bidding on a landscaping project for my backyard. When he entered my modest house he asked how long I had rented. He was obviously shocked when I replied that I had owned the home for eighteen years. With a jolt and wide eyes he whispered in his lilting Irish brogue, "Imagine that! An Irish woman who owns her own home in America!"

His statement prompted me to carefully examine the scripts imposed on some Irish people of my age. Though I didn't suffer the financial limitations of the kind of Irish woman this man imagined, I was surprised to realize how limited I sometimes felt. I recalled my mother's favorite phrases: "They may be rich but I'll bet they are not happy" and "Money only brings misery." Poverty consciousness is sometimes hard to detect, but it may be powerful in one whose ancestors have come from a poor or oppressed country. This scene with the Irish gardener occurred many years ago, but it springs into mind, unbidden, at times when I am threatened by the script of financial limitation played out by my parents and ancestors.

The effects of cultural scripting are most easily seen in people in extreme social positions. In America, the spectrum runs from the oppressed and forgotten to the socially, educationally, and financially privileged. Powerful cultural scripts strongly shape the possibilities for most individuals who live them.

Hidden rules and regulations are created by religions and other institutions within each culture; the more aware we are of them, the greater our ability to sort through and choose among the valid, beneficial values and beliefs offered by our families and cultures. As you will see in the studies that follow, our dreams often guide us in this valuable choosing and sorting process so that we then can create an original script of our own design.

CHAPTER FOUR

Script or Myth?

With their PBS series in the 1980s, Joseph Campbell and Bill Moyers brought to mainstream America the importance of the mythic level of human experience. Campbell and Moyers dramatically presented the myths that have created and continue to create our cultures and impact our personal values and beliefs.

Since the early 1980s the shelves of American bookstores have grown heavy with titles including the word *myth*. Springing from the mythologies of many cultures, we find books on gods and goddesses, and on many types of heroic or mythic journeys. American television has presented several miniseries spectaculars based on myths and fairy tales. Every day our youngsters watch and play in this realm, for cartoons and video games are based on mythic creatures, the archetypes of good and evil in myriad forms, from mice to robots to entire virtual galaxies. Campbell showed us that myth has always been the foundation of our lives. It seems that many Americans are now examining what that means.

If you hang out with dreamers for any period of time, you are likely to hear the word *myth* used liberally. We speak of mythic dreams, mythic characters, mythic symbols, and mythic motifs. Many dreams mirror folktales and fairy tales, elemental parts of this mysterious realm of the myth.

A *cultural myth* is a story that illustrates the beliefs of a certain group of people, and often tells how the world and her creatures were created. It addresses what is important about life and how best to maneuver through times of transition, showing rituals that foster support, and modeling acceptance of the inevitable stages of human life. Myths highlight values and illustrate the choices of the ancestors. They also reflect the basic patterns of the human mind itself. Myths symbolically reflect the psycho-spiritual patterns on which conscious thought and feeling rest.

To live mythically is to live with the invisible, the mysterious, the archetypal, the gods and goddesses, the patterns of life that affect all people at all times. The mythic life is full of feeling and purpose; of guidance from special sources; and of intuitive knowing, synchronicities, and miracles. The mythic realm is deep and profound—and repetitious. The life journey is mythic, repeating the same stages and experiences in all cultures: birth, growth, and development; union and separation; challenge and accomplishment; success and failure; joy and tragedy; and aging and death. These are all existential experiences that are mythic—bigger than any one person and common to all.

Part of my research for this book involved interviewing, writing to, or chatting casually with many of the dream writers interested in myth. I received a variety of answers to the query about the differences between *myth* and *script*. All agreed that both motivate our behavior and create our worldview. There was consensus that the more aware people are of the myths they are living and the scripts they are playing, the more free choice is available to them. Some of the experts suggested that the differences between myth and script are insignificant. But many believe that a dream symbol that recurs for years is probably connected to the dreamer's *personal myth*.

Personal myth refers to the stories we tell to describe who we are and how we came to be who we are. What repeats within our dream world is likely to be from the mythic realm, inviting us to undertake the heroic journey of a life lived reflectively, consciously, in cooperation with the dream and other forces far grander than any individual.

Because the terms *script* and *myth* have been used interchangeably, I want to differentiate between them. It seems to me that each creates a different level of influence in a human life. The difference between script and myth is the difference between a daily soap opera and the trials of Ulysses. The first appears to be mundane and the second is obviously transpersonal and universal. A soap opera is the "he said, she did" level of human experience, fairly boring once you recognize the plot. Myths, on the other hand, are full of the greater energies, including the gods and devils, far larger in power and scope, far less predictable and controllable.

Jungian theory tells us that myths are lived by archetypes. According to the theory, all humans fall into various patterns of behavior (archetypes) at one time of life or another, or throughout an entire life. We hear stories from people proclaiming a knowing or a calling to a particular career from a very early age. "By the age of five I knew I would be a doctor and I've never veered from that." Or, "It seems I was born to have a military career. That is all I've ever wanted to do." The first example could represent the *healer archetype* and the second, the *warrior archetype*. The families in which individuals are raised influence that inner sense of self. Often addiction or accident alters the path. Sometimes the individual lacks the will to manifest his or her inner yearning, to make real the calling, as if a lack of character sabotages the myth that wants to be lived. But no matter how it may be deflected or repressed, a truly innate longing will be seen, often repeatedly, in dreams that can frustrate and then energize the individual to follow his or her inner psychic code and, eventually, live the myth that seems intent on creating the individual.

In other words, the mythic level creates us; we do not create the myth. In contrast, once conceived, we are written into the script by our previously scripted parents. Even before we are born, our parents may begin to define our roles—and their expectations: "She will be a dancer and a poet," or "This one is a great ballplayer! Feel him kick!" Cultures define us as well, dictating through subtle and direct means what is appropriate and acceptable for males and females to do, what is expected of the first-born child, and so forth. These notions, hopes, projections, and expectations affect our lives, usually without our becoming aware of them. And, of course, we do have choices. As creatures with free will, we make unique decisions in response to the dictates and modeling of parental figures. To a great extent, we co-author our scripts. Thus, it is possible to reject or abandon the roles chosen by families and culture.

There are many reasons for altering or even abandoning the suggestions or orders of the parental or cultural directors of our lives. One reason for an extreme rewriting of the script is the power of the myth that is creating us. In the mythic realm, we are dealing with forces or energies far more powerful than our parents. When directed by my own myth or personal archetype, I feel that I am being carved out of my script at the same time I am surrendering to a mighty river as it carves and polishes me. In this sense, myth is pro-active, while script is re-active.

The mythic level is broader, deeper, higher, and more encompassing than the level of script. The mythic leads us through life and defines us at our greatest and also at our most base or horrible. The mythic self precedes consciousness but can be made conscious by observing what we ultimately do with life. The mythic level feels and acts like destiny. It is usually stunning, out of the ordinary, illogical, and unavoidable. When myth breaks through, it is stunning, startling, terrifying, or exhilarating. In most cases, the myth succeeds by overpowering the script.

By contrast, the scripted level feels like attending a rehearsal. We are not surprised by life because we are familiar with the script. Some part of us, though it seems to be acting unconsciously, is compliantly aware of the role that we play.

In dream histories I have heard, there is a mythic type of dream that is so amazing it is best described as an epiphany. Sometimes this life-altering dream is experienced as a horrifying nightmare, or in my case, a "griefmare," which shatters one's sense of self and world so completely that, eventually, everything changes. My epiphany resulted from an image that rendered me helpless to resist: a magnificent eagle caught and dying in a monstrous spider's web. This experience began my conscious dream life. Extracting the eagle from the web became my life task. By breaking each strand of the web that bound the eagle, I was escaping from the many sticky, destructive aspects of my family script. In working out this struggle, my deeper myth gave me the strength and courage to "rewrite" my family script.

The mythic realm is often heralded by a big dream, and when the myth takes over, it may greatly impact what we feel and do. We are shocked and shaken. Yet we are sure of the rightness

of what has happened. One of the blessings of this psychic earthquake is a complete lack of doubt. Like it or not, we see the way
that is meant for us and we follow, sometimes with confusion
and even terror of the unknown, but with a clarity of purpose
that is very reassuring to even the most upset part of us (or our
incredulous families and friends). It is, therefore, extremely beneficial that there is little room for doubt at the mythic level.
Within the scripted level we hear many voices, often conflicting.
At the level of myth there is a sense of predetermination, destiny,
and fate, which leaves no doubt, only surprise.

We create our script by the choices that we make as we
develop. My script—familial, cultural, personal—dictates to my
personality. To a great degree, I will likely look and act like most
of the people in my socioeconomic/educational/racial strata. At
this level, most of my dreams seem mundane and ordinary,
driven by ambition and material possession, status and security
or fear. My myth, however, creates my deepest soul and highest
spiritual self. It does not follow the mainstream and will likely
conflict dramatically with the expectations of my family and culture. It is not rooted in security and does not follow the rules that
are so familiar to my personality. Often the only map I can follow comes from my dreams, assuring that what seems insane to
others is true and correct for me. The dreams will warn, as well,
with great clarity, when I am falling off the path of my higher
and deeper self, of my myth.

Myth and script either intersect or clash. If, for example,
the myth that leads me wants me to be a great artist but my script
disallows free-flowing creativity, the clash may result in physical
and/or psycho-spiritual dysfunction and chaos. Often it is this
very crisis of conflict, manifested in physical or emotional illness,
that weakens the ego/personality sufficiently so that the individ-

ual can now hear, see, feel, and allow the mythic realm its due. When this occurs (as it often does through the study of a recurring symbol), all one's resources of courage and honesty are demanded. Throughout the studies that follow, you will see people reaching for their own, very personal truth. What are truly my values? Who am I, really? What am I meant to be? How do I blend with the world while maintaining my authenticity? Who and what are the best and worst of me? These questions are asked from the deep mythic realm.

As I worked with my recurring symbol of Victor Biento, I crashed into brick walls as long as I asked, "What does this Victor symbol mean?" Finally I began to ask, "What does Victor Biento want from me or for me?" Then the walls came down and the importance of the symbol become obvious. By asking what the symbol wanted from me, I began working at the mythic level; I let the dream symbol lead me instead of perceiving it through the limitations of my scripted and limited self. I let my psyche unfold me, rather than following the dictates of my awake ego.

The mythic level of the dream reveals itself when I am being transformed beyond the resolution of the awake state or issue. My script presents the problems to be recognized and resolved; then my myth forces me to rewrite the script, thus leading me to the intention of my life. The script deals with the persona and developmental ego tasks in order to allow me to reach the mythic level and the unfolding of the authentic self, the growth and eventual flowering of my personal archetype. After I revise my personal script, I am ready to manifest the goals that the unconscious holds in store, to be implemented when freed from the constraints of the unconsciously compliant self. With the cooperation of a healed ego supporting the dream, I move ever closer to my authentic, individuated Self.

This seems like a tall order and, of course, it is not a simple or even goal-oriented experience. The journey, the hero and "shero's" process, is multidimensional, often vague, sometimes stalled, and frequently mislaid. But it is hard to lose altogether because the part of self that is not lived creates such a fuss in so many ways.

The mundane scripted life is more grooved than groovy, often stagnated by repetition. It is predictable and lusterless. In contrast, the mythic realm is never boring. Indeed, it can be terrifying to go over the edges of acceptability and expectation. The journey often feels like driving a car at top speed, safe—paradoxically—only when ego's hands release the steering wheel. Those willing to accept the challenge, offered repeatedly by psyche through recurring symbols, will find a great sense of peace in this tumultuous process. Ultimately, nothing feels better than finally arriving home.

PART TWO
Case Studies

CHAPTER FIVE

A Mother Series Creates a Contender

Dreamer: Caroleena
Recurring symbol: biological mother
Length of dream series: 10 years
Number of dreams presented: 9
Script messages addressed:
  "Surrender your calling to serve a demanding, negative
  mother."
  "You have no right to be a contender in life."
Benefits to the dreamer:
  Increased self-esteem.
  Developed emotional freedom to claim and promote artistic
  talent.
  Increased ability to fully engage with others and experience
  life.
Summary: A 42-year-old woman replaces a vicious inner mother
with gentle, loving acceptance of self and new ways of being in
the world.

As the group quietly gathered for the early Sunday morning
ritual, I appreciated the air of conviviality that had developed
during the weekend dream retreat. I counted heads, hoping for
the presence of all group members. Alas, the slender, attractive

woman who looked a decade younger than her forty-two years was absent. I extended the group meditation as long as possible and then, regretting Caroleena's absence, began the candle-lighting ceremony. Finally, about fifteen minutes into the opening lecture, she appeared, sliding into the room, almost literally hugging the walls. I was so fascinated by her almost imperceptible movement that I had difficulty focusing on my talk. After every few sentences, I paused to spot Caroleena. Eventually, as if walking on cotton and blending into the paint on the walls, she made her way around the room and sat behind a huge potted plant. I doubted that anyone else in the room knew of her presence. I wondered why such an attractive and obviously bright woman felt the need to be so circumspect. The dreams I had heard Caroleena share were eloquently, even poetically written. She seemed deeply connected to her dream material.

Caroleena remained essentially alone for the rest of the day, and I grew more intrigued by her mysterious aloofness. I noticed that she always walked alone. She glanced at people in a sideways fashion, as if afraid of being caught looking openly. Unless sharing a dream, she volunteered nothing of herself.

Three years later, Caroleena answered my call for case-study participants for this book. As she shared with me her four-year-long series, I began to understand her behavior during the dream weekend.

We held our first interview for the series study on a sunny spring day at the rural home Caroleena shares with her husband, Gerry. We began by strolling around their extensive informal flower and vegetable gardens. As we settled with mugs of hot tea in Caroleena's art studio, we were serenaded by the raucous screeches of peacocks mating in a neighbor's yard. Doing our best to ignore the cacophony, we began our work with Caroleena's initial dream in what she called her "Mother Series."

Dreams are often obtuse and confounding, so we may be startled when a piece presents a clear and straightforward statement of a problem and, by implication, indicates a path for healing. The first dream that Caroleena ever recorded, hurriedly written on the back of an envelope, was just such a dream. Many therapists and dream professionals take particular interest in the first dream presented by a patient or client because this initial disclosure from the unconscious often exposes the major issue confronting the dreamer. So it was with this piece, the first of what would become the Mother Series.

The Contender

I am passionately screaming at my mother in the driveway of my family home. "I could have been an artist! I could have known dynamic people! I could have traveled to interesting places! Instead I have wasted my life trying to please you, to make you happy, to avoid your displeasure!"

My mother listens to me. Then, from the house, she retrieves a gift for me. It is a very old perfume bottle in the shape of a pyramid.

"Do you know why you titled this dream 'The Contender'?" I asked.

"Oh, yes!" Caroleena responded enthusiastically. "The word comes from one of my favorite classic movies, *On the Waterfront.*"

I asked her to tell me about it. Paraphrased, this is what I learned:

"Marlon Brando plays a longshoreman who does petty jobs for the Mafia. He blindly follows the directions of his Mafia bosses and his brother, who also works for the Mafia. Brando plays an average fighter, a boxer. Apparently he had some talent and might have earned a title or two—but he tossed his career by throwing a critical fight so that the Mafia bosses could win some bets.

"At that point, he doesn't seem to care or even really notice that he has relinquished his one chance to make something of himself. But later, as the movie develops, Brando's character falls in love, opens his eyes to the corruption surrounding him, and realizes that if he hadn't complied with the Mafia bosses he could have been a contender. I remember vividly how touched I was by that statement when I saw the movie thirty years ago. The fury that I feel in my own contender dream is how I feel when I see the film, even now."

We returned to the dream. The calmness with which Caroleena had read "The Contender" dream was replaced by a rising voice and flushed cheeks as she shared her associations and reconnected to the strong feelings generated by the dream. "It felt great to yell at my mother. I have never come close to doing that in real life. It seems to me that I have always been afraid of my mother," Caroleena explained. "She's ceaselessly critical and domineering, cold and judgmental. She seems unable to touch or be touched by anyone. I cannot imagine her holding me as an infant. I have no memories of nurturing or comforting from her, even when I was a baby."

Caroleena described the ways in which her mother controls others with a strident, demanding voice. "She dominates all conversations with her acutely pessimistic view of the world. She is aggressively opinionated and never allows room for doubt, possibility, or discussion. Anyone who dares to suggest a different view is verbally attacked into silent submission."

I was remembering Caroleena nearly crawling into the group room during the weekend seminar when she added, "Being completely quiet and unseen was the only way to be safe around my mother. Now, drawing attention to myself feels like a deadly dangerous thing to do. The more hidden I am, the safer I feel."

"And yet," I offered, "it seems that there is a part of you that passionately wants to become a contender."

"Right. I can almost literally feel her [the contender]. She's still hiding, but I think she wants to emerge," Caroleena responded.

I could see this vibrant Caroleena in the art that surrounded us. Her studio is a place of creative honesty that reveals a bold and gallant woman in every piece of work. Looking back at the dreamer, I could see this authentic individual peeking through her fear. I suspect that anyone brave enough to do serious dream-work has the gumption to be a contender in the external world.

Caroleena explained that, though she had physically lived apart from her parents for twenty-four years, she had never felt independent of them. She had always been severely punished for any act considered a transgression by her mother, so Caroleena had, of necessity, sidestepped the developmental stage of teenage rebellion so vital to healthy maturation. And so, by the middle of her life, Caroleena had only begun to discover and activate her authentic self, the self hidden under layers of compliance to and fear of the mother who dominated her spirit and much of her life.

Studying the first dream of this series seemed to free Caroleena and spur her to action. She responded to the call from her psyche by joining a weekly dream group. She taped and repeatedly listened to my weekly radio dream show. She and Gerry shared, discussed, and researched every dream retrieved by either of them. "Engaging with my dreams nearly every day provided the first therapeutic work of my life. I began to read dream books and many psychological and spiritual books to which my dreams led me. My sense of myself and my potential changed slightly with every arduously examined dream."

Caroleena's dreams helped her to see herself anew, to recognize her limitations and her needs. Through daily communication with her unconscious, she began to actively rewrite the life script she had unknowingly followed for her entire life. To write our own life story, we must separate from our parents and develop our personal view of the world. Before we can begin the heroic journey of slaying dragons and creating our own castle in our own kingdom, we must actively sever the psychic umbilical cord.

Caroleena responded dramatically to "The Contender" dream by severing her waking life relationship with her mother. This was something she had wanted to do for many years. Though she hoped to someday develop enough strength to feel emotionally safe in her mother's presence, the following dreams convinced Caroleena that distancing herself was imperative. These stunning dreams allowed her to see her mother more clearly and to feel how unsafe she was.

> I sit opposite my mother, watching her talk. I observe a bizarre physical transformation as Mother changes from a well-dressed, normal-looking woman to a banshee-witch with a contorted face, hurling wrathful incantations. Mother is oblivious to these bizarre shifts.

And in another dream:

> Mother shows a magazine picture of a room she
> thinks is fabulous. It is black and white op-art. It's like
> a carnival house-of-mirrors, deliberately distorted to
> create fantastic illusions that are terrifyingly disorient-
> ing. If I go into this room I will be trapped. There is
> no way out because the floor is constructed to allow
> descent but not ascent! I feel panicked and awake
> screaming, "Get me out of here! I'll do anything if
> you get me out of here!"

In her journal Caroleena wrote, "When in the presence of
my mother, I always feel as if I'm plummeting to hell. It's like
quicksand. I get sucked in and lose all hope of escape. I have no
sense of direction. I feel so disoriented by Mother's vile perspective that my life feels literally threatened."

Each of these dreams strengthened Caroleena's resolve to
remain separate from her mother despite many attacks of self-
doubt and shame. "I often feel like a really bad girl. I am breaking so many of society's rules by not playing the role of dutiful
daughter. When I recall these dreams I see clearly why my decision for separation is valid."

In a healthy relationship parents consciously help their
children leave the nest. Responsible parents model and teach
the skills, attitudes, and beliefs necessary for their offspring to
succeed on their own. In these ways, a nurturing and helpful parent is internalized, allowing the youngster to develop into a
mature individual capable of self-nourishing and self-support. If
this inner dynamic is not instilled by the parents, a developing
person must consciously create this inner parental energy.

Caroleena clearly needed to learn self-care skills if she was to become an adult capable of contending in the modern world.

Identifying admonitions and belief systems—dictated by authoritative people from our past—is vital to recovering the authentic self that is buried inside us. These internalized voices control how we play our roles and act out our scripts. Caroleena's experience with that task was addressed brilliantly by the following dream:

> I find a reel-to-reel tape recorder perpetually playing the droning voice of my mother. I try to turn up the volume to make Mother more conscious of the inflammatory content she repeatedly spews forth, poisoning her environment. However, I am unable to control the volume and feel nervous and powerless once again.

Psychiatrist Eric Berne identified the presence of such repetitive inner voices as *parental tapes*. Caroleena needed to identify the internalized beliefs of personal worthlessness and universal hopelessness that controlled her. "I need to turn up the volume on the inner mother so that I can become conscious of the absurdity and exaggeration of her destructive perspective of the world." We all remain imprisoned by similar limiting beliefs until we make them conscious by turning up the volume. Until we are aware of these destructive tapes, we may well feel inexplicably nervous and powerless, as Caroleena did in this dream.

Caroleena had been a silversmith and oil painter for many years, selling her unique work in shops and galleries. Despite this, she did not consider herself a serious artist. "My mother's first husband was a Bohemian—a self-styled artist, charming, irresponsible, and unfaithful. Mother decided that all artists were like him. She did everything possible to squash my interest in art, so I always hid from her what I considered the best of myself. I guess because I'm still hiding my art from her I continue to hide it from the world at large." The following dream addressed the need for Caroleena to confront her mother's negative attitude about artistic talent.

> An exotic couple knocks on my door to ask if I know where they can perform in order to promote themselves. In the kitchen I hear my mother grumbling about not wanting to feed these people. I charge into the kitchen and shout at my mother, "Cease and desist!" She is shocked speechless. I tell her to have a large glass of wine. I feel in charge as the dream ends.

When the performing artist boldly presents itself, the negative mother is activated and rejecting. But dream ego has now become strong enough to control her. "Cease and desist!" Dream ego directs the mother to go unconscious (have a large glass of wine), thus freeing herself to tend to the newly entered creative energy.

I applauded dream ego's actions by saying, "You were certainly able to contend with the mother who is unwilling to nurture the artistic performer."

"Right!" Caroleena replied. "Though I hadn't really thought of that meaning for the word before." We then began to probe this word so important in Caroleena's struggle with her external and internal mother. The dictionary defines a contender as one who strives in opposition to, one who is able to deal with an enemy and is competent in the act of arguing. These were important skills for Caroleena to develop after years of repressing her own ideas, feelings, and needs in order to protect herself from her domineering mother. If she was to mature into an empowered adult, she would need to contend with others as well. "This is happening in my awake reality," Caroleena volunteered. "I have been surprised by how easily I now know and state what I want. I'm even willing to argue to get what I need."

While Caroleena was extricating herself from the dictates of her negative mother, she was able to create a loving inner parent so necessary for healthy living. That development is reflected in the following dream:

> I'm standing in a circle of women. I am telling the true story of the typical ways my mother rejected me. A warm, friendly sixty-five-year-old psychotherapist is quiet and reflective after she hears my story. She finally says she has decided she wants to mother me. I'm very pleased!

One of the many benefits of any kind of support group, including dream groups, is the freedom to tell our true story to receptive ears and compassionate hearts. When we admit the truth to ourselves and to others, we make space for a healing energy to nurture us.

Another dream showed Caroleena's progress and personal growth:

> An articulate male politician is being attacked by his mother as he gives a speech to a large gathering of people. He ignores his mother's attack, which so enrages her that she hurtles something at him over the

heads of the crowd. Without missing a beat, he calmly and precisely catches the object and silently watches as his violent mother is removed from the group.

The significance of the male politician was clear when Caroleena defined him as "the masculine intellectual able to formulate and articulate policy and laws." Apparently a new, inner ruling force is taking power away from the abusive mother as Caroleena proceeds with her struggle for independence. In her journal she wrote, "I really like the politician's ability to ignore his mother because my mother's attacks always leave me speechless and devastated. In addition, I have never been able to speak comfortably in public or even in a small group. I can see that during the year away from my mother, I have been develop-ing a powerful ruling inner force that, when the time is right, will allow me to speak out. Hopefully, the next time I confront Mother I will be as cool as this guy."

Dreams in which we observe or exhibit admirable but for-eign behavior allow us to experience new and empowered feel-ings. It's as if these dreams allow us to rehearse a new role, a more healthy way of being, before we actually need to perform it. Connecting to the new possibility is powerful motivation for the continuation of change.

Many dreams from Caroleena's study cannot be shared here because of space limitations. Be aware that she doggedly and assiduously wrangled with hundreds of dreams during the four years preceding these final pieces. We chose the next two dreams because they highlight the healing and growth resulting from this dream series. Both of the remaining dreams echo themes already presented.

> It is night. I'm in the attic of my parents' house
> unplugging the wires from a tape recorder on which
> my mother's voice is recorded. This is a very defiant
> act. I must leave quickly and forever when my task is
> accomplished. I am also loading preserves into a bas-
> ket to take with me. These home-canned goods are
> intended to sustain me after I make my escape.

This dream presented an important healing aspect often experienced by those working through issues of former abuse. At some
point, most people begin to recognize positive aspects and times
from the past. After a certain amount of healing and strengthening comes a time to acknowledge the value and nurturing that
occurred during an abusive time. Despite Caroleena's severe difficulties with her mother, her parents' attic (intellectual
processes, beliefs, and values) contains sweet nourishment
(home-canned goods) that will sustain Caroleena for the rest of
her life.

I loved the reference to the defiant act of permanently
unplugging the old tapes. It is a brilliant example of dreams
performing subversive activities—that is, of dreams breaking
down the old structure that no longer serves, to make space for
a new more functional and mature way of being. The part of
us that is comfortable with the original script experiences this
as a supreme betrayal; but we will not achieve the power and
freedom necessary to recreate ourselves unless we commit
such acts of defiance. And when that happens then we must
deal with inner authorities of profound importance. Here is
the second scene of the dream about disconnecting the
mother's tapes:

I see a table of old men and women sitting like a panel of Supreme Court Justices. I join my husband and our black children to perform a ritual in which we all dance to the center of a square. This is done to reassure the authorities who watch us that we are truly fine. They acknowledge our reformation and allow us to leave.

This scene presents the powerful archetype of the supreme inner judge who in this case applies the stamp of approval after *reformation*—reforming the past—has occurred. Greatly appreciating the ritualistic dance of wholeness (center of the square) with her inner family (Caroleena and Gerry have no children), the dreamer wrote this in her journal:

Now that the hated negating tapes have been silenced and I have symbolically left my mother's abuse forever, an integrated inner family (Caroleena and her husband are Caucasian; the dream children are African American) can celebrate in ancient, ritualistic form. Even the scary old judges are content. This dream really feels like a pat on the back from my dreaming self.

For the purposes of our study, Caroleena and I needed to identify the last piece we would work together. Though we would label it the ending dream, we suspected additional mother dreams would occur in the future. I was fascinated to see that the final dream of Caroleena's study included the symbol of a pyramid, similar to one in her very first series dream; the Contender dream had ended with "My mother listens to me. Then, from

the house, she retrieves a gift for me. It is a very old perfume bottle in the shape of a pyramid."

Caroleena titled her final series dream "Big Development
at the Top." In it, her biological family is driving in a powerful
new truck, ascending a mountain road.

> At the top I am quite astonished to see huge equip-
> ment moving the earth in an ordered way. Enormous
> trenches have been excavated. The whole project
> reminds me of a Mayan pyramid. I am quite excited
> by this huge development. The view is spectacular
> because there are no obstacles; the area is cleared.

Clearly, new development is being undertaken in Caroleena's
psyche, which excites her. She examines this newness with her
family after accomplishing a difficult climb made possible by the
powerful new vehicle. During our final interview Caroleena
connected to the pyramids by saying: "These ancient structures
guaranteed an Egyptian ruler's journey to the other world, to the
afterlife. In the Aztec and Mayan cultures, pyramids were essential to rites of passage and to encouraging the gods to serve the
needs of the people."

"What is that for you?" I asked. "What rite of passage is necessary for you to serve the needs of the people?" After several
weeks of pondering these questions, Caroleena's answer became
obvious. She quit a variety of "survival jobs" that had financially
supported her avocation of art. Caroleena and Gerry began promoting and marketing her art. This action said to the world, "I
am an artist and I shall embrace my art as my only vocation."

In 1990, Caroleena declared her deep desire to be a contender, to authentically engage with her talents and with life.

Developing the psychological maturity to do so required separating from an external domineering, repressive mother while creating loving and supportive inner nurturing. Caroleena's entire series dealt with the multiplicity of issues and personal internal developmental tasks necessary to accomplish this. At the beginning of the journey she was presented with the gift of the pyramid from the repressor. Five years later the pyramid is clearly under construction. Can it be that our greatest gifts come from that which forces us, often painfully, to activate previously emaciated, undeveloped parts of the self? In Caroleena's study, this appeared to be the case.

After the "Development at the Top" dream Caroleena was finally able to present her authentic self to the world. The rites of passage suggested by the pyramids had been accomplished. Like the pharaoh, this transported Caroleena into another world, that of actively promoting her art work. In this new role, authored by Caroleena and her dreams, she must contend with fears of judgment and rejection, as well as anxieties that accompany success. But she is now strong enough to cope with this, for Caroleena has become a contender.

Six months after the completion of this study, Caroleena experienced a major shift in consciousness vis à vis her parents. She writes:

> A brief but debilitating illness confined me to bed for two weeks. During this time it is as if my normal ego defenses were burned up by the fevers I was experiencing. After one particularly surreal episode of dreams, and perhaps even awake hallucinations, I suddenly felt overwhelmed by an intense feeling of universal compassion. During that moment of grace,

I was instantly able to unconditionally embrace and accept my mother. Understanding and forgiveness replaced anger and fear, leaving me with a desire to reconnect with both of my parents.

After my physical recovery, I wrote my parents, inviting a reconnection and suggesting some guidelines for a new relationship. Our first meetings were tenuous and short in duration. But during the past six months my husband and I have shared many long meals and celebrated several special days with my parents.

Both my mother and I have changed. My mother's attempts to bait me are rare and ineffective. For the most part, I am no longer influenced by what she thinks or feels about me or anything else. The first time she pulled out her metaphoric gun to blast away at something, I stopped her before she got off her first shot. She has not tried again.

My energy remains high before, during, and after the visits. The awful days of toxic hangovers following an encounter with my mother are gone. By consciously maintaining my personal boundaries and acknowledging and expressing my needs, we have finally created an adult relationship of healthy, mutual respect.

I feel as if I literally grew up during the months I spent studying my mother series. Now I am at peace with my parents and happy to be reconnected to them. In addition, I have finally claimed my talent and abilities as an artist and am able to make the living I deserve, need, and enjoy.

CHAPTER SIX

Searching for the River

Dreamer: Darian
Recurring symbol: river
Length of dream series: 17 years
Number of dreams presented: 19
Script messages addressed:
   "As a member of this church, you must abandon all your
      individual thoughts and feelings in order to survive."
   "You are stupid and evil."
Benefits to the dreamer:
   Acquired an appreciation for her unique courage.
   Confronted and reevaluated her former religious
      training.
   Recognized the value of living drug free.

Summary: A 48-year-old woman escapes from the bondage of her spiritually abusive past and from substance addiction to live the life she wants.

Because of the bold handwriting on the envelope, I imagined its writer to be both honest and interesting. Inside, on plain blue paper, was written: "I'm responding to the request I heard on your radio show for case-study volunteers. For seventeen years I've dreamed about the same river. It is not a river I've ever really seen. I would like to know what the dreams mean." The letter continued: "You might be interested in another recurring theme about the escort/outcall/massage parlor business where I worked for twelve years. I was a working woman and managed five parlors in San Francisco until eight years ago." I appreciated the directness of her letter and sent Darian the initial interview packet for case-study participants. A few weeks later we had our first face-to-face meeting.

Darian, an attractive forty-eight-year-old woman, and I chatted casually before directing our attention to her dreams. I liked her directness and gentle humor. She expressed great enthusiasm for the dream and a definite bias for pursuing the river series. Dreams containing rivers have always been significant to me, so I agreed. The most interesting element about her river series emerged immediately with this statement: "The first river dream occurred in 1980. It was a short dream, but it contained very unusual feelings of peace and bliss. I loved this beautiful river so much. But I have not been able to reach it since the first dream."

"Why was being at the river so important to you?" I asked.

"At the time I had this dream I was thirty-three years old. The dream gave me my first feeling of peace, safety, and complete joy," Darian replied. "My life has been pretty chaotic and unhappy. The dream was really my first encounter with a way I would like to feel. It calls to me like a promise of hope. But I have never been to the river again, even though I have had sixteen more dreams about it."

I watched Darian shuffle through the many dream papers she had prepared for our session. She appeared to be quite organized, so I was surprised by the self-recrimination in her next words. "I'm sorry about the way I write. I rented a typewriter for this project but it can't correct my bad spelling and I don't use words well. I can never say what I really feel. You will have to be patient with me. I've always been a bad student."

Considering how she berated her identity as a student, I decided Darian's educational experiences might be a strategic place to begin. "Talk about your schooling," I suggested, looking for a way into her life story. "Did you enjoy school?"

I was surprised by Darian's immediate loss of composure as she approached my question. Her voice, filled with emotion, began to tremble as she described her very first day of school. "From the start, I was terrified of school. I resisted getting on the bus to go to public school. I was expecting to see horrible things. My parents had told me I would meet the 'infidels' who would try to teach me wicked things. They warned me that my teachers and the other students would try to hurt me because they were the evil servants of the devil. Can you imagine what those words do to a five year old?" By the end of this amazing disclosure, Darian's voice was filled with anger, her eyes brimmed with tears.

Darian's answer astonished and frightened me. I had never before heard such language. Recovering my composure, I responded that infidels and "evil servants of the devil" were unusual thoughts for a little girl.

"Not if the little girl is raised in a radical Christian cult," Darian explained.

A radical Christian cult. Images of the tragedies at Jonestown and Waco flashed before me. What little I knew about such communities I had learned from media coverage of those two events. When I told Darian this, she continued by saying that a mother and two children from her original religious community were consumed in the flames of the Branch Davidian fire. Suddenly I was immersed in a crash course on a religious sect that believes in the imminent, literal ending of the Earth as God's punishment for evil human behavior.

Clearly emotional now, Darian continued by sharing her childhood fears about Judgment Day. She had been taught that on the appointed day, True Believers would ascend to Heaven, unscathed. All others would "suffer the fates of the damned at the uncontrolled hands of Satan and his forces." Darian described her time in church school as filled with horror. "Our coloring books and children's stories all contained terrifying tales of horrible punishment, destruction, and hideous death to the infidels."

Darian explained that much of her childhood pain resulted from feeling totally different from other members of her family and her church community. "My 'good' brother and sister were unaffected by these ideas (in the coloring books). But I knew, from age three, that I was one of the 'bad' people. I did not belong with my family. I lived in fear that the truth would be discovered and my family would throw me away. All of my childhood years I knew I would spend eternity with the damned, as pictured in the books."

I took a moment to examine this thin, delicate-appearing woman with nearly translucent skin. Her long dark hair curved softly around her shoulders, enfolding a perfectly heart-shaped face. Dressed in a thin, modest cotton dress, she seemed to me physically vulnerable. Though the weather was warm, I wanted to place a wool shawl around her for protection.

Darian's apparent vulnerability concerned me at the beginning of our work together. I worried about her ability to cope with the feelings and memories that would inevitably surface as a result of this study, especially when she said that she had never told anyone her entire life story. She was not affiliated with a support group and had little experience with any form of therapy. This was to be her first in-depth look at her past. Because of this, we moved very slowly while I took constant barometric readings of Darian's coping skills and stability.

My fears were unfounded, for the inner strength that had permitted a tiny girl to rebel against an entire community protected Darian as we worked. As her story developed, I could see that this seemingly fragile woman was supported by a core of steel that had allowed her to escape from a cultural dominance very few have had the courage to abandon.

During the months of our work together, Darian told me many stories about her early years. Looking back at her past, she now understood that she had dealt with her terrors by acting out in ways very unusual in a culture that demands complete, unquestioned compliance. As a result, Darian was considered a bad, rebellious girl from early childhood. She was constantly compared to her siblings, who complied with the dictates of the church with apparent ease. "I was the opposite of everyone else. I hated the twice-daily family Bible studies. When I begged to go outside and play, I was always told that those yearnings put my soul in jeopardy."

To add to her feelings of alienation, after a short time in public school Darian began to trust and enjoy the townspeople. This was considered a terrible sin. "We were told to shield ourselves from the people outside our community. But I liked these free and easy folks. Many of my teachers—the so-called infidels—were funny, relaxed, and warm."

From the school playground, Darian watched town children playing with and loving pets, which were not allowed in her community. She envied the couples who kissed or hugged each other as they walked around town, seeing them not as evil but as genuinely loving. "I could not obey the teachings to hate people of color, and I did not revere the leaders of my church. I simply didn't belong, and I lived in terror of being found out."

I learned to steel myself when Darian preceded her descriptions of the church community or her parents with a statement like "They were good people but..." or "They meant well but...," because I knew I was about to hear more upsetting details of common practices she had suffered. Darian told of the searing pain she experienced from shunning, the dominant form of discipline in her former church. In high school Darian had been completely ostracized for several weeks at a time. "No one was allowed to speak to me or to even look at me. I felt as if I was totally invisible."

She earned severe punishment for a variety of teenage "crimes" common to the outside world but strictly forbidden within her community, such as smoking. Showing her creative potential, Darian regularly forged the name of the dean of students on excuse slips, selling them to classmates for a dollar a copy. She cut a cavity in a book to hide a transistor radio so she could hear rock and roll music. She refused to do class assignments and earned the reputation as the worst academic student in the history of the school. Such a perverse student was she that Darian had to retake an IQ test—the high scores she received on the tests were not congruent with failing academic grades!

Though these rebellious acts are understandable and even laughable to most people who understand teenage developmental issues, the view from Darian's perspective was very different She often was called insane, wicked, and evil. This sense of self would restrict and direct Darian throughout much of her life.

By age seventeen, Darian's fear of her church had turned to hatred. Despite her academic failure, she was forced to attend a church college on the East Coast. Her roommate was a girl with similar feelings toward the church and more worldly experience than Darian had accumulated. Together they plotted and executed their escape from the college and the church.

They survived quite happily as carhops until they were found by the friend's parents. Darian's parents were immediately contacted and sent her a ticket to return home. Darian sold the ticket and continued to live on her own. During this period, she discovered the writings of Henry David Thoreau and was excited by *Walden* and *Civil Disobedience*. She had encountered her first worldly hero, and "for the first time I realized that freedom from oppression was both possible and valuable. I was thrilled to finally see the depth of soul and talent in a human being. Thoreau stimulated me and filled me with hope. Then I read Edgar Allen Poe and felt a kinship with his dark fears. I couldn't believe someone else had felt the way I had. I read as many old masters as I could, amazed that reading what I chose could bring such joy."

During these first years of her independence, Darian completely rebelled against her childhood religion. "When I saw a Bible I would shake and turn red with rage. I developed a passion for persuading people to turn against religion. I used my knowledge of the Bible to convince people that God did not exist. I was very good at this. I converted many people to atheism during those years," she said with great force and a touch of pride.

So eager was I to hear the fascinating details of Darian's unusual life that I almost resented using our time together to study her dream material. But psyche had presented us with a specific curriculum, so we finally began the first arduous and exciting steps into the world of Darian's dreams.

Darian's first series dream took her to the river and to the sublime feeling of peace and joy. After that, all of her attempts to return to the dream river were futile. That theme provided our primary focus. What dream events, people, or feelings separated her from her desire to reach the river? What was psyche presenting as obstacles to attaining the peaceful state of mind she sought?

In her first seven dreams Darian knew of the presence of the river but made no attempt to reach it. In one of these dreams, Darian knows the river is close but she cannot follow her desire to reach it because of three demented religious men who are attempting to kill everyone she loves. As she frantically runs away from the place of probable slaughter, she is surprised to find an infant in her arms. She hopes she can save herself and the baby even though the others will be killed. Darian felt that the three religious men portrayed her distrust and hatred of the religious leaders from her past. Though these feelings might kill what she had loved from her past, she escaped from these prior threats with a baby—a new sense of self or a potential way of being in the world.

All of the river dreams from the first nine years of the series imaged the tumultuous life Darian was living. "I sense the presence of my river a long way off. While trying to reach it, my children and I are nearly overwhelmed by a violent storm as we try to cross another very wide stream. I cannot see the end of the rickety footbridge we are on. I feel so frightened that I wake up."

During these stormy years, the peace and bliss that Darian wanted were rarely evident. "I made some really bad decisions and had to live with the consequences," she said. One such decision was her relationship with a convicted felon. Darian married Mickey in the penitentiary where he was serving a fifteen-year sentence for burglary. When he was first released from prison, Mickey seemed to be a good husband, committed to their relationship and an honest life. However, shortly after the birth of their daughter, his moods became violent, as did his choices for making a living.

For the next six years, Darian managed an explosive marriage and a dangerous business. She created financial security as a prostitute but quickly became disenchanted with the lifestyle it demanded. Anxiety and discontent grew into chronic depression. "Life was a mess in all areas. I was using drugs, heavily at times. I became addicted to cocaine, speed, and marijuana. I was an alcoholic and smoked cigarettes every waking hour."

Eight years after her first river dream found Darian totally separated from the peaceful place she wanted to experience. Her chaotic life was traumatic for both her and her daughter. "Finally, in 1988, I knew I could not go on. Planning my suicide became an obsession. One desperate night I was amazed to find myself praying to any source of help I might be able to contact." Darian's hopelessness and despair took her to a place of such need that, despite her cherished atheism, she prayed for help with an intense desire. She was amazed by the image that came to her.

"Suddenly I saw Jesus knocking on a heart-shaped door and remembered the words, 'Knock and it shall be opened unto you. Seek and ye shall find.' I felt a force or a power that was tremendous. I sensed that I had been contacted by a supreme power filled with love, and bringing me peace." Darian then experienced what she called a miracle, one that is not uncommon to addicts who have truly hit the bottom in their unhappy lives. "I had no desire to use heavy drugs from that moment on, though I continued to smoke cigarettes and marijuana. Within the next six months, I quit the prostitution business and left my husband. My daughter and I began a new life."

This miraculous experience and the changes it brought created a desire in Darian to visit her childhood church. She needed to know whether the image of Jesus was directing her to "return to the fold." It was immediately clear that that was not the case. "I felt as uncomfortable and angry when I returned as when I had left twenty years before." The unconditional love and acceptance Darian had felt during her profound spiritual experience could not be reconciled with the paranoia, hatred, and generalized fear promoted by her parents' church. Darian found herself in the place of many present-day spiritual seekers: "I have no words to explain or understand my visit from Jesus, but I know it had nothing to do with the terrifying teachings of my childhood. Because I cannot trust any organized group, I must create my own religion, find my own truth. It's hard and confusing, sometimes even scary, but that's okay with me."

The next dream in her series occurred two years after her life-altering spiritual episode. The dream metaphorically reflected Darian's experiences and feelings as she pursued her own path. Going beyond the sense that the river was nearby, this dream showed her first attempt to reach the river since her first serial dream ten years before. Both Darian and I were awed by the symbols from this significant dream that took her to the depths of her being, just as the perceived visit from Jesus had raised her to the heights. The metaphors it contains, though specific to Darian, seem universal as well. The dream begins with an arduous journey descending into the Earth.

My Deep Descent to the River

I'm deliberately trying to reach the river. I want to feel the peace and bliss it brought me before. I know I can be creative by the river. I can paint and sculpt whatever I want, in peace.

> I know that the river is underground in a cave beneath an old, nearly abandoned building. I pass through the crumbling building to go down very narrow stairs, level by level.

As dream ego descends to the river, she meets old women from her parents' church. They are afraid to go with her but they admire her courage. Darian was surprised by the women's approval. She felt this represented a great deal of inner healing, freeing her from original religious admonitions and dictates. "It's as if the old women know I'm doing the right thing. Even though these women are from the past, I don't feel judged and wrong, as I always did as a child."

Dream ego continues her downward journey, passing many people (who seem to represent different stages of her life). She is very excited knowing that her river is so close, until she suddenly is overtaken by a feeling of tension and dread.

> The stairway has become even more narrow and dangerous. The steps change, becoming very steep with no railing. One wrong step and I'll go over the edge. Coming toward me, up the stairs, are the oldest people I have ever seen. They are helping each other. I am convinced I cannot get around them. I'm frantic and look for another way down.

Although she has overcome judgment and blame, Darian may still be stopped by other *very old obstacles*. In the past when a dream turned into a nightmare, Darian's fear had always awakened her. Perhaps bolstered by her spiritual experience and awake-life development, she now had the strength to continue the dream and her descent.

> I try to work my way around the old couple. It becomes very hard because I am so far out there. I am afraid of falling. I don't know what's below me. Suddenly, a woman appears in a window above me. She encourages me, saying that I can make it if I turn myself around backwards and boost myself up.

As is often the case in a mythic "shero's" journey, just when the challenges are too much and no options seem possible, help miraculously appears. The process of letting go and trusting the unknown seems to be a requirement for those on the journey into the depths.

"As soon as I do what the woman advises, I am sitting on the threshold of a doorway in a sunny room that leads outside. I know the river is through the door. I feel very, very happy anticipating my reconnection to the river." When dream ego trusts the voice of the woman in the window and turns herself around, she finds herself at the place she wants to be. This would have been a great place for the dream to end but, alas, as in awake life, just when we think we've arrived, more is yet to come—or to be overcome.

> When I go through the door I see a huge garbage dump. Though my joy turns to disgust, I decide to go through the garbage dump, avoiding poison dripping from above. I find a relatively clear path that seems safe enough for me to proceed, even though I am barefoot.

Darian was particularly struck by the image of her bare feet. She thought it signified her willingness to continue on her path despite a lack of support (shoes). In spite of her willingness to continue, an obstacle awaits her.

> Then I hear a male voice shout, "Hey!" A big garbage man wearing hip boots yells, "You are not supposed to be here. This is lethal." Pointing to the building behind me, he says, "Specific instructions have been left in that structure that no one is ever to come down here. You leave here right now and never come back again!"

Darian was immobilized with indecision and frustration when she awoke.

And so, though she had come a long way to reach the river, dream ego is stopped by the "keeper of the garbage." This made complete sense to Darian when we connected it to another repeating element within her series. In more than two-thirds of her series dreams, Darian is unable to reach the river because night falls, forcing her to turn back. She understood this to mean that her hopes of achieving peace and joy are impossible because darkness—the inability to see, unconsciousness—ends her journey.

Darian was clear about the meaning of this metaphor. Despite her recovery from life-threatening drug use, she had continued to smoke pot every day, taking refuge in this deliberate form of unconsciousness. For many years she recognized that she used her addiction to avoid the garbage that lay at the depths of her being. Garbage—that which we discard, reject, throw away—is a common and potent symbol for what must be dealt with as recovery and development continue.

As we worked with the dream, years after it was given to her, Darian still became immobilized by hopelessness as she reflected on its meaning and on her continuing addiction to marijuana. Several times in the past she had tried to put down this crutch but literally had been overwhelmed by the strong, disgusting feelings—the garbage—that had surfaced. During these attempts, she had become so deeply depressed that she could not cope with daily tasks.

Even frustrating and disgusting dreams lead to healing. The dreams that showed Darian's inability to reach the river motivated Darian as much as they upset her. In one, dream ego cannot begin her trip to the river until she finds a tin container that holds her marijuana. In another, "A crazy man steals my car. I argue, telling him I must go to the river. He takes my car anyway." Darian described the crazy man as "the desperate and determined way I feel when I want to smoke. Once my energy (car) is stolen, I have no desire to go anywhere."

Another dream—very long and frustrating—describes many detours on the way to the river. In the beginning of the dream, dream ego cannot decide on the best way to get to the river. She eventually sorts this out, is finally sure of the way, but is thwarted for another reason: "I sit in the driver's seat. When I put the key in the ignition it feels squishy. I take it out and see that it is broken in half. I put my fingers into the ignition and search for the other half. I feel the jagged edge but can't get a grip on it. So I keep the half I am holding, abandon the car and the trip to the river, and walk to a hotel."

Darian felt that a key to her recovery (and the way to the river) would be found in therapy or support groups. She realized that her inability to get a grip on this squishy key was due to her fear of organizations (even support systems) and "authorities" (even therapists). "After my experiences with my parents' church, I cannot risk losing control of my life again." She saw that as ironic when she admitted that her addiction caused her to feel out of control. Just as she needed to discover her own spirituality, Darian knew that she needed to develop her own individual path to overcome her addiction to marijuana.

Darian's inability to choose a process that would get her to the river was reflected in the following dream:

> I am sitting behind the wheel of a car stopped in the middle of a big, busy highway going into the mountains. I know the river is on the other side of the mountain. I see a big lightning storm ahead of me. On my left is a narrow road winding around steep jagged cliffs down to the ocean far below. I can't decide which road to take. I wake up frustrated.

The big storm between dream ego and the river seemed to be another deterrent, like the garbage dump. Few can make important changes in life without "going into the storm" and "through the garbage." The decision to do so demands a great deal of courage and, for most of us, significant and trustworthy support.

In the next dream in the series, the trip to the river is halted when dream ego realizes that she must take a shower before going on.

> Before I can go to the river I have to get cleaned up and change clothes. Then I realize that the only clothes I have with me are the dirty ones I am wearing. By the time I find clean clothes it will be nearly

> dark. I feel hopeless. I know I will not be able to go on
> to the river.

Darian felt sure that the need to get clean meant to become drug free. "There is no sense in getting clean if the old identity is put on again, if the old unclean attitudes and behaviors continue."

The following dream repeats and combines the conflicts stated above: The river is close but it is getting dark. Darian's car is unreliable. She could take another car but she is unfamiliar with it and unwilling to risk driving it. Darian thought the other car represented the unknown self that would materialize if she chose recovery instead of addiction. This is an intense conflict for people who are considering significant life or behavior changes. Darian summed up the dilemma I've heard so often from people on the edge of a major decision: "I've been a pot smoker all my adult life. Who will I be without it? Is it worth the risk?" Until this conflict is resolved, it is unlikely that an individual will choose to change.

Much to our mutual surprise, the process Darian needed in order to begin her recovery was supplied by doing this study. At the beginning, neither of us envisioned the healing that would result from the many hours of reflection, association, autobiographical writing, and soul searching necessary to accomplish this work. Besides the awareness and realizations resulting from her individual work, Darian experienced herself anew as she shared her story with me, the first person to hear her complete life history. As we dug through the many levels of meaning contained within her seventeen dreams spanning twenty-five years, I was repeatedly struck by the courage and strength that had guided Darian from age three. Over and over, in her life experiences and in her dreams, we saw an innate and irrepressible ability to survive horrendous experiences.

It was clear from our first session that Darian had never seen herself as clever, courageous, and even heroic. I was frequently unable to suppress a gasp as Darian related the horrors and the accomplishments of her life story. We would have to stop our work while I explained to Darian what caused my strong response and how truly amazed I was by her courage and ability to survive. Darian took my viewpoint to heart, often commenting in a subsequent meeting how my shock or delight influenced her sense of her past and herself. Clearly, I mirrored a perspective never before imagined by this woman who had been so whipped by judgment, ridicule, and rejection.

As a new self-image came into focus, Darian was touched by new feelings. Instead of seeing a disobedient, stupid, and evil little girl, she was able to visualize the spark of love and fearlessness that so desperately sought something different from the dictates of her family and religious community. Finally she was able to see the strength it took to escape from her repressive childhood and from her abusive marriage. Add to that the courage and faith required to extricate herself from a lucrative but destructive career as a prostitute. Eventually, the image of an amazing child who had grown into an unusual woman shone through Darian's grimy self-portrait from the past.

Seven months after our study began, Darian apparently had mucked barefoot through enough lethal garbage to free herself from the protective benefits of marijuana. At this writing, she has been "sober" for seven months, never feeling the panic that had overwhelmed her in other attempts at abstinence.

Darian is delighted that her freedom from addiction allows her to more fully experience her creativity, which harkens to the

"Descent" dream: "I know I can be creative by the river. I can paint and sculpt and create whatever I want in peace." From early childhood Darian had loved painting and drawing, but her religion considered such activity Satan's work. Her creative abilities were disallowed, but her desire to express them never diminished. After quitting the business of prostitution, Darian desperately wanted to try her luck as a working artist. She tried a variety of art jobs and projects while augmenting her income with house cleaning and sales. After three addiction-free months, Darian found the job of her dreams, working as a full-time artist in a small design firm with a salary commensurate with her ability and adequate for her needs.

Darian and I worked on her study over the course of nearly a year. Much to our surprise, during this period she had no additional series dreams. This absence of fresh material confused us until, during our last interview, we postulated that Darian is now at the river. All of the healing changes brought about by the study (or at least during the study) have created the feelings Darian has yearned for throughout the last twenty-five years. We think it is safe to say that she is finally living peacefully by the river's edge.

CHAPTER SEVEN

Bodies and Bones

Dreamer: Griffin Rose
Recurring symbols: skeletons, corpses, body parts
Length of dream series: 25 years
Number of dreams presented: 21
Script messages addressed:
"The options of women are limited."
"The feminine principle has little value."
Benefits to the dreamer:
Connected to and activated the deadened parts of
herself.
Accessed new personal power, resulting in profound transfor-
mation.
Summary: A 46-year-old woman connects to the creative power of the collective unconscious and acknowledges the value of her inner knowing.

While searching for case studies for this book, I invited members of ongoing dream groups to submit intriguing series. I was delighted when Griffin Rose showed an immediate interest in studying what her group lovingly had come to call the "Bodies and Bones" series. During a four-year period, the series had both intrigued and frustrated me. I was fascinated by the stunning images of skeletons buried in walls, body parts strewn about, butchered corpses, desiccated and abandoned bodies, creatures drained of life, and ghosts rising up to meet the living. My personal favorite was the dream of forming a Dead Rights organization to protect and honor the dead! Though Griffin Rose had worked nearly a dozen such dreams in group, we had never grasped psyche's movement from dream to dream, nor the overall intent of the repeating symbols. I hoped an in-depth series study would alleviate our frustration.

In addition to my interest in these dreams, I suspected that working with Griffin would be exhilarating and rewarding. She had been an enthusiastic group participant, offering helpful insights about the dreams of others. She approached her own dreams with intelligence, sensitivity, and openness. In four years Griffin had rarely missed a session. She always had prepared her material with serious forethought. She was well-read in dream studies and clearly committed to the value of consistent dreamwork. I expected to learn a great deal from her study.

After extracting all the dreams containing the symbols of bones and bodies from her journals, Griffin Rose was surprised to discover the extent of this theme throughout her adult life. The first dream of the series, "Grandmother's Deeply Buried Rose-Covered Corpse," occurred in 1973 when Griffin was just twenty-one. As we read the dream together, sitting on the deck of Nepenthe's Restaurant on California's Big Sur coast, Griffin and I suspected the dream was a rite of passage for a young woman beginning independent adulthood. Like many of the dreams of this series, it takes us into and beyond Griffin's personal life to the depths of universal human experience. The awesomeness of Griffin's first dream in the series was enhanced, appropriately, by migrating whales that rose from the depths to dance below us as we perched on the coastal cliffs. To fully appreciate the power of the images we read the dream aloud to each other.

1973: *Grandmother's Deeply Buried Rose-Covered Corpse*

I am wandering through an old, vaulted, underground chamber, browned with age. Diffuse golden sunlight pours through openings high above.

I am alone. It is extremely quiet. I can see particles of dust dancing in the light as I listen to the sound of my footsteps echoing on the stone floor. I walk through room after empty room, each as silent and warmly lit as the next. I feel oddly safe and secure.

I discover an ornate iron stand in the middle of a room. The stand supports a large wooden box that is illuminated by another light from above. My curiosity leads me forward to see that the box is actually a casket of finely polished wood. It is lined with white satin.

I see a body inside. It is my maternal grandmother. The lines and wrinkles of her very old skin look like a road map. Though clearly dead, she appears to be only sleeping. Her body is completely covered with fresh red roses that envelop her in a sweet fragrance. The combination of the scent, the brilliant colors of the roses, and the glowing light surrounding her body creates an awesome feeling of life and vitality in the darkened stillness of the room itself.

Griffin loved this dream because it evoked feelings of aliveness and oneness with the universe, a hint that we were dealing with a profound level of the collective unconscious. It also reconnected her with the grandmother for whom she was named. Griffin felt that she needed this dream because it connected her to the archetype of the ancient feminine principles of intuition, wholeness, and the sacred. "These characteristics were not valued by this culture when I was entering adulthood. I was not taught to extol the inner skills of listening, being still, accepting, allowing. Our society does not honor introspection and introversion. Therefore, as an introvert, I never had felt that I fit or could successfully compete. Now, it seems to me, this dream, this initiation, wanted me to remember and integrate the heritage of my true feminine self as I began my journey to maturity."

Focusing on the image of the grandmother as an internal part of herself, Griffin realized that her psyche wanted her to know, at age twenty-one, that something sacred was buried within her. This is a marvelous example of our dreams presenting an image that allows us to see what we need at a specific time in our development. Whether we can understand, and therefore consciously utilize these images and the archetypes they represent, is dependent on many factors. Like most of us, all that Griffin was able to do was record the dream and continue to live her life without the benefit of cognitively understanding the dream.

During her young adult years Griffin Rose utilized her introverted personality to engage in a process of consciously sorting and identifying the personal values necessary to write her own script as a woman. She deliberately separated herself geographically from her family to allow the development of her individuality. She was happy with her progress because she was able to shape her life to reflect her deeper nature. She experimented with life, tested her intuition, tried on different roles, and developed a sense of herself as a unique being. At age twenty-nine, she fell in love and married.

Griffin's sense of self and her desire to maintain a sense of individuality became blurred within the marital relationship. "I had just become comfortable and secure with my single life when we married. Suddenly I felt the loss of the me I had been creating. I actually suffered mild anxiety attacks during this time. I examined other marriages, wondering how I could become a wife different from the polyester-clad, hair-curled, passionless frumps I saw in grocery stores."

Assuming the new role of spouse pulled Griffin into the very behaviors and feelings she wanted to avoid. Complying to an extent beyond her conscious desires, she was soon living according to family and cultural scripts that dictated how to be the kind of wife she didn't want to be. Despite her intent to expand and further develop herself, she began to contract and withdraw from the exciting authentic life she sought. Griffin's need to clarify her role and to participate passionately in life is reflected brilliantly in the following dream, the next in her series. Notice the recurring sense of underground power.

Undiscovered Talent

I've responded to this ad in a newspaper. "Wanted: Undiscovered Talent for a New Dramatic Production! We are looking for people who are spiritually alive but have not yet discovered their innate talent. Apply only if you are willing to transform through renewal at the source."

I excitedly report to the site of the production. It is a graveyard so full of buried dead that there is literally nowhere to walk without stepping on graves. Paradoxically, the ground seems to be undulating with life beneath the surface.

> I push aside one of the gravestones and descend
> a stairway leading to an underground cavern tiered
> with well-preserved bodies. These dead ones appear
> to be only sleeping. This underground place is
> infused with a great light that seems to be coming
> from the bodies.
>
> I see another bright light at the end of a corridor
> down which I am walking. Illuminated at the end is a
> huge valley that seems to hold a large sunlit city.

Thus far this dream repeats images and themes from the grand-mother dream. Both take us to the depths to find well-preserved dead bodies surrounded by grand light. In both, dream ego feels safe and at peace, and the dead seem to be only sleeping. The "there is light in death" theme seems to underscore the idea that transformation requires the death of one way of living/being in order to move onto another and that this is part of "enlighten-ment." But here the second dream shifts dramatically, presenting astounding images and metaphors.

> This amazing underground place is a large generator
> that serves as the source of life for the people living in
> the city above the surface. Each dead body is one cell
> of the generator. Each body provides a life force for
> one individual living above ground. It is important I
> understand that this is the source of individual energy.

Artists often describe the thrilling experience of creating from a source beyond ego, beyond acknowledged, conscious knowing. This creative experience is an occasion of being overtaken by or surrendering to a power greater than the known self. The source of this power is often felt to emanate from a deep repository of ancient creativity and wisdom. Some call this the *collective unconscious.* The scene in Griffin's dream supports this notion of regenerative power provided by the underground. It was important for Griffin to understand that the life force that sustains the individual emanates from, and is replenished by, a larger universal source. The necessity for and use of this energy are evident as the dream continues.

The next scene of the dream focuses on the performers aboveground. These people wish to discover their *innate talent.* Griffin Rose defined innate talent as those qualities special to each of us that make us unique. "We each have different, special gifts to develop and nurture. Talent implies something precious and valuable."

The dream continues, further clarifying the purpose of the performance in the graveyard. The performers are engaged in the drama of transformation. The dream says that the role the performers choose to play will determine the level of consciousness they will manifest. Here psyche provides Griffin with a brilliant exposition of options for the human journey. In retrospect, Griffin now understands that this dream occurred during a time of change and upheaval because she needed to see, at the personal level, that she had choices about the way she lived her life.

The dream defines three types of roles. The first is the *role of total remembering.* Actors playing this role may choose to perform with others in the graveyard while being regenerated by the dead bodies from below. By doing so, they make a commitment to live in constant consciousness and transformation. This is described as a state of total remembering because the connection to the source of memory (the underground bodies) is constant.

In case that seems too demanding, one can choose the *role of partial remembering.* This role allows one to transform more slowly by resuming activities in the drama of the city while continuing to remember. This means that the actor can take some of the regenerating energy from the graveyard while continuing to live a mundane life. In this case, one is sometimes conscious and sometimes unaware.

Finally, the dream presents the role that most of us play most of the time: the *role of total forgetfulness.* The actors in this role participate in the mundane world with no awareness that other options are possible. These actors know nothing of the underground source and have no interest in transformation. Because the actor has no knowledge of even participating in a play, this role is devoid of awareness and self-consciousness.

The dream ends with the presentation of these profound possibilities. Dream ego is simply given the options but makes no decision about which role to play. Indeed, Griffin Rose did not work with the dream until our study began fourteen years later. Her subsequent dreams and life experiences suggest that, like most of us, she chose the third role by default. When we fall into the usual patterns of habituated living, our innate talent may remain hidden as we slosh through our days, dazed by what life does to us. We seem to wander around, succumbing to temptation. In this state we are prisoners of unconscious cultural and familial dictates.

I'm reminded here of the comic strip *Family Circus* by Bil Keane. He frequently shows a bird's-eye view of the process of a little boy, Billy. Let's pretend the youngster is told to take a spoon to the neighbor. He skips off in the right direction but then spots a spider's web on the neighbor's garage. He follows the spider as it slides to the ground on a silken thread. Next to the spider the boy sees a kitten inviting play. Their game of tag leads to the end of the block. The boy/kitten team then encounter a dog, who trees the kitten. Firefighters need to be called to rescue the kitten from the telephone pole. The neighbor finally gets the spoon the next day when the boy finds it lying beside the spider's web.

The cartoon character illustrates how easily we are distracted from a specific focus and direct path. Unending possibilities invite our attention. A plethora of mundane needs constantly vie for our time and energy. Though our intention to attend to our innate talent, our true nature, may come into clear focus from time to time, our ability to remember our ideals long enough to manifest them may be as difficult for us as getting the spoon to the neighbor is for Billy.

And so it was for Griffin Rose. Despite her desire for a unique union, Griffin's marriage was not a happy one. In addition, she struggled with the common problems of ailing parents, difficult jobs, bothersome chronic physical problems, and depression. That her passion for life was deadened and replaced by anxiety clearly registered during her sleep time. At this point in the series, the friendly and generative corpses were replaced by violent images of crime scenes strewn with mutilated and abandoned bodies. Griffin was plagued by nightmares of gruesomely murdered people. In several dreams, dream ego was a detective. Over and over, psyche presented Griffin with images of vital energies that were severely threatened and in need of her detection.

Her first dream of this type showed a dead body with a detached head. The face had been completely carved away, leaving a structure without ears, eyes, nose, or mouth. Both arms and legs were also missing. This pathetic image suggested loss of movement as well as the facial elements vital to human interaction and communication. What had been murdered was unidentifiable and separated into many parts. With hindsight, Griffin saw that her wholeness had been severely threatened. Two parts of herself were distinctly divided: thinking (head) had become separated from feeling (body). The face, that which allows us to be recognized, had been removed. Griffin's identity had been stripped away. This powerful warning dream was recorded in her dream journal but not understood or utilized.

Over the next eight years, Griffin's warning dreams continued but were unheeded. This is one of the most common phenomena I've found in researching serial dreams. Perhaps because our culture does not widely value the wisdom of the dream, we rarely recognize the nightly help offered to us. Many people respond to an inner pressure to record powerful warning dreams, but lack the ability or incentive to work with them, so the dream message is unrecognized. This precludes the possibility of playing the role of *consistent remembering* and *transformation.*

But so it was for Griffin. For eight years her dreams presented images of homicide victims. The dead were unknown, suggesting that Griffin was disassociated from the threatened parts of herself. However, after she began therapy and dream-work, the following dream surfaced, showing some progress in awareness:

> I have been killed. Nobody knows it because my body is missing. I am floating around in a spirit state, trying to locate either my body or my killer. I notice something lying on the ground that looks familiar to me. It is a small manila envelope holding my library card and other personal identification.
>
> I join a man who is attempting to help the police find my missing body. We all walk to the nearby

woods where we find my old body lying on the ground. As we watch, vines and flowers begin to grow over and through it.

By this time, Griffin Rose was consistently working with her dreams, and wrote the following in her journal: "A clue to discovering the murdered part of me is contained within issues of personal identity (the envelope). To find what is lost, an unknown masculine energy is needed." These messages urged Griffin to stay focused (masculine energy) on her dreamwork (her spiritual practice) in order to recover her lost identity. This was a pivotal dream in Griffin's series. Referring to the vines and flowers that begin to grow, she wrote: "When made conscious and acknowledged, the deadened, lost self becomes the source of new life."

As the series continued, Griffin Rose reconnected to the images from twenty years before:

I'm visiting a historical site where war has been waged. As I walk, I think about all the people who have been killed here. The ground beneath my feet feels full of something moving, as though the blood of the dead is congealed in certain places and is still alive and calling to me.

This continues the theme of the underground source of life, the collective unconscious. As with other dreams from this series, the dead are still alive and things are definitely moving below the surface.

The surface of the ground becomes transparent, allowing me to see the bodies of the dead, somehow still alive, clamoring for my attention. I walk around

> until I find a large puddle of blood underground. I
> stand there and feel its energy coursing through me.

Having once again connected to this vital life force (blood) reaching upward from the depths, Griffin Rose is confronted by a disgusting element she would normally reject: "While standing in the puddle of blood I am embraced by a friend who confirms the value of this spot. I am embarrassed and upset because my friend smells bad. When I tell her this, she smiles. We embrace and walk off together."

Accepting, embracing, and being with the elements of our being that stink, that repulse us, takes us to a profound level of healing and integration. This heralds the raising of the dead, so to speak, for in the next piece Griffin finds ways to bring the dead back to life.

What has been dead and buried now begins to resurface in many dream scenes. In one dream, Griffin finds skeletons washed up on a beach near her home. In another, she walks among the dead. The following stunning dream occurred in 1995 while Griffin was on a trip with a merry band of dreamers and me. We had traveled to Canyon de Chelly in northern Arizona. Perhaps stimulated by this spectacular Navajo and Hopi site, the original home of the Anastazis, she recalled the following dream, set in the Canyon of the Dead (Canyon del Muertos), an area we had toured the preceding day. She shared it as we all sat in our large four-wheel-drive vehicle perched on the edge of the canyon. Lulled by the patter of rain on the car roof, we were transported to an altered state by this beautiful piece.

> I am walking along the riverbed at Canyon del
> Muertos. A part of me rises to the top of the canyon.

The Higher Me observes the Walking Me as a small, moving element in a huge expanse of land and sky. From above I can see that ghosts are rising from the imprints of my footsteps on damp ground. My walking releases the ghosts from the Earth. The released ghosts follow me through the canyon.

Soon, the path behind me and the cliffs around me are filled with the ghosts. The Walking Me can sense but not comprehend the ghosts. Only the Higher Me can see them clearly.

I continue walking and find myself in a room of dreamers. I listen to a woman telling a dream about being afraid to enter a small dark room. I thoroughly identify with the woman's fear until the group leader intervenes, pointing out that the dream itself does not give any indication that the dark room is unsafe. It is the dreamer's fears that seem to be creating the barrier to entry. Suddenly, I see the room described by the dreamer. Although I feel uneasy, I am able and willing to enter the room with a relatively neutral mind. I let go of preconceptions and let the place speak for itself. My fears are still with me but they no longer possess me.

This stunning dream deserves careful scrutiny. As we often do in dream groups, we will examine this dream bit by bit.

"I am walking along the riverbed at Canyon del Muertos." Here she is, the skeleton-and-bones lady, in the Canyon of the Dead.

Next there is a split in her consciousness, allowing Griffin to simultaneously be both witness and participant. Paraphrasing

the dream for clarity, Griffin wrote this interpretative addition to
her journal:

> A part of me rises to the top of the canyon. It observes
> the Walking Me as a small, moving element in a huge
> expanse of land and sky. From above I can see that
> ghosts are rising from the imprints of my footsteps on
> damp ground. The ghosts are following me through
> the canyon, as my walking releases the ghosts from
> the Earth.
>
> Soon the path behind me, and the cliffs around
> me, are filled with the ghosts. The Walking Me can
> sense but not comprehend the ghosts. Only the
> Higher Me can see them clearly.

Griffin continues walking until she finds herself in a room
with dreamers. She listens to a woman telling a dream about
being afraid to enter a small dark room. Griffin Rose thoroughly
identifies with the woman's fear until the group leader intervenes:

> The woman leading the group tells the dreamer that
> the dream itself does not give any indication that the
> dark room is unsafe. It is the dreamer's fears that
> seems to be creating the barrier to entry.

This statement impacts dream ego powerfully, allowing her to
see the truth in the statement and the dream. She enters into the
scary dream room herself.

> Although I feel uneasy, I am able and willing to enter
> the room with a relatively neutral mind. I let go of

preconceptions and let the place speak for itself. My fears are still with me but they no longer possess me.

The waking-life trip to the canyon seemed to initiate an essentially fearless "opening" for Griffin. While there, and in the days following this dream, she sensed that she was at a profound turning point in her life. Indeed, within weeks of her return from the trip, Griffin Rose sold her house and prepared to change jobs. That accomplished within two months, she soon began putting her attention to the avocation she deeply wanted to develop. Before the passage of two more months, she had begun a dream resource center and a bimonthly dream publication. In addition, she volunteered as a news director of another dream magazine.

During this frenzy of awake activity, Griffin seemed to expand before our eyes. It was as if all the wizened, atrophied parts of herself inflated into a brilliantly colored and highly active entity. Her dreams changed dramatically, showing scenes of very personal connections to the resurrection process, showing images of what had been deeply buried connecting with dream ego. A progression of dreams shows the following: In one dream the dead rise up to the surface. In another, skeletons wash up on a beach. Then dream ego engages in a research project to reuse dead bodies in constructive ways. Dream ego takes on a new role as a Dead Rights Activist to ensure that what has died will be identified properly and treated with respect.

Griffin Rose identified the final dreams in the series as *transformation/integration* dreams. In the first of these, she sees what at first appears to be her own reflection. It is, in dream fact, a skull surfacing from the ground. She unearths the entire skeleton, slings it over her back and takes it with her. She writes: "I am able to see myself in the symbol for the first time. I accept the responsibility of taking this skeleton, this essence of who I am, and making it a part of what I consciously carry through life."

After this powerful reuniting with the long-dead essence of herself, Griffin Rose is able to become a healer. In this dream, called "The Boneworker," dream ego cuts deeply into her leg to touch her living thigh bone. In her journal, Griffin wrote, "I am committing myself to getting into the deepest parts of myself and to working with them in a healing way."

The skeletal images become more personal and even animated and useful as dream ego purchases jewelry containing skeletons to accompany a newly designed outfit (persona, sense of self). In her next series dream, dream ego purchases a skeleton-shaped telephone to enhance communication. Finally, she adds a wonderful new piece of furniture to her home, a rocking chair made entirely of bones! Not only do the bones allow her to communicate (telephone); they also support and soothe her!

In the twenty-first dream of the series, we are brought full circle to the original dream by profoundly and beautifully reconnecting to roses once again. Both Griffin Rose and I felt that this awesome dream should be admired, appreciated, and accepted without interpretation.

> In a forest I find a skeleton covered by moist dirt. As I watch, a rose begins to grow from the mouth. Within the rose is a glowing crystal that reaches out, like a snake, to wrap itself around the rib cage and through the eye sockets.
>
> The rose-enshrouded skeleton rises up and enters my body. Now the rose is moving through me like blood in my veins. Suddenly the rose reaches out

from within me. As it wraps around a tree, I become the tree. Now, inside the tree that I am, I see Deep Woman emerging from the shadowy internal bark, her skin dappled with all the colors and lights of the earth and forest.

As this astounding piece continues, the scene shifts to dream ego, still contained within the skeleton, becoming aware of a doctor/healer called Lily. Lily instructs dream ego/skeleton to lie upon the leaves under the tree where the skeleton was originally found. "I do so and feel the skeleton inside me shifting, aligning itself once again with the ground. My stomach begins to glow. Lily tells me that something is growing there. I am fearful but she assures me that everything is fine. Although I am anxious, I continue to lie there, feeling a baby within me. I realize this is all part of the great cycle of birth, death, and rebirth. I feel at peace."

Thus ends this phenomenal series of dreams that has taken us below the surface of the conscious realm into the depths to reconnect with the ancestors and to enliven what has been dead and buried. It is impossible to prove that working on this series had any connection with the amazing shifts in mood, sense of self, and awake-world activity experienced by Griffin Rose. However, those of us who watched her transformation during this period had little doubt that what was brought to the surface during this study activated Griffin Rose in profound, life-altering ways. Would the same transformation have occurred if Griffin had not spent time and energy weaving together these twenty-one dreams? There is no way to know that. Perhaps dreams of this magnitude will do their work without conscious involvement. Personally, I doubt it.

CHAPTER EIGHT

The Significant Other

Dreamer: Carla
Recurring symbol: former lover
Length of dream series: 25 years
Number of dreams presented: 57
Script messages addressed:
"A woman is nothing without a man."
"Doing is more important than being."
"You will never be fully accepted by the patriarchy because you are a woman."
Benefits to the dreamer:
Overcame her fear of upsetting dreams about a former lover.
Learned that distressing dreams contain information that leads to healing.
More fully recognized the healthy development that resulted from leaving a destructive relationship.
Acknowledged healthy and unhealthy aspects of her inner masculine (ways of thinking and doing).
Dream approaches: Examining the progression of dream ego throughout a lengthy series.

Summary: After decades of fearing her distressing dreams about a former lover, a 60-year-old woman is able to see the important inner development that these dreams encourage and reflect.

"Oh, no! Not him again!" Dreams containing images of a former lover, spouse, or other significant relationship often leave in their wake a burdensome dream hangover. These emotionally charged dreams may create a wide spectrum of feelings, from anger or depression to hope and intense joy. For years we may feel haunted by dreams about a person who was once cast as a star in our awake-life drama. It's not easy to understand the significance of this dream character, because a former lover or important friend carries a broad range of associations: the stronger the emotional connections in the awake realm, the greater the complexity of possible meaning in the dream world.

When sharing these dreams with friends we tend to say, "I had a dream about Fred last night." This statement may or may not be accurate. The Fred character may refer to a biological person named Fred, perhaps reflecting information about his condition at the time of the dream. Perhaps such a dream mirrors the dreamer's feelings about Fred at the time of the dream. Examining the dream character imaged as Fred may lead the dreamer to identify something formerly recognized about her relationship with Fred, bringing a surprising "aha!" reaction. Or the dreamer may identify a previously unrecognized aspect of Fred's personality. All of these possibilities present objective information—aspects of an actual person named Fred—about an external reality, former or present. And there is yet another facet of good old Fred: a representation of some aspect of the dreamer. For example, women often learn about the condition of their own inner masculine principle when examining a dream "about" a male partner, past or present.

In my practice clients often present dreams featuring people with whom they are having or have had a relationship. I often find that these dream characters reflect both inner and outer aspects of the dreamer's life or state of being. Let's pretend that Joe and Fiona are lovers. When Fiona's dreams contain a character identified as Joe, the dream may be reflecting something about the actual person Joe, and about their relationship as it exists at the time of the dream. These *interpersonal dreams* often contain information vital to the health of the relationship. If the relationship becomes dysfunctional, dreams may help the dreamer identify the problem and repair or prepare to leave a relationship. After a relationship has ended, dreams may help to process the grief of the loss and/or to clarify the mystifying aspects of the breakup. Dreams may address such questions as: What really happened between us? How do I deal with it now? What do I need to know to protect myself from making a similar choice in the future? How did I participate in the creation of the problems that led to the dissolution of the relationship? What could I have done differently? How do I heal and prepare myself for my next intimate connection?

It's also possible that dreams depicting a former partner may be *intrapersonal*, telling the dreamer something she needs to recognize about herself. If the dream lover is pictured at a specific age, perhaps twenty years younger than he is at the time of the dream, psyche may be presenting characteristics of who Fiona thought Joe was twenty years before. On the day of the dream Fiona may need to be reminded that she is now acting or feeling as Joe did twenty years before. For example, if, during their relationship twenty years earlier, Joe withdrew every time he became frightened, his presence in Fiona's dream may indicate that Fiona is dealing with the world in a fearful, withdrawn, limiting way. If the dream shows her "married to" or "in bed with" Joe, the dream may present a warning about her present intimate embrace with fear.

A good, clear look at a lover can be a gift brought by the dream. I recall a client besieged by dreams of a former lover for whom she still yearned. The man was considered a sleaze and a scoundrel by nearly everyone who knew him. However, to the dreamer he was the incarnation of all that was holy—that is, until her dreams showed her beloved in the stark light of truth. In a short and potent series, the adored one appeared as an obnoxious clown, as a snake swishing through the grass, as a greasy-haired, gun-toting, Mafia hit man, and as a pathetic young child with a chest wound that could never be healed. By looking at all of these dream images with complete openness, the dreamer was able to admit that she had blinded herself to her former lover's glaring faults and betrayals. As a result, she was able to stop yearning for someone who did not exist.

The language used by the dreamer to define the significant other in the dream is extremely important. The character is likely to be described in strongly emotional terms. When asked to describe the former lover, the dreamer may respond with, "She was the love of my life," or "No one ever victimized me like this man," or "She was someone I loved who never loved me in return," or "He was all I ever wanted." The dreamer may use several paradoxical definitions to describe the same person because some love relationships (or love-hate relationships) are multifaceted. The specific dream content, or the dreamer's mood when approaching the dream, may cause one particular aspect to shine most brilliantly, revealing wildly contradictory definitions of the same individual in different dreams.

A female writer described a former lover as "the love of my life" and their relationship as "the most passionate and joyful experience I've ever had." Her dreams containing this character became clear when we applied those definitions, seeing the dream lover as a representation of her awake-life passion at the time of the dream. The following dream illustrates this approach.

Due to family crises and business trips, Molly—an author—had been separated from her writing projects for many months when she dreamed the following about her once-beloved Steve.

> Steve has finally divorced his wife. I prepare for his return, thrilled that he is now free to join me. While in a bookstore buying a book on flying, I see Steve and run to him in anticipation of a joyful reunion. He ignores me. I hear from others that he is deeply in love with a beautiful Native American woman. I can understand his love for her, but why didn't he return to me before he found her?

Molly awoke feeling devastated. "It's as if I have had another chance for real happiness and lost it," she reported.

First we looked at the meaning of Steve leaving his wife. (This was a symbolic statement, Steve's marriage being very much intact.) The biased dreamer defined Steve's wife as whiny, demanding and controlling, and insecure. "She guards Steve as if he were a prisoner. She has a bunch of dysfunctional kids, always in crisis, who really keep Steve locked up."

Feeding back this information, I said: "So the love of your life has finally left a whining, controlling, insecure feminine force that has kept it imprisoned for a long time."

"Well, I can see that the description of the wife is a reflection of me during the past months! My kids have been in crisis, I've been whining about all their stuff while determined to control their lives. All this chaos has kept me separate from what I really love—that is, my creative work. I understand that it is important to leave or divorce this part of myself. I recently told a friend that I am determined to return to my book regardless of what happens within my family."

I asked why dream Steve ignored dream ego and chose the Native American girl. Molly explained, "Even before my affair with Steve I always loved writing. I really believe that I am most natural and authentic when I write. In a way this is my native nature." After some reflection, Molly continued: "This dream tells me that the part of me that is the love of my life, my passion for writing, is not interested in my martyred mother persona. Instead, it chooses my native talent, the writer!"

As we sat in silence appreciating the brilliance of the dream, Molly added: "I just realized that a great day of writing or painting is as filled with passion and fulfillment as making love to Steve. At the end of such a time I go to bed feeling a peace and joy similar to my best years with Steve."

It is easy to see why dreamers become confused and frustrated with dreams showing former lovers and spouses. This was certainly true for Carla, a former dream client, who had been bothered by her "Andy Dreams" for twenty-five years. The need to understand which one of the plethora of possibilities he represented motivated her to begin a series study. As is usually the case at the beginning of such an undertaking, Carla could not find her way through the immense forest of possible associations to see the individual tree identified as Andy. "He represented so much to me. As my boss, he was a professional mentor. During our good times, he was a sophisticated, funny, and wonderful lover. During the bad years, he was an alcoholic and a womanizer. Throughout the entire relationship, Andy was a prodigious and productive worker and business leader. He was the most influential person in my life. I thought of him as my savior until I could see that his addiction to alcohol and other women was totally destructive. How in the world can I see who he is in each of the hundreds of dreams that I've either recorded or rejected during nearly a quarter century?"

How, indeed? The first suggestion I offer to dreamers beginning such a daunting study is to go forward unhampered by preconceived notions. As you record and begin to examine each dream, admit that you have no clue who or what the significant other represents in this piece. Be willing to detach yourself from the emotions that overtake you as you consider each dream because, if unchecked, they will snap you back to the feelings of the past which may or may not have anything to do with the message of the dream.

This last piece of advice may be disturbing to therapists who use dreams for the purpose of activating *catharsis*, a strong emotional response to a former, unrecognized, or unprocessed trauma. This may be a valid use of the dream within a therapeutic setting. However, working with dreams in leaderless groups or with a lay dreamworker is usually a very different process from working under the guidance of a trained therapist. Unbridled emotions have the potential to sweep away the significant content of the dream, destroying the awareness and healing it provides. Like an avalanche in the high country, emotional storms can bury the dream's intention to reveal another way of seeing oneself or the significant other. Therefore, setting aside the knee-jerk response to "that nasty-so-and-so" or "my savior" is conducive to producing very useful and growth-enhancing insights.

In my practice, the most dramatic example of this need to get past the emotional reaction to the dream began with a call from a woman who was sobbing so that I could barely understand her. An "abusive" dream involving her former husband rendered her nearly paralyzed. When she arrived for her appointment (driven by a friend), Jane was still in a nearly hysterical state. She had been so upset by the dream that she had not been able to write it. Believing that a written form is essential for full understanding, I sat with Jane as she committed this dream to paper. She then read it to me through her tears. Essentially, the dream was a life-giving piece loaded with eight specific, valid, empowering suggestions for dealing with her former spouse if he should verbally attack her in the upcoming mediation sessions Jane so feared. Buried in the avalanche of her fear, Jane was unable to see these brilliant ideas, even while reading the dream to me. I wanted her to recognize the rescuing qualities of the material so I slowly read the dream to her. The light bulbs began to flash from the very first sentence as Jane moved from her patterned old feelings and literal interpretations to symbolic awareness, from emotion to metaphor, from seeing the dream through the eyes of a victim to looking for the healing it supplied. In the following months, Jane clung to the suggestions from her dream, which served very well in situations with her former spouse. This valuable guidance would have been lost had she been unable to extricate herself from the powerful emotional storm the dream evoked.

Though it is difficult for people to be objective about former "heartthrobs" or "victimizers," an unemotional examination of the dream is essential. This category of dream is fraught with the pitfall of literalism into which so many dreamers fall, preventing understanding of the dream's intent. Step back, be objective, and ask the same kinds of questions about a former lover or spouse as you would about a stranger. Take into account the locale of the dream and the age the characters seem to be. Carefully examine the attitudes and behaviors of the dream character represented by the significant other. If, for example, the former love is acting immature and whiny in the dream, this may be an accurate reading: "I am dealing with an immature and needy energy that betrayed me in the past." You may then see a part of yourself or another person who is betraying you in your present life.

Carla and I began her dream study by e-mail but found this unsatisfactory. I flew to her home in Arizona so we could physically join forces in this complex and important dream exploration. Despite her experience as an avid dream student in previous years, Carla fell into all the pits so common in this emotionally "loaded" type of study. We hit one wall after another as Carla sought literal interpretations for each dream scene.

When doing intense dreamwork it is easy to recognize hitting a wall or a dream dead end. The feeling is one of simply roaming in circles, baying at the sky like the coyotes outside the walls of Carla's home. After a long period of probing the dream for associations, we would look at each other like two giant question marks. So what? Where does this lead us? No connections had been made. When, after examining the dream for a while, Carla had realized nothing new about herself, her former friend, or her relationship with him, we assumed that we were experiencing "dead end-itis." Even banging our heads together was ineffective until we devised the following strategy.

Carla and I created a simple list of questions designed to determine what the dream was not. This allowed us to swing in another direction, using the list to move quickly through the myriad possibilities and achieve a sharper, more productive focus.

Possible reasons for dreaming about a former spouse or significant other:

1. Process dream:
   a. Evoking emotions necessary to resolve grief.
   b. Evoking emotions necessary to resolve trauma.
2. Warning dream:
   a. A former destructive dynamic is repeating in another relationship.
   b. A former destructive dynamic is recurring within the dreamer.
3. Awareness dream (removing the rose-colored glasses and acknowledging the shadow):
   a. Finally recognizing the truth about the other.
   b. Finally recognizing the truth about self.
4. Symbolic dream:
   a. The other represents an inner aspect of the dreamer.
   b. The other represents a project or way of doing or thinking (if the dream character is male) or a feeling or way of being or feeling (if the dream character is a female).

When Carla and I ran each dream through this sieve we were able to separate the seeds from the juice. Here is what we found.

Carla recorded her first Andy dream in 1976 when they were still an active, but unmarried, couple. It was at this time that Carla first suspected Andy of being unfaithful. The dream seems a clear warning of what would happen if the relationship progressed into marriage. As is often the case with the first dream of a long series, Carla had quickly jotted this piece in a journal but had no idea how to work with or heed its warning.

1976: Ocean House without a View

Andy and I, recently married, have moved into a house on the ocean. I am anxious to show off my house to my women co-workers. Everything is perfect when they arrive until waves begin breaking over the top of the house, throwing wet sand against the windows. I know there is no immediate danger but the view is obscured by the wet sand. The women are alarmed and leave.

I tell Andy what happened but he is unconcerned.

Examining the dream through the lens of hindsight twenty-five years after it was recorded, Carla clearly saw the warning it contained. "When I commit to [marry] a person who is lying and cheating [Andy at the time of this dream], I am overwhelmed by emotions [waves] that thoroughly obscure my vision. In addition, this dream reminded me that I had thought of my relationship with Andy as something to show off, as a way of gaining respect and increasing self-esteem. I was still ruled by the notion that a woman is nothing without a man. I thought that the more powerful and admirable the man, the more I rose in value. Naturally, Andy is unconcerned about the crisis that is threatening [the waves]. He did not care that our relationship was in the terminal stage. I was the one feeling all the pain."

Eventually, Carla gathered the courage to end the affair. She went on to important new work, professionally and personally, and married a loving and committed man. During these years Carla recorded the frequent and upsetting dreams that created the "Andy" series. From 1982 to 2000, Carla recorded fifty dreams in which Andy was a character. She estimates that she had at least that number that she had not recorded. "The dreams always depressed me. I just wanted to ignore them and get on with my life." But eventually, rather than continue with the tyranny of this dream experience, Carla hoped that confronting the dreams would either cause them to stop or render them harmless.

Like the other dream series presented, this one has more aspects than can be discussed here. Therefore, we focused on the transformation of dream ego as the series advanced, and the emergence of four categories into which dreams fell. We start with the transformation of dream ego because that most clearly reflects the important role a dream series plays in the area of psycho-spiritual development.

Like many people in the midst of a crisis, Carla was compelled to record these dreams, though she was unable to consciously understand their important messages. (The act of writing such painful dreams provides relief for those suffering from loss and confusion.) Nor did Carla work with these dreams when they occurred. For the first seven years of the series (which began two months after the end of the relationship) most of the dreams symbolically presented Carla, dream ego, as experiencing only painful emotions. In chronological order from the first to the seventh recorded dream, Carla *avoided* conversations about breakup and *felt panicked* about her transition to being a single woman. She *felt terror* about the separation, using these words to describe her myriad reactions to either Andy or the dream situations: *hurt, used, rejected, confused, pissed,* and *burning mad.* Two dreams showed Carla as *displaced,* having no place to sit, not feeling accepted by others. Three of these dreams described Andy as getting married, as moving on in one way or another, leaving Carla *feeling rejected, lost,* and *angry.* Andy had not married, so these dreams seem to fall into the category of process dreams, expressing feelings (including wanting to scream and cry) that needed to be expelled.

In the first dream signifying growth, Carla experiences many familiar, upsetting emotions but shifts her awareness when she realizes that "It is only my ego that is hurt." This provided a sense of another self, an observer self, with awareness of emotional options other than pain. The following dream is the first in the series that indicates a sense of self-determination, of taking charge and moving on. This dream occurred seven years after the end of her relationship with Andy and one month after Carla joined her first dream group.

In this powerful dream Andy and Carla are together, stuck in an elevator. Carla decides this will not do and takes action to remedy the situation.

February 4, 1989: I Won't Stay Stuck!
I'm in a high-rise office building reminiscent of where
Andy and I worked together. We are having a farewell
party as our division is shutting down. The elevator we
are in shakes and rattles to a stop. We are stuck and on
a tilt. We are told it will be a long time before help

will arrive. I say, "I will not stay here. I'm going to try something." I push the number four button. The elevator goes up from the second floor and then stops. There is a stained glass window, like a church, on the side of the elevator. I break out one section, making room for me and my grandson to escape.

This dream says that it is time for the old ways of working with Andy to end ("We are having a farewell party as our division is shutting down"). A sense of being stuck and unbalanced still exists. Unlike previous dreams, this one shows dream ego refusing to be victimized by these circumstances and taking charge. Accompanied by a developing masculine (Carla's grandson was five years old at the time of this dream), Carla will not remain stuck on the second floor. In an Eastern symbology familiar to Carla, the second level of consciousness, or *chakra*, represents relationships; the fourth level represents both wholeness and the beginning of spiritual development. Thus, Carla breaks through the stained glass window to escape to wholeness with her developing potential (grandson), leaving the old relationship behind.

That accomplishment seemed to invite a new perspective from psyche, for the next dream in the series depicted Andy looking like Einstein (whom Carla equated with revolutionary thought) and urging Carla to forget him and move on with her life!

This was the end of the sequential dreams showing Carla as a victim. There were, however, three more in the series, each with milder affect. It seems that these dreams continued to discharge the negative emotions connected to the actual demise of the relationship. It amazed Carla that this grieving and raging process lasted for seven years. We speculated that the victim dreams were triggered by awake-life events that threatened

Carla's sense of self, but cannot corroborate that, as Carla recorded only dreams in her journal.

The tide began to turn from overwhelming despair to self-empowerment when Carla actively and consciously engaged with her dreams by joining a dream group. Speaking to this coincidence Carla wrote, "By working with my dreams I stopped being a victim of them and the unhealed inner dynamics they portrayed. After years of casting myself as the rejected victim in relationships and seeing that self-image so clearly in my dreams, I was really ready to have a positive shift in my life. I think that recording the dreams, even though their meaning was veiled to me at the time, began to heal my inner masculine and my sense of self. By more consciously engaging with these dreams I have been able to develop in many ways. To a great extent, I feel as if this work is helping me to grow up, an odd feeling for a woman of my age!"

Though odd to Carla, her feeling of growing up is common for middle-aged people as their dreamwork advances. As we have seen with other studies in this book, the discipline of regularly recording and working with dreams both activates and develops the masculine, which brings with it a sense of personal power. Dreamwork often leads to action that resolves problems in the material world. This, too, exemplifies masculine energy. (By contrast, simply worrying or imagining solutions with no behavioral follow-through is characteristic of the feminine principle divorced from the masculine.)

The following dream illustrates additional determination and growth.

November 16, 1994: Farewell to Andy
Because I'm going away, Andy and I are getting together to say goodbye. I am giving him three pictures:

one of me as a baby, another of me as a little girl with my father, and one of me as a grown-up. Andy arrives late and drunk. He seems disinterested in what I have given him. He gives me a used card! This is the last straw. I prepare to leave, once and for all. Now that I am leaving Andy is getting amorous. I just want to get out of here.

This dream has three important elements: the pictures of Carla maturing ("one of me as a baby, another of me as a little girl with my father, and one of me as a grown-up"), the image of a drunk Andy, and Carla's response to Andy. The three pictures show Carla at various developmental stages, from dependency to maturity, suggesting that personal growth is necessary to separate from a painful and dysfunctional past.

"Drunk Andy" became a theme within the series. These dreams encouraged Carla to remove her rose-colored glasses about the actual Andy, and alerted her to the need to eliminate her own addictions. Because Carla does not suffer from substance or activity addictions, we suspected that the "Drunk Andy" dreams arose when she was in danger of activating some aspect of unconscious, destructive relationship behavior. This form of addiction was vigorously activated during her last years with Andy.

"Farewell to Andy" shows Carla's refusal to stay and play the old games with Andy, the addicted part of her psyche. Dream ego becomes determined to escape from the uncaring and unconscious masculine. (The importance of this decision is seen in the final dream of the series.) The remainder of this dream is about a journey through a cactus field, suggesting that bidding farewell to formerly destructive relationships, from others or from parts of our selves, is a prickly aspect of the journey to health.

In addition to the recurring sub-theme of "Drunk Andy," a majority of Carla's remaining dreams fell roughly into three other motifs: "Yearning for Andy," "Rejecting Andy," and "The Other Woman." (The rest of the dreams defy categorization!) The recurring motifs in this type of series are quite common, so we will briefly describe the salient elements of each.

"The Other Woman" theme began two months after Carla ended her relationship with Andy. The theme continued for fifteen years, appearing in seven dreams. The first three dreams, which occurred within a year of the breakup, could have been reinforcing the fact of Andy's infidelity, helping Carla to reconcile the separation. It would be easy to dismiss these dreams as just reliving the anxiety from her past, but that would do a disservice to the dreams. We could also diminish the dreams by suggesting that each dream popped up when Carla felt rejected or threatened in her awake life. Let's probe a little deeper by remembering the words of Jeremy Taylor: that every dream comes in the service of healing and wholeness. Given that, what else might psyche want Carla to learn about herself from dreams of Andy involved with other women?

Let's break into this question by examining a dream that came just a few months after the breakup. Carla dreams that Andy is getting married. She feels hurt that he is moving on so quickly, is not mourning the loss of her. Does this simply reflect that men usually put former relationships and problems behind them more quickly than women? (Psychologists suggest that is one reason that more women than men tend to suffer with depression.) That awareness is not particularly helpful to Carla, so let's examine this dream from the theory of the animus, the masculine principle. If Andy represents that principle within Carla, and if the masculine is about doing and thinking, then perhaps for her betterment, psyche is suggesting that Carla get "married," develop an inner integration needed for her to develop without Andy. If integration is called for then we must see what is apparent about the feminine (the feeling and being component) in these dreams.

In three dreams, the other woman was described thus: "about my age and quite average; dowdy and unattractive, warm and responsive, surprisingly gray, and slightly overweight." Carla remarked that none of these dream women threatened her in any way. Compared to them, she, Carla, was far more attractive and appealing. So, is psyche trying to show Carla that her emotions (the woman/feminine) were quite ordinary and average, not spectacular in any way? That they were indeed gray and heavy? That they need not threaten her? This line of questioning brought the "aha!" response from Carla. Like most people raised in post-World War II American culture, Carla valued characteristics of the masculine far more than those of the feminine. "Feelings just get in the way of living a successful life. They take time and interfere with getting the laundry done and raising the kids." (She had raised two daughters.) Carla thus rejected her feelings by judging them as somehow wrong. This limited her ability to process her emotional reality. For many, the preference for doing over feeling limits development. If Carla could recognize the ordinariness of her feelings she could embrace them and move on.

One of the other women was described as "the inheritress." By coining that word, was Carla asking herself to look at what she had inherited as it related to Andy and relationships in general? Did it invite her to examine what beliefs and ideas she had inherited about moving on or being emotionally stuck? Unfortunately, with dreams this old, we cannot answer these questions. If you are dealing with dreams like this, however, I encourage you to engage with all the details of the dream instead of discarding "the other woman" dreams as simple (or complex) anxiety.

"Yearning for the lost love" is a common theme for this type of significant other series. Such dreams are often discharged as a literal longing for the former times. However, in Carla's case, this made no sense. "If Andy showed up at my door I wouldn't let him in. I have no desire to reconnect to who he was in any way." And yet the dreams persisted, off and on, for nearly two decades. Remembering that Andy represented so many various qualities, both negative and positive, provides a direction, or at least some good questions. For what would Carla be yearning that Andy had to offer? The only qualities that were never tarnished by inappropriate or addictive behavior were Andy's business skills. Because he was very focused, he accomplished a great deal as an extremely successful businessman. As Carla's mentor, Andy was a model for business excellence. After leaving Andy, Carla hit her stride as a successful businesswoman. Shortly thereafter she remarried, retiring from her field to enjoy a more leisurely life with her new husband. Carla is a woman of many talents, and it is possible that her retirement was premature and kept her from realizing the full benefit of her training and ability. The yearning dreams, then, may have reflected this loss of masculine or doing energy in the world. In addition, after leaving her field Carla found it difficult to follow her involvement in hobbies and other interests to a satisfactory conclusion. She became passionate about something only to wander away from it before it reached fruition. As in her frustrating and upsetting dreams, she was left yearning for something she seemed unable to have.

Thus, the "Yearning" dreams bring balance to the "Other Woman" theme, highlighting the search for equilibrium so obvious in many dreams. A healthy psyche is a married psyche, an integrated whole of both doing and feeling, thinking and being, logic and intuition. Of all of the studies in this book, I think Carla's is the best example of this important inner dynamic, which is discussed further at the end of this chapter.

The final category, "Rejecting Andy" dreams, usually showed Andy as either drunk or disheveled, looking awful in a variety of ways, or driving vehicles ready for the junk heap. In several of these dreams, Carla felt the familiar yearning but then realized that Andy was no longer desirable. The dreams ended with her desire to escape from Andy. The pertinent question in this category of dreams is, "What am I rejecting and from what do I wish to escape?" Because we are always growing and changing, therefore, what we once sought—what served us in the past—changes and must be discarded so that we can move on. This type of dream may have surfaced when Carla needed to be reminded that something she once valued was no longer desirable and needed to be dismissed.

Due to the wide variety of associations to, and projections about, a significant other, the character may play as many dream roles as the flesh-and-blood person does in the awake world. In addition, a woman's partner may represent the masculine principle—ways of doing, thinking, accomplishing in the world. Therefore, the dream feeling of betrayal may well be warning the dreamer that she is not being true to herself in these ways. Correspondingly, the other woman may show the development

of a new way of feeling or relating to others, the feminine principle, the ways of being with oneself and others.

In many of Carla's dreams Andy represented her masculine
aspect, which went through many incarnations in this long
series. Late dreams from this series show growth and transformation in this significant other character, reflecting Carla's inner
development.

> *March 3, 1999: Andy's New Office in Hawaii*
> A group of us are walking across a freshly plowed field
> in Hawaii to see Andy's new office. I feel the warm,
> moist earth between my bare toes. The office building
> is the very attractive mission style. Andy looks very
> good as he shows us his office and indicates that the
> office next door will be mine. I am surprised to hear
> this. I don't think I will be working here but I say
> nothing. As I leave the offices I see they are in the
> center of a house. I wonder why these people choose
> to live in a house with an office in the center. I exit
> through the baby's room.

According to the dream, this masculine is clearly not disrep-
utable in any way. He is working in a fertile place ready to welcome and nurture new growth. If this represents Carla's thinking
process and/or her ability to accomplish life goals, this is a positive image. The attractive mission style may refer to life mission,
spiritual goals, or even the individuation process, also suggested
by the reference to center, as wholeness is thought to be at the
center of the Self. The notion that the workplace is the same as
the living place further connotes the lifetime work of personal
growth and development. Ego is not ready to work here and exits

through the baby's room. Is an escape from such a commitment infantile? It is often true that the ego or personality lags behind other aspects of the psyche. Or it may be, now that the masculine is healed and working in a healthy way, ego can move back out into the world through a new project (baby).

About this Carla wrote, "The dream suggests that I still have some fear of joining the masculine process in this growing place and thus decline the offer because I'm not quite ready for partnership with this healthy way of doing business. I guess I have to exit through the baby's room because a little more ego growth is needed."

Dream ego's reluctance seems remedied in the next dream, which occurred twenty-five years after the first recorded dream and shows wonderful healing and perhaps the purpose of this important inner work.

> *January 2000: Boogie Dream*
> I am having a great time dancing wildly to boogie woogie music. Andy steps into the circle and begins to dance with me. We dance together with abandon— he throws me over his shoulder and between his legs, performing all the great boogie steps as we dance with great abandon, like champions. As Andy turns to leave the circle he says, "I just wanted to show you what partnership looks like."

What a great transformation occurred from the beginning dreams about "Andy the Sleaze" (who abandons Carla) to the dreams about an Andy who demonstrates and encourages partnership. And in the end, that is the point of dreamwork: creating a marvelous partnership with the parts of our own psyche by which we have previously been hurt or from which we have been separated. Working with these often painful dreams of lost love or abusive relationships is vital to our healing and wholeness.

Carla wrote, "One of the interesting elements of the boogie dream is that I am doing very well on my own, having a great time, ecstatic in my solo dance. But when the masculine partner appears the dance is richer, fuller, and more complete. This has been evidenced in my awake life. When I am needy I fall victim in relationships, but when I am complete, functional in my own right, I attract what is healthy and joyful. Another interesting element is the dream language: 'Andy steps into the circle.' The dream never defines the circle but it sure feels like coming to wholeness. To me, the word *partnership* means joining forces to accomplish a common goal or purpose.

"In addition, I have recently been able, without concern, to speak out when something bothers me, in my personal and social life. I am finally fighting for equal rights for women in my small community. I am working with needy children, a job that takes a lot of determined masculine energy. As I write this I can feel a sense of accomplishment, self-pride, and personal value that seems far more mature than rejecting the job in the Hawaii dream. I really do feel more mature, never mind that I'm in my sixties!" It is surely never too late for the development of the Self.

Nearly two years after the Boogie dream Carla presented another dream that begged to be included in this study. She felt the dream contained a broad, archetypal truth that clarified the patriarchal cultural script that had, to a degree, limited her and created many of the problems addressed by the Andy dreams. Carla described this last piece as unusual because it was more like a philosophical overview than a drama.

Prior to bedtime on the night of the dream, Carla had been very energized by a television program about the unfair treatment of American women prior to laws prohibiting sexual discrimination in the workplace.

> *November 2001: The Hatred of the Fathers*
> Andy is ignoring me in a public place and I'm feeling rejected and angry. Suddenly Andy becomes a combination of every man, including my father, with whom I have been in relationship. The feeling of rejection intensifies and I turn to leave this place, unable to bear the humiliation I feel once again. Something compels me to return to this Composite Man to ask him what I have to do to make myself acceptable to him. I am really asking what it would take to be loved by this rejecting and judgmental character but I cannot bring myself to ask that.
> Composite Man is very sympathetic and replies it is not him but his father who will not accept me. I know by this that he means all the Fathers throughout history. I feel profound grief realizing that there is no way to be loved by the Fathers.

The grief of the dream followed Carla into her awake state and mingled with thoughts of the television program she had viewed the night before. As she ruminated about the dream, the program, and her past, she was assailed by very old, deep feelings that had been her response to the "patriarchal society in which I was raised." Carla recalled a variety of experiences from her past in which she had been discounted, ignored, overlooked, rejected, bullied, or betrayed by men, including her father. Her

emotions ranged from the sorrow of being discounted and belit-
tled to the rage evoked by violent treatment of women throughout the ages and continuing to this day. She felt intense anger
against all men throughout history who had been responsible for
shoddy treatment of women.

Carla wondered why this dream surfaced when it did. Was
it just a response to the television program, offering her an
opportunity to process old emotions? Was this piece particularly
potent due to the current media coverage of atrocities against
women in Afghanistan and other countries? Although both of
these possibilities are valid, the dream evoked deeper emotions
than would be warranted by these explanations. Searching further, Carla realized that the Composite Man carried the feeling
of an archetype, and the dynamic between him and dream ego
suggested the universal pattern (addressed throughout her previous Andy dreams) of the masculine and the feminine principle.

Our exploration of the dream led to discussion about the
widespread distrust/hatred of the feminine principle, the inner
qualities that bring so much meaning and value to life. As
reflected by nine other dream studies in this book, this bias is
confronted by both men and women who are striving to live life
consciously. This outer and inner bias is addressed more often
than any other in the dreams that I hear in my dream practice.
It appears that there is great need to confront society's denigra-
tion of the feeling realm, of intuition, of inner work in general,
and of being receptively in the moment.

I find it amazing that the need to rewrite scripts that deni-
grate the feminine principle and alter the masculine principle
was a significant part of more than two-thirds of the studies for
this book. (The studies that address this issue are listed in the
introduction.) As is obvious in all of the studies in this book,

strenuously engaging with the unconscious by studying a recurring symbol uncovers a wide variety of beliefs that must be examined and ultimately rejected. Thus, the common need to balance the masculine and feminine seen here provides hope, since scripts that remain unconscious and unchallenged continue to abuse. Carla wrote: "I am determined to continue my own work on this masculine/feminine dynamic. I must be free of the seemingly eternal pressure to *do* rather than to *be* so that I can live in peace within myself and in harmony with others and our planet." The goal of wholeness is to equally honor and appropriately utilize all parts of ourselves, including the feminine/masculine components. Each aspect provides valuable elements of this important inner dance so necessary for a productive and meaningful life.

A deeper look at Carla's dream leads us beyond the grief evoked by historic rejection of the Fathers to see a hopeful crack in this old pattern. The Composite Man has grown enough to experience compassion for the feminine (he "is very sympathetic and replies it is not him but his father who will not accept me"). This signifies a shift in an old, destructive paradigm and suggests hope that the future can be transformed by the "sons," by what is developing now in the collective consciousness.

I was particularly struck by this sentence in the final dream: "I am really asking what it would take to be loved by this rejecting and judgmental character but I cannot bring myself to ask that." Ten of the dreamers in this book are asking that same question and they are finding their own answers. Like Carla, they have all been willing to face the schism between their own masculine and feminine dynamics. The ultimate result of this courageous work is the integration that leads to balanced, full-flavored living, healing, and a profound self-love.

CHAPTER NINE

What's a Tom Selleck?

Dreamer: Janice
Recurring symbol: Tom Selleck
Length of dream series: 18 years
Number of dreams presented: 10
Script messages addressed:
  "Ambition, work, and logical thinking are all that
    matters."
  "Relaxing, playing, and intuiting are ridiculous."
Benefits to the dreamer:
  Learned to be comfortable with intuitive knowing.
  Learned to balance a dominant work ethic (masculine) with
    feeling and being (feminine).
Dream approaches: Working with a dream celebrity
Summary: A 46-year-old woman develops a relaxed way of being
within her self and in the world.

"I hope you don't mind me calling you," the voice whispered on the phone. "I listen to your radio show but could not talk about these dreams on the air. I've had the same dream for more than twenty years and I hope you can tell me what to do about it."

Thus began one of the most bizarre dream conversations of my career. Sensing that this would be an unusual discussion, I grabbed a pen and began taking notes. The caller took off like a Learjet, flying through her monologue without pause, until she landed on what was, for me, very swampy ground. This sad woman's perception of the dream world exemplifies a tragic mis-use of the dream. Her series was "about Paul Newman."

The woman's diatribe continued: "Paul Newman wants to marry me. He has for more than twenty years. In my dreams he is always knocking on my door. I don't know why he doesn't find me. I've written letters to his wife telling her to let Paul come to me but I guess she won't. Should I go see him in person? That would be really hard for me because I'm agoraphobic. In fact, I haven't left my house for twenty-three years. I don't know what to do. It is definite that Paul wants me. We're getting older now. Pretty soon it will be too late. Should I call him? How would I get his phone number?"

Dream teacher and author Jeremy Taylor uses a term that perfectly identifies the problem expressed by this haunted woman: *mistaken literalism*. (The seriousness of this woman's skewed beliefs might suggest deeper problems than that.) Every dream professional has to address the common problem of mis-taken literalism in order to help dreamers understand the sym-bolic and metaphoric message of the dream. Without this shift in perception, very few dreams can be understood deeply enough to be truly beneficial.

The study titled "The Significant Other" showed how dif-ficult it may be for a dreamer to make the perceptual shift from literal to symbolic understanding. Dreams featuring movie stars or political figures are often as emotionally loaded as those pre-senting a former mate. The similarity between the two may lie in the intensity of our projections on those characters and the emotions they bring forth. Perhaps you have witnessed the heat that can be generated in conversations about the merits of a character from a TV series or a movie. It is as if some unconscious identification takes over, causing normally sane, rational debaters to defend or promote their perceptions/projections about "stars" beyond all logic. It is that realm, whatever it is, from which a dreamer may need to escape if a series containing a media or sports star is to be understood.

The process of understanding a famous dream character, particularly a movie star, is complicated because the dreamer may be pulling from two sources—feelings and information— when defining the dream character. If the dreamer knows a lot about the actor (as reported by the media or, less likely, from personal experience with the actual celebrity), psyche may have pulled this character from that pool. For example, the dreamer may report, "I read that she is a really arrogant, controlling person." In a case like this, such a dream character may be warning the dreamer of similar character traits within her or within someone in her life.

I've had the opportunity to help dreamers wrangle with dozens of dream characters of "star" quality. One dreamer came to see that Rush Limbaugh represented a vocal, vitriolic, and conservative element within her. Conversely, Eleanor Roosevelt embodied an active inner element determined to defend the underdog, a part of the dreamer that was being neglected. Because of his very visible support of the Dalai Lama, Richard Gere depicted one who fights for the freedom of the spiritually repressed or expelled; this dream occurred when the dreamer was joining a church despite her parents' extreme objections.

Two dreamers may apply identical associations to a personality but arrive at very different conclusions about the meaning of the dream character. For one dreamer, former National Rifle Association leader Charlton Heston stood for one who defends the constitution and the personal right to bear arms. Another dreamer defined Heston as one whose action promotes violence on American streets and in schools; because of the way this dreamer was dealing with a rebellious teenager, she understood that her "inner Heston" was a force in her battles with her son. The content of his dream led a third dreamer to recall Heston's role as Moses in *The Ten Commandments*, representing the ability of a human to receive the Word of God.

Because of the heroic levels to which we lift them, celebrities in dreams often represent an archetype, a pattern of behavior of mythic proportions. The dreamer must be the one to define the essence of, and therefore her projections onto, the character. We will see this in the Blonde Woman study with the character of Marilyn Monroe. For the dreamer, Monroe clearly represents the exploited feminine as well as the sexual exploitation of women.

Is it possible that a dream featuring a movie or musical star is precognitive or literal, as the woman who dreamed about Paul Newman hoped? Anything is possible in the dream world, but where famous people are concerned, those possibilities are highly unlikely. Unless the dreamer has a personal relationship with the movie star, it can be assumed that the famous person is a representation of something the dreamer needs to understand about himself or herself or someone close to him or her.

And so we proceed to a series of ten fairly short dreams featuring Tom Selleck. Notice that I do not say these are dreams *about* Tom Selleck, because they are not. These are dreams about the dreamer and what she needed to develop in her movement toward healing and wholeness. The dreamer and I glimpsed this probability during our first interview just by defining a role, played by Selleck, in a television series.

I met Janice, a beautiful forty-something woman, when she attended one of my workshops in Colorado. She had been involved in dreamwork for nearly a decade and wanted to understand a dream series that had begun in the early 1980s. "At the time of the first dream [1982] I knew nothing about Selleck, the person, but I was intrigued by a character he played on a TV series called *Magnum, P.I.* The character was laid-back, relaxed, and fun loving. He often used his intuition to guide him. He had lots of friends, loved living and playing in paradise [the TV series was set in Hawaii], and reveled in his lack of ambition."

Janice considered why some of those traits might have been important to her at the time the series began. "I was just beginning to realize that my life was not working. I was in the middle of a divorce and examining myself to see what I really wanted from life. What I did not want was the life of my parents. My father was a very successful surgeon, driven, ambitious, impeccably logical, always serious, rejecting fun and leisure like the plague. I was dissatisfied for many reasons, tense, lonely, and searching for a better life."

It makes sense that a masculine role portrayed so differently from her father's script would intrigue Janice. "I was just becoming aware of the unhappiness caused by my propensity to be overly serious and driven. It seems that this first Selleck dream wants me to get a look at another way of getting the job done, of being in the world." This first dream shows Janice as being intrigued but just previewing a possible new way of being.

September 2, 1982
I am previewing a not-yet-released movie with Tom
Selleck in it. The setting for the movie is a place like
Casablanca or New Mexico.

It is said that some dreams are rehearsals for the future. This
dream suggests that Janice, in her twenties, was willing to look at
a new way of getting the job done, of thinking, of being in the
world (Selleck as the masculine principle), but was not yet willing to let it be seen in public ("not-yet-released movie"). As this
experienced dreamer looked at the Selleck character with the
clarity of hindsight, she said, "It's as if I was considering a masculine energy that was independent, intuitive, self-directed, and
determined to enjoy life." Because Selleck played a private
detective, he also represents one who is able to uncover and discover clues and follow them to a resolution. As a private investi-
gator, he had many interesting and unorthodox ways of getting
necessary information. About this Janice said, "I was just beginning my own inner journey at the time of this dream, trying to
understand the mysteries of my own life, both inner and outer. I
was willing to consider intuitive ways of understanding and perceiving which were in drastic opposition to my father's strict logical process. I loved dreamwork and was using my dreams as a
great source of knowing." A successful dream detective must be
open to many nonrational realms of knowing, so using her
dreams as a tool for understanding herself and her world was
ridiculous to Janice's logical father.

Why did this first dream occur in a place like Casablanca
or New Mexico? "I think of both places as exotic, far away,
unknown, adventurous, and romantic. For my own healing at
the time of this dream, I needed to go to such inner places in my

own psyche, to see life from a more romantic, less practical perspective than I was familiar with from my own script." The next series dream shows that contact has been made between the Selleck character and Janice.

September 16, 1983
> I'm with my dog at the beach. We meet T.S. He is attracted to me. We talk and flirt a bit. Selleck and I keep interacting. He matches my eagerness. I am not nervous or immature.

Water and land merge at the beach, making this a place where, metaphorically, the unconscious and conscious realms blend. By this second series dream, Janice was more conscious of the masculine traits that intrigued her and was willing to flirt with this new and lighthearted lifestyle. She was not nervous about the connection. The connection between dream ego and Selleck deepened in the next dream.

September 22, 1983
> I am in line on a tour with about twenty-five people. Tom Selleck is at the end of the line, looking at me. With each look I feel a deep connection. His eyes are special.

Now the animus (masculine) figure and ego are "eyeing" each other. The homonyms "eye" and "I" suggest that Janice is now identifying ("I-ing") more deeply with this Selleck energy. In addition, Selleck and ego are aligned (standing in a line). The progression of connection between dream ego and Selleck that develops in these three short dreams clearly illustrates the direction in which psyche wants Janice to move. This kind of awareness is one of the great advantages of studying dreams in a series. The next dream continues that development.

September 26, 1983
With others, including Tom Selleck, I'm out in nature, training as a part of a team of martial arts experts. We are studying Tai Chi Chuan. Tom Selleck and I are friends and are very attracted to each other.

To be "out in nature" in a dream can suggest a process that is natural or authentic. The martial arts consist of a variety of Eastern-style physical and mental defense disciplines. Unlike Western modes of overpowering with direct force, a martial arts expert incorporates a philosophy of harmony and oneness with the opponent. Incorporating the concept of energy fields, a martial artist will work with ideas of blending with rather than fending off or attacking the other. Tai Chi Chuan is a form of movement intended to activate energy within the practitioner to heighten physical, mental, and spiritual health. Therefore, in this fourth dream of the series, dream ego is working with the Selleck energy in a natural way, learning to deal with processes of defense that blend and combine rather than separate and attack. These images suggest that a new and foreign form of integration is taking place within Janice/Selleck. At the time of this dream, Janice had been studying Tai Chi. She was learning to avoid futile confrontations with her father and no longer tried to defend her new lifestyle and independently chosen worldview.

Janice did not record another series dream for seven years. During those years she was altering her life dramatically by studying Chinese medicine, learning a variety of healing arts considered alternative by American standards and "ridiculous and stupid" by her mainstream father/doctor. Janice was indeed learning to live life in a way very foreign to her upbringing. The Selleck character in *Magnum, P.I.* was becoming a model for her new way of dealing with the world, both internal and external.

During the years of her dream series, Janice remarried and had a son. Her need to relax and enjoy life intensified with the demands of marriage and child rearing. Perhaps because of this, a deepening contact between dream ego and the Selleck character are seen through the symbol of marriage in the next Selleck dream.

November 1990

My husband (Tom Selleck) and I are detectives. I have taken some photos that are helpful to the case we are on.

I am upset to discover that my husband is gay. I feel as if my life is ruined. Tom is not affected by my emotions. He cares about me but doesn't feel badly. He accepts this fact about himself without judgment. He is very masculine with a lot of presence.

It is interesting to see a shift from a macho Selleck to a gay man. This acknowledged Janice's need to continue softening her masculine processes. The dream shows further integration in that both ego and Selleck are detectives, looking together for clues to the mysteries of life. Dream ego seems to be getting the picture! ("I have taken some photos that are helpful to the case we are on.")

As is frequently the case when embracing new ways of being, a behavioral backslide seems to be reflected in the next series dream:

June 6, 1996
Tom Selleck and I are lovers, though we have not been together for a long time and our time together is intermittent. Amidst a happy group of partying people, I make sexual overtures to Tom. We leave the others to go to a private area. We connect in such a way that I feel very loved. Tom is very present in his embrace.

The dream says that Selleck and ego have not been together. Janice saw that this way: "In my journal I had written about returning to a compulsive way of doing things. I felt as if I had forgotten everything I had learned about living a nurturing and balanced life. I was driven, nearly frenzied, in my need to complete many unnecessary activities." That is certainly suggested by the dream fact that ego and Selleck have not been together for a long time! However, all is not lost, as ego reconnects to her Selleck masculine energy, fully enjoying the experience. The sense of presence ("Tom is very present in his embrace") provided a very real feeling of joyfully relaxing into the Selleck/Magnum way of living. By contrast, being obsessed with accomplishment, with achieving life goals, or with getting the chores done, diminishes the moment. Being present in the moment (a strong trait in the Magnum/Selleck character), rather than hurrying toward the future, brings balance very necessary for Janice.

Another reconnection between Janice and Selleck occurs in the next dream.

February 1, 1997
I'm visiting some friends when I meet Tom Selleck in a hallway. It's great to reconnect with him. We chat

amiably. I discover that Tom has been enjoying recreational sex. It doesn't matter to me.

Janice had always felt like a loner, on the outside, not included in most peer groups. "I've always been uncomfortable with others. My extreme introversion and natural shyness have created distance between me and others. Overcoming this discomfort has been a major goal in my healing work." Relaxing her serious nature and driving ambition was necessary so that Janice could develop tolerance for recreation. Metaphorically, sex may represent social intercourse and/or intimate connection, and recreational sex may suggest a form of intimacy that recreates in a casual, pleasurable fashion. Thus, the Selleck dream character blends two of Janice's needs for transformation.

The next dream, short and not so sweet if misinterpreted, is the kind of dream that can cause great confusion unless the metaphor of death is understood. In dreams, to die often signals an ending of some project, process, way of being, aspect of the self, or even a relationship. Remember what Selleck has represented so far in this series and then assume that there is a need for something to die. Given the dreamer's history, you can probably guess why there might be such a need.

April 9, 1999
Tom Selleck stabs and kills me.

At the time of this short but potent dream, Janice had been suffering from a great deal of back pain. (The back is behind us, and therefore can metaphorically represent the past.) As she reflected on the period during which she had this dream, she saw that her former script (back/past) had regained too much power, forcing the return of her syndrome of extreme busyness. "I have been inappropriately busy," she wrote in her journal. "My back is raising a fuss but it is hard for me to stop and rest without feeling guilty or inadequate. Thus, the laid-back Selleck character, the balanced masculine who is 'gay', blending both masculine and feminine traits, needs to do me in!"

Because this study focused on development of a healthy animus (masculine principle), let's consider one model of individuation that postulates that a woman will embrace four types of animus figures before achieving full integration of her inner masculine archetype. This model suggests that a woman's inner development may be reflected in the kind of man she finds attractive in the awake world, as well as the types of masculine characters appearing in her dreams. The first stage of animus development is seen in a physically macho character (athlete/hero), followed by an intellectually powerful animus (successful businessman, teacher/mentor). She may then be attracted to some type of social transformer (a politician or innovator), and finally her desire turns to a masculine source of spiritual power. Let's see how that theory applies to this series by carefully examining the final dream, which provides a surprising twist.

February 18, 2000
I am exercising and having fun when it becomes evident that my car needs to be moved. It is magically lifted up and travels some miles away through the air.

The first statement of the dream repeats a focus of this study: the exercise and recreation theme. When ego exercises her ability to have fun, she needs to alter her source of power, her drive, what moves her (car). As if by a state of grace, the car or process moves on its own ("it magically lifts up"). This sense of a magical shift is common in dreamwork. To ego, it seems that something just happens, though psyche has been working toward this particular transformation for years.

As the dream continues, we see a new transforming vehicle delivered from the depths by something that is also transforming:

> I see the ocean from an aerial view. An ocean liner is rising to the surface, bent in half but reforming to its normal shape and structure as it rises. I know that my car will come from it.
>
> The dream continues inside, in a room, an interior space that needs cleansing and clearing: I light a large stick of healing incense to smudge a room in order to cleanse and purify it, marking an ending and preparing for something new. The ash at the end of the incense is a blue goo which I wipe on my breasts for healing.

It is as if the arrival of the new process (car) deserves a ritual to mark this momentous transformation. The smudging becomes part of the healing of the feminine (breasts), of Janice's way of being, feeling, relating, and nourishing, imperative to support a new way of being in the world (the vehicle). That done, the recurring character appears: Tom Selleck arrives in three ways. It is as if he is present in three different and simultaneous ways:

1. He is just here.
2. He arises from the water.
3. He has always been here, like a carpenter or some other kind of helpful man.

The new vehicle and the repeating masculine figure arrive by the same means, rising from the depths. In addition, the healed masculine has always been present, although it seems to arrive at a specific time. This force is now perceived to be a practical and helpful force (carpenter). The dream continues with the completion of the ritual.

> After my car arrives from the water, I wipe the blue goo on the foreheads of the intimate friends who are present, myself and Selleck included. This is a type of blessing.

Dream ego, the aspect of the self that makes conscious choices, anoints those in attendance, a representation of her wholeness. And now, the surprise ending:

> Later, at a celebratory dinner, my best friend is making a toast. I walk past Selleck as he listens. Ignoring him, I scoot through a narrow opening in the crowd and leave.

After eighteen years of developing a dream relationship with the Selleck/Magnum energy, dream ego ignores him and moves on. It is as if psyche is suggesting that the Selleck energy no longer needs attention. As this series shows, from first dream to last, a goal of Janice's transformation was to meet, greet, get to know, and finally become intimate with a new way of acting in the world, the masculine as represented by the Selleck character. Could leaving him at this juncture be explained by the theory of the developing masculine presented above?

The Selleck/Magnum character certainly fits the first animus type, the macho man. In the television series *Magnum P.I.*,

Selleck's character is extremely athletic, playing team sports, surfing, swimming, and rescuing damsels in distress. Janice identified the next element, the intellectual, as Magnum's intuitive ability, which provided the television detective with valuable insights. There is nothing of the social transformer or the spiritual, the third and fourth forms of the animus, in the Selleck/Magnum character. This limitation may be why dream ego passes by Selleck in the last dream—he can no longer provide the model she needs for growth, although the transformation he has represented thus far has been extremely valuable.

Indeed, in her awake life, Janice has bypassed the Selleck/Magnum character. By learning ways of acting in the world that are different from the dictates of her family script, Janice has become a social transformer as a practitioner of several types of Eastern healing arts. The spiritual component of the animus has also developed in Janice's personal practice and professional teaching. Therefore, having learned from and embraced this laid-back, fun-loving, intuitive masculine, Janice is now living a life that reflects a full integration of the masculine, one very different from her father's script. From the final dream of the series, it appears that it is now time for her to move where this Selleck symbol of her animus cannot go. Surely a new series is just around the corner.

Dreamers sometimes complain that they have no time to simply enjoy a series that seems complete. Over our lifetime, recurring symbols address all the areas of our lives and evolution, so when one aspect of our inner house is cleaned and reordered, another suddenly is in disarray. As one client said, "After years of working with my series I seem to have finally resolved it. On Monday, I celebrated (what seemed to be) the final dream of the series, but that very night found myself searching for a clean rest-room stall, needing to relieve myself yet again!"

And what of the woman waiting for Paul Newman to rescue her from a life of isolation and agoraphobic imprisonment? I never heard from her again and can only hope that, in some way, she too was able to embrace a powerful way of acting in the world, as Newman and Selleck represent to many female dreamers.

CHAPTER TEN

The Internal Strangers

Dreamer: Jessica
Recurring symbol: unknown boys and men
Length of dream series: 8 years
Number of dreams presented: 21
Script messages addressed:
> "You are emotionally safe only when your kids are safe. Therefore, you must accept excessive responsibility for your children."
> "Being safe is more important than exploring your personal power in the world."
> "Being dependent within a marriage provides security."

Benefits to the dreamer:
> Strengthened independence and personal power, leading to a career.
> Developed ways of fostering independence within her marriage.
> Created healthy emotional detachment from grown children by healing a wounded inner feminine.

Summary: A 57-year-old "smother-mother" develops new ways of thinking and doing (masculine), empowering herself and enhancing her relationships.

The first dream recorded by an uninitiated dreamer is likely to herald something significant to his or her health and development. This was true for seven of the dreamers contributing to this book. Each began dreamwork with the dream that eventually became the first of the series presented here. So it was with Jessica. "The image in my first written dream was so bizarre it demanded my attention. I wrote it on a piece of scratch paper and, amazingly, never lost it." Following is a very unflattering picture of an aspect of herself that Jessica desperately needed to acknowledge.

Mid-1980s: The False Nun

I am wearing a traditional nun's habit. Friends and family are gathered at a banquet table. I'm busy shoving people into an old-fashioned gas oven. I [the nun] am suffocating all of these people under the guise of spirituality.

"I was horrified by what the nun was doing," Jessica said. "My first impulse was to reject the dream, but that was impossible when I realized that I was the nun! Even though I knew little about dreamwork at the time of this dream, I actually had a body hit when I examined the dream."

Presenting a dramatic, and sometimes horrifying, snapshot is a powerful way for a dream to awaken us to something vitally important. Having the courage to acknowledge the truth of such a *shadow* image (unknown or unflattering aspect of our personality) marks a true spiritual seeker. Distressing as it was to admit this flawed character, Jessica did just that, thus beginning her transformation.

What "habit" did Jessica need to acknowledge at the time of this dream? What spiritual guise hid enough rage to damage family members as imaged in this dream kitchen? The specific language of any dream provides one of the most valid clues in dream detecting. Notice that the poor folks stuffed into the ovens are not burned to death but suffocated. This, combined with the nun's habit, suggested that Jessica had unconsciously succumbed to an erroneous notion of spiritual purity and service, which resulted in the habitual suffocation of family members.

About this Jessica wrote:

As I reflected on the "nun," I knew that my habit of caring for others was, in fact, killing them. At the time of this dream, my son's drunken rages led our family into therapy, forcing us to face our problems. During these years of turmoil, I was prone to outbursts of anger, depression, and general emotional instability. I came to realize that I felt most powerful and secure when I controlled family situations and, god-like, "fixed" the problems of others. I felt that this was my "calling," but like a nun stuffing people into an oven, I was doing more harm than good. After all, as a Jewish woman, I come by this predilection culturally! I do have a great deal of loving Jewish mother tendencies. All my close friends tease me about this dimension of my personality. However, there is a drastic difference between nurturing and suffocating. I'm grateful I finally realized that by "solving" the problems of others, I was robbing them of their own power.

This suffocation of others is often described as *smothering*—mothering that does not allow others to breathe for themselves. Jessica was determined to heal this smothering dynamic.

Altering one's identity by assiduously searching for behaviors harmful to self and others is a heroic endeavor. When such a commitment is made, psyche—our internal healer—will shine light on an alternative path. This happens in dreams suggesting the balancing factors within our personality that could be enhanced or enlivened. Like clearing a garden of weeds, we must create psychic/spiritual space for a healthy self to grow. Jessica realized that, in order to change her attitudes and behavior with others, she would have to use her time and energy differently.

Thus, over the next ten years Jessica shifted her focus away from the lives of others by devoting time and attention to her own development. She began taking classes in an ancient form of Chinese bodywork called *acupressure*, which examines and realigns energy systems within the physical body. In addition, she continued to pursue her passion for oil painting and sculpting. She joined a weekly dream group. All of these activities provided emotional release and supported her personal growth.

As Jessica's dream studies continued, she noticed and became intrigued by dreams containing unknown male characters, both human and animal. Studying acupressure and reading Carl Jung familiarized her with theories of internal energy. In the simplest terms, she understood that all people have two different ways of thinking and working, of dealing with everyday life—either a masculine or a feminine approach or process. The masculine principle or archetype (power, drive, or energy) is perceived as: logical, linear thinking; goal orientation; accomplishment in the material world; focus and direction resulting in the completion of tasks. Without this inner ability, both men and women wander around in circles, having many laudable and enjoyable experiences, perhaps, but ending with no substantial accomplishment to call their own.

For example, without sufficient masculine energy a book cannot be written, a house built, or a new school of thought presented to those who need it. Great artists might circumnavigate fabulous ideas swirling in their brains, but a tangible sculpture, painting, or symphony would never reach the public.

Jessica decided to collect and study all of her dreams containing unknown male characters. The series begins in 1989 with an image of an unknown baby boy locked in a car while his mother attends a therapy session. This suggests that Jessica's masculine is not free to develop (locked up) until the mother experiences sufficient healing. That is, until Jessica altered her smothering habits, an alternate form of being could not manifest (get out of the car).

For the next two years Jessica continued pursuing the several strands of recovery and therapy mentioned above. She committed to a course of study that resulted in her eventual certification as a teacher of acupressure. Her resultant growth seems evident in the next dream in the series. It contains unknown male characters, both animal and human.

November 5, 1991: The Giraffe Balloon

When I turn on the garbage disposal at my kitchen sink, a tiny giraffe balloon emerges from the drain opening. I take the giraffe [a male] in my hands to breathe air into it. This feels like a monumental task. The fully inflated giraffe is enormous, like a high floating raft. I am thrilled! It belongs to the boy next door. We decide to keep it between our houses and share it.

Symbols that transform within the context of a dream may represent what needs to change, and how. This dream shows the emergence of something that has been treated as garbage. Instead of disposing of this something, grinding it up and flushing it away, dream ego rescues it and breathes life into it.

What has emerged? In her journal Jessica wrote: "Because of its long neck, the image of the giraffe seems phallic or masculine. Because a giraffe is able to reach and receive nourishment from high places, stretch, and still be grounded, I see this as a model of healthy masculine functioning."

To Jessica, reaching high for nourishment felt like bringing the spiritual into the material world, thus grounding what was unbalanced and destructive in the "False Nun." Reflecting on her life at the time she had this dream, Jessica wrote: "Compared to the time of the nun dream, I was in much better shape emotionally. My children and I had established good boundaries. I was a certified acupressure practitioner. I had done a considerable amount of inner work, and had more strength, stability, and direction. I was involved in artistic endeavors as well as acupressure. I was staying focused and productive, so my masculine energy must have been developing! But sharing the giraffe with the young masculine next door tells me that I was not yet ready to completely own this powerful, new transformation.

"One last thought about the dream is that psyche may be warning me about ego inflation. I will have to keep my eye on that." Because the giraffe/balloon was blown-up, inflated, Jessica was wise to question the common human dynamic of thinking better of ourselves than is warranted. However, in this case, it seemed that Jessica needed to consciously interact with the development of another way of being, to actively inflate it in order to balance the overactive mothering behaviors that had been destructive.

I asked Jessica why her masculine energy might have been put into the garbage disposal in the first place. She reflected that she had been very focused in college. In fact, she recalled becoming quite obsessed with ideas and projects at that time. This obsession went beyond the passion of a normal young college student into unhealthy extremes. "Perhaps I unconsciously decided, at that time, to abandon my masculine rather than learn to alter it," Jessica suggested. The next dream provided another possibility by showing another version of this kind of too much energy as it connected Jessica to some unhappy childhood experiences.

August 13, 1992: Against the Wall
In a small room a large elephant is pushing me against the wall. I feel like I am being crushed. After I struggle to push it off of me, a man comes and pulls it away.

Jessica wrote in her journal: "As I studied this dream I remembered that my father gave me a toy elephant when I was a small girl. An elephant is a powerful instinctive force, considered very intelligent but known to crush those who get in its way. This is a perfect description of my father. Though I loved him dearly and know that he loved me, he was a very controlling man. There was no sense in arguing with him. When I tried to engage with him I often felt up against a wall, hopeless. If I'm still being constrained by beliefs of powerlessness, I need a strong, still unidentified masculine energy to free myself."

Women who have overwhelmingly powerful fathers or husbands may reject their own masculine energy to avoid becoming like their feared, masculine role model. Developing the ability to make choices, to construct an alternative, healthy way of being in the world, is essential to remedy this loss. For Jessica, healing and strengthening the self that had been overpowered was vital in developing a healthy inner masculine. The next dream in the series highlights this in an amazing way.

> *October 10, 1992: The Man on the Flying Trapeze*
> I am on a very high trapeze among city buildings. On the trapeze with me is a woman dressed in a beautiful white gown. She begins to bleed severely. I know her life is threatened.
>
> Suddenly a man in a black suit appears and says we can save her. He has a towel twisted into a rope and instructs me to grab hold of it. It seems incredibly difficult. He says, "Tell me that you can do this." Though feeling weak and doubtful I say, "Yes, I can do it." Then he takes away the bleeding woman, leaving me alone on the trapeze.
>
> I am swinging widely, feeling terrified and exhilarated at the same time. I fly under a building and back, feelingly very unsteady on a thin bar, fearing I might slip off at any moment. Though in a highly vulnerable state, I stay on the bar.

About this Jessica wrote: "I think that the wounded feminine is my inclination to overnurture others. I now realize that, by focusing only on others, I have been able to avoid my own pain and my own healing. I can see that this dream was calling me to the task in a most powerful way."

In this dream Jessica must consciously decide to engage with the unknown masculine to deal with the wounded feminine. That is, ego—her sense of her self, her present identity—must say yes, no matter how scared, tenuous, or vulnerable she feels. When she agrees to help the wounded woman (feminine), then she is left alone on the trapeze, feeling both terrified and exhilarated. That combination of heightened emotion often accompanies a leap into a new phase of life, creating a feeling of the thrilling vulnerability of flying on a trapeze without a net! Doing so opens the door for interesting rewards, as the next dream validates.

July 21, 1994: Cooking with the Man I Adore
I am in the kitchen with an absolutely fascinating man. He is tall and thin, with searing blue eyes. He lives with his mother and sister. They are very nice and ask me to help make the salad. This wonderful man stands by me, smoking occasionally. Though he is quiet, I can sense his incredible love. When we kiss lightly, his look and attention transport me. Our connection makes me feel complete. My love for him is so intense that I can hardly contain myself. Our conversation is about the inner world. When we talk of the integration of the masculine and feminine, I am totally blissed out!

This dream, which takes place in the kitchen, shows much more healthy activity than stuffing people into the oven in the "The

False Nun" dream. The masculine in this kitchen lives with sister and mother, suggesting a kind of integration needed to protect Jessica from the obsessive-compulsive masculine energy of her past. An inner integration is implied by the strong love between the male character and dream ego, and by their discussion about the masculine-feminine dynamic.

Reflecting on her awake life at the time of the dream, Jessica wrote: "As my inner masculine develops I feel more confident in the world. I am doing many things I never could have imagined five years ago, such as teaching groups. In this work, and in other ways, I am very conscious of the value of the masculine characteristics of logical thinking, focus, and emotional detachment. In addition, being less emotionally involved (smothering) with my children has allowed us to develop healthier relationships. This dream confirms the changes that were taking place in my psyche."

Jessica's internal masculine displays superhuman powers in the next dream.

1994: The Amazing Car Mechanic

I'm trying to drive a small station wagon into an auto repair shop when I get stuck. The shop owner, a muscular, stocky man, picks up my car and leaps over the edge of the shop parking lot on to the street. He jumps down a considerable height. I am amazed that he doesn't hurt himself and am in awe of his physical strength and courage in taking such a risk.

Like the two preceding dreams, this one shows the strength of the masculine, a new development for Jessica. It also describes superhuman courage and risk-taking. How clever of psyche to identify this force as that which repairs energy systems (cars). Jessica related to that this way: "Within months of this dream I surprised myself by teaching far more than I had previously anticipated, traveling out of state or country five months in a row. For me this seemed 'superhuman.' These were huge risks, as I had always been afraid of flying, of traveling alone, and of facilitating any kind of group outside my family. I am convinced that the integration of the strong masculine energy is responsible for my ability to take risks and to fly, metaphorically and literally! I've come a long way from the trapeze dream!" As I reflected on this transformation I noticed that, by flying so much, Jessica is now literally "up in the air," as was the giraffe she worked so hard to inflate.

The next dream in the series presents another powerful masculine character, this one named but not personally known to the dreamer.

> *May 3, 1995: Joe Louis, the Champ*
> Joe Louis, world champion boxer, is shooting baskets.
> He is doing all kinds of trick shots with great ease. I
> am outside in a parking lot where Joe's trucks and cars
> are displayed. One of his cars may be a Saturn, like
> ours. A radio announcer says that his material assets
> have great value.

It is always interesting to notice how dream facts differ from awake-world reality. In this case, the solitary boxer is participating in a team sport requiring five players on each side. Jessica laughed when she recalled that she was on a team of five acupressure teachers! The dream says that Joe owns a car like hers, suggesting that these two energies travel through life in a similar fashion. Jessica wrote: "Joe Louis was certainly a hero. I feel that the more I own this hero in myself, the more I can be in the world with ease and skill. In addition, the rigorous training and practice of professional sports figures demands strong commitment. This now seems true for me, as well."

When we focused on the rather startling last sentence ("a radio announcer says that his material assets have great value"), Jessica appreciated its truth. "As a result of my teaching, I am now earning more money. At the time of this dream, my husband and I moved to a beautiful new home that has served as a place for workshops and gatherings. I do appreciate the value of these material assets, which feels very balancing to the austere life of the nun in the first dream! ['The False Nun'] There is no question that my life has undergone big shifts." In addition, the assets of inner growth are of great value to Jessica and all others in her life.

As our dreams reflect the transformations we are experiencing, they often point out a truth about the unhealthy aspects of the self from which we are escaping. One of the values of the individuation process is the development of a self that has unique texture, shape, and nourishing characteristics. Jessica's dreaming self created a wonderful symbol to image that development.

April 25, 1998: The Transformation
from Oatmeal to Bread
I am babysitting for a family of five children. I am drawn to the youngest child, Cameron, a boy around twelve. He is big and chubby with broad shoulders. I think that he might become a football player. But now he has the baby-fat look, pudgy, precious, and very sweet.

> Outside, I am preparing oatmeal for Cameron. As I scoop it from the pot it falls to the ground, suddenly looking like a loaf of bread. I tell Cameron not to worry, and I slice two-thirds of it, leaving the crusty bottom part in contact with the ground. Now it is like slices of oatmeal bread that he seems to enjoy. I am amazed at this transformation.

In a dream group, Jessica enhanced her understanding of the transformation from oatmeal to bread through a process called *gestalt*. The dreamer closes her eyes and assumes the identity of a symbol, allowing a better connection to the remembered image. Jessica began the process by saying, "I am a bowl of oatmeal. I ooze and flow to fit the shape of any container. This feels comfortable and familiar but a bit runny, uncontrolled, without boundaries, insubstantial."

Staying in this slightly altered state, more connected to the feelings of the dream than to intellectual associations, Jessica "felt into" the bread and reported quite a different sense. "I am a solid loaf, equally nutritious as the oatmeal but firm. I stand by myself. I can be cut into pieces that maintain a distinct shape." At this point, Jessica grinned and opened her eyes. She had experienced the body hit, the "aha!" that usually indicates a bridging of awareness from the dream to the conscious self. "Yes, this is true. I feel much more independent, solid, with more appropriate boundaries in my relationships. In the past I would easily lose my own sense of self, getting swept into the emotions of others. Now I am much more detached from other people's psychological state. Physically I am more aware of being 'in my body,' feeling centered and at peace."

It is interesting to note the symbolism of bread in spiritual development. Spirit is often referred to as the "bread of life." This association connects with other spiritual images occurring within Jessica's series. There is more on this dynamic below.

Jessica suspected that the twelve-year-old child in the dream represented the number of years she had been developing her new career. "Perhaps his name is Cameron because I feel so exposed and spotlighted when I teach, as if the *camera* is *on* me. When I am performing at such times, I must be nourished by my own specific shape and sense of independence and boundaries, like a piece of bread."

Indeed, the performance theme continues in the next dream, showing hesitation and withdrawal as well as willingness. In an excerpt from this dream, Jessica decides to hide behind some houses to watch the filming of a movie starring William Hurt.

> When the camera crew arrives I hide my face. Finally the big scene takes place. I notice that the actors are suddenly filled with tremendous energy. I had seen William Hurt pacing up and down for hours, quietly preparing. Now he is ready to express himself.
>
> Suddenly, I realize that I have left my purse in the bar. I am worried about the loss of money and credit cards. Later I find my wallet and have to prove my identity to an official.

Jessica wrote, "Despite my willingness to teach, sometimes I feel shy when called to be in the limelight." This is clearly not a problem for William Hurt, the professional masculine way of acting, that is very well prepared and ready to express himself within the dream. About that Jessica said, "One of the most important aspects of my new way of being shows up in how I plan. Planning, being prepared, thinking through, and mentally rehearsing for professional and social events are new for me. I have learned that it is extremely valuable to my peace of mind and to the execution of the event." All of these practices are aspects of a highly functional masculine.

Transformation is never a steady forward movement. One step forward, two steps backward may be an overstatement, but certainly we all get to a halting place, if not a stuck place, now and then. At that time, our dreams often reflect fears from the part of the self that is more comfortable with the status quo than with growth and change. Thus, the last paragraph in this dream reflects ego's fears. "Suddenly, I realize that I have left my purse in the bar. I am worried about the loss of money and credit cards. Later I find my wallet, and I have to prove my identity to an official."

The theme of losing wallets and purses is very common when a dreamer is feeling insecure, unclear about being able to prove his or her identity. As we evolve we must be willing to experience this uncomfortable loss of self until the developing identity has clearly taken shape, until the bread is baked and can stand on its own.

Jessica had nine more dreams featuring unknown male characters before the final dreams presented below. These nine dreams show Jessica doing the following:

1. She observes a powerful doctor performing precise surgery.
2. She observes young parents emerging from an underground dwelling with a robust, ten-pound infant baby boy.

3. She needs to choose between three brothers who represent very different values. She chooses the middle brother who is balanced and open to growth.
4. She watches a dentist operating on a molar.
5. She observes two brothers, one evil and the other good.
6. She observes a doting father caring for his new baby girl.
7. She flies in an airplane with a Chinese Grand Master and his thirteen-year-old son.
8. She distracts a male carpenter while he is building a new church.
9. She baby-sits for the president's infant son.

Throughout all of these dreams, dream ego seems to be clarifying her values and making positive choices. It is as if ego needs to see and evaluate many different aspects of her active masculine.

To date, Jessica's series ends with two amazing dreams. The first weaves in the spiritual theme once again.

November 25, 1998:
The Man who Conceives a Baby by God
I see a movie scene in which a man is lying on an elaborate gold altar in Egypt. With his legs spread apart, he is mystically impregnated by God. Later we see him with the child. The movie critics say that the movie is bad but I don't agree with them.

Later, I have a procedure in which my nipples are removed from my breasts. Little dark holes remain.

Why does this potent image of the man being impregnated appear in a movie? Movies either reflect or create collective and cultural beliefs and attitudes. As we transform personally we may well challenge long-held cultural mores and expectations. When that is the case, we must deal with the judgments of the critics in the culture. In this dream Jessica clearly decides to go against the collective critics by approving of the film showing the blending of spirit and human, of the masculine and the feminine (the man's ability to become pregnant), and of the masculine with the divine.

The dream says that God impregnates the masculine. Therefore, it appears that Jessica's psyche is suggesting that her transformational work has created a product (baby) with spiritual significance. As Jessica is a person committed to her spiritual life, this dream validation reassured her that her developmental process does more than serve her ego. Regardless of the cultural critics, Jessica favors this development, this new birthing and, by implication, the image of the masculine as mother.

During the 1950s, when Jessica had formed her persona as a wife and mother, her culture demanded that women be relatively powerless, if not actually subservient. The way to stay safe and be accepted was to embrace "womanly" attributes and leave accomplishments and personal power to the men. Contrary to that cultural belief, the dream suggested to Jessica that the masculine attributes and processes she had embraced result in divine creations.

This amazing dream evoked much emotion and thought. Jessica wrote: "The altar is gold, which indicates transformation, the goal of the alchemical process, of psycho-spiritual growth and development. Journaling and working this incredible dream gave me a sense of the validation of my authentic self, the gold or true value within me, even though the collective perception (the bad movie review) does not always support what I value. All of the work of developing a masculine aspect of my personality seems to culminate in this image of mystical conception. In addition, the removal of my nipples, the symbol of maternal nurturing, feels like a final statement by psyche that my role as the mother has come to completion." There may be a when-then aspect to this dream: When the masculine is impregnated, then the mothering aspect can be released.

Over the years of this dream series, the masculine has altered its presentation substantially—from an infant stuck in a car while its mother receives therapy, through several heroic figures, to an integration with the divine. The most recent dream takes us back to the mundane and a challenge of more work in the future.

May 2, 1999: The Garbage Man
A very large, stocky black garbage man comes into our bedroom. He wants us to pay him immediately. He proceeds to lie down on my side of the bed while I write out the check. I am somewhat frightened since he has most obviously invaded our space. I wonder if he might be planning to hurt us, but it seems that he just wants his money. When he gets it, he leaves.

About this Jessica wrote: "Because this dream takes place in the bedroom is it suggesting that I need to be more intimate with the masculine energy that can clean out and remove literal clutter? Or, metaphorically, that the part of me that clears out old thoughts, beliefs, patterns that no longer serve me is determined to be paid." Each is a valid question based on the dream content. Jessica doubted that the suggestion was aimed at the literal level of physical clutter. More likely, as with most dreams, the message was metaphoric and symbolic. Recognizing that allowed Jessica to further examine the deeper levels of the dream.

The garbage collector clearly invades the bedroom, the place she shares with her husband, the place of intimacy, privacy, dreaming, and rest. The dream shows that the masculine — the goal-oriented, focused energy — that takes away the garbage is intent on getting his due from both her and her husband. ("He wants us to pay him immediately.")

Exacting payment is an interesting issue in dreams. There is indeed a price to pay for doing the kind of cleaning, sorting, and disposal that results from consciously dealing with the dreaming that occurs in the bedroom. For instance, if a dream causes a dreamer to suddenly realize that his or her job is harmful or unproductive, he or she may begin to seek other employment. To the part of the self that values stability and the status quo, change — even positive change — is a high price to pay. Over the years in my practice several dreamers have quit their weekly dream groups when they realized that the price they would have to pay to follow their dreams was more than they could tolerate. At least the decision is a conscious one. Saying no with awareness is far better than saying no from a position of denial. Awareness always opens the door to potential movement when time, circumstances, or personal strength are more favorable.

There seem to be two important levels to "The Garbage Man" dream. The first message, appropriate at this stage in the development of Jessica's own inner masculine, suggests that it is time to further confront some issues in her thirty-five-year marriage. We arrived at this conclusion because the dream language clearly placed the garbage collector in her marriage bed. Jessica wrote the dream with these pronouns: our bedroom, *my* side of the bed, invaded *our* space. If the dream had been about Jessica's personal development, the scene would have been set in *her* bedroom with the garbage man demanding payment by invading *her* space.

Payment is usually expected after the completion of a job. Therefore, we looked at the transformation already experienced by Jessica, much of which has affected her strength in her marriage, her role as a wife. As she has developed and changed, her husband has had to adapt and adjust to his "new" wife. (He teases that he lives with a woman who has been reincarnated many times since he married her.) Some spouses might feel that the price for such alteration is excessive.

Metaphorically, the marriage bed might suggest the blending of the masculine and the feminine. Such integration has been the overall goal of this dream series, as well as Jessica's conscious focus, for many years, and it appears the time has come to receive payment for all that work. Considering the garbage man as a shadow (unconscious or unlived) element within Jessica suggests that it is time for her to pay for all the clearing out and cleaning up that has occurred. Now that Jessica has a fully functional masculine component to her personality, she will undoubtedly be expected to use it, to pay the bill tendered at the end of this potent piece of individuation.

Where this work will lead her is unknown, of course. Dreams present what is necessary and possible, but only our awake egos can commit to the changes that are suggested. Great strength and conscious commitment are necessary to "pay the garbage man" what he (the dream) deserves. But Jessica is willing to commit to the following: " I am determined to continue using my newly developed masculine energy in my career and in everyday life. Now that I feel, and my dreams seem to confirm, that my masculine is integrated, I expect to continue to access left brain skills such as logic, planning, and judgment. I am on the alert to detach from excessive emotion and from overreacting. This, of course, is an ideal scenario, but even as I write, I feel a sense of renewed commitment to keep the masculine activated. Should I 'fall off the wagon' I expect my dreams will alert me before much harm is done!"

CHAPTER ELEVEN

The Unknown Young Man

Dreamer: Tom
Recurring symbol: unknown young man
Length of dream series: 5 months
Number of dreams presented: 5
Script messages addressed:
   "To be safe, you must accept responsibility for your mother's
      feelings and needs."
   "All work and no play is the formula for success."
Benefits to the dreamer:
   Escaped emotionally needy and demanding maternal script.
   Broke free from a compulsive work ethic by embracing a
      more feminine process.
Summary: A 73-year-old retired businessman learns to embrace
himself and life with a gentle spirit.

This chapter and the following one contain studies from
members of the same dream group. As group leader, I was able to
watch the recurring symbols come into focus and work with the
dreams when they were fresh. These two studies are similar in
that each features recurring images of a person unknown to the
dreamer and of the same sex as the dreamer. Each seems to show
a clear re-creation of both gender role and self-image. Both

involve healing of the past to create a more healthy sense of self and, by extension, healthier present relationships. Despite the age and gender differences, both dreamers are working through similar developmental issues. We hope that these stories will show the value of short recurring studies and the brilliant healing provided by dreams regardless of the dreamer's age or his or her issue.

Tom is a vibrant seventy-three-year-old man who has committed his life—both professionally and personally—to the processes of human transformation and organizational change. He received an MBA and a doctorate from the Harvard Business School, was a professor there and at the UCLA Graduate School of Business, and worked as a business consultant in the United States and Europe for over thirty years. He also practiced as a California certified organizational psychologist.

Tom had never before participated in dreamwork, but from his first group meeting he felt he had "come home." Within a few weeks of Tom joining the group, we noticed the recurring presence of an unidentified masculine dream character. Was there a connection, dream to dream? If so, what was developing within this series and how would it impact Tom, a mature man committed to inner exploration, who appears comfortable with himself and accomplished in the world? What could a man who had spent so many decades on personal growth and development harvest from dreams strung together by this recurring dream character?

These questions intrigued me in light of Jessica's study. During my years of dream tending, I have grown aware of the need for women to develop a functional inner masculine archetype. With Tom's study I was eager to see what a similar development would mean to a man who had already retired from a successful career. I suspected Tom's dreams would not address the manifesting and goal-oriented mechanism of the masculine, since Tom had clearly integrated that energy successfully in his twenties. Then what did this young, unknown masculine force want, if anything?

From his emotional response to each dream featuring an unknown male character, we had no doubt that the series was valuable to Tom. Intuitively, he felt that something very important was unfolding within him, leading to a more natural, uncomplicated way of living. Due to his unusual worldly success, Tom had always lived life on a "grand scale." In contrast, Tom said, "This young dream character feels closer to my nature and feeds my desire to be simple, to lead a less complicated life." Perhaps this dream character would lead Tom to a certain balance still necessary for his healing and wholeness.

As we began to work with the dreams as a series, Tom's feeling was borne out. The first dream, "Held Up at the Border," showed Tom and "an unknown young, male business associate" in a German train station, trying to get to Paris in order to fly home. Tom is unable to find his passport. The young man "goes swiftly through Immigration and Customs to get the train for Paris." Dream ego feels "very frightened that without a passport or a ticket home, they will not let me through."

Recurring dreams often show us the ways we are "stuck" by presenting images of characters who are not. This seemed to be the case in this piece, suggesting Tom was stuck in Germany and unable to leave. And what is Germany as a symbol? Dream settings often represent states of mind, so we examined both of the geographic locations in this dream. Tom described Germany as "highly task-oriented, where family is subordinated to work, which, in my experience, was very serious and technical." In contrast, Tom defined France as "a place where aesthetics and good living are emphasized, at home and in the family. Rigid boundaries are placed around the time and energy devoted to work, keeping it in its proper place."

The unknown man in the dream carried a great emotional charge for Tom. He said, "It's as if this competent young man is capable of making significant transformations in states of mind. He goes swiftly through Immigration and Customs, from a serious work attitude (Germany) to joie de vivre (France). Though he is unclear as yet, I want to get to know him, to make him a more conscious part of myself."

Because the dream began in a train station, we wondered whether psyche was suggesting that Tom had been *trained* in a significant way that continued to keep him separate from his identity (passport) and from more relaxed and joyful living (France). If so, the dream suggested that his training kept Tom locked into a production-oriented, disciplined, and controlled mindset even though he was now retired. An important goal for both men and women in their later years is to balance lives formerly devoted to achieving both status and financial success.

The dream says that Tom cannot go home until he proves his identity (recovers his passport). For Tom, the meaning of going home carried a strong emotional charge. "Home is the place of authenticity and of peace. I guess we are all searching for that feeling within us. In addition, home has deep spiritual connotation for me, referring to a place of peace after death. At my age, that is significant!"

Often one series dream presents a problem and another provides a solution. That seems the case with the issue of identity, which reappears in another dream later in the series.

Two weeks after the first series dream, Tom dreamed about "an unknown young man taking up the white ceramic kitchen tiles" laid by Tom and his wife only a month before.

> The replacement tiles are one and one-half inch thick, soft cork tiles. We ask the woman who hired the young man, "Are you taking up the tiles so you can have softer ones?" "Yes," she replies. We think it is odd she is taking them up after only a month but we also understand that she wants softer ones.

This dream's potential for leading to a resolution of being "stuck" lies in the significance of the flooring. Tom immediately resonated to a definition of floors as "what is under us as we stand"—representing *understanding*. How we understand the world greatly affects our ability to move in it. How we understand ourselves influences our options. Continuing to work with the symbol of the flooring, Tom said, "White ceramic is bland and hard on the feet, whereas cork is warm, soft, multicolored, and multitextured. I'd far prefer to understand life and myself from a soft, accepting, comforting, varied perspective than from the hard, practical, sterile white view. The speed with which the tiles are being torn up (a month after being laid) suggests that a rapid change is taking place." After a pause he continued, "I'm standing on the cork floor. It feels forgiving, easy on the body even after a long day in the kitchen." Later reflections on the dream led Tom to see that the white tile represented "a hard, brittle, persistent judgmental stance I have toward myself, particularly in regard to my relationships with women. A great deal of forgiveness is necessary if I am to heal this old pattern, originating in my relationship with my mother."

At this point, we get our first glimpse into Tom's script. The relationship issue with Tom's mother shows up in an interesting way in the very next series dream. "Due to an impending but undefined attack I join others in the front closet of my childhood home, where we wrap ourselves in coats as shields." This sets the stage for dealing with a sense of vulnerability from the past (childhood home). The solution is to wrap up in protective clothing (coats) that protects us from threatening, chilling environmental conditions. In Tom's case, this referred to the chilling moods of his unhappy mother.

The dream then shifts scenes to an even colder environment, an ice skating event outdoors in winter. Enter the unknown man, who helps Tom clarify his identity:

> Skating beside me is an unknown young man, a powerful skater who asks, "Is it Tom or Bob? Oh, I see. It's Tom," he says, looking at my nametag. "OK, Tom, let's go." With that, I skate down the hill very fast, with the young man at my side. At the bottom I know there'll be a big banquet or feast but I still wonder about the attack.

The young man asks dream ego his identity, Tom or Bob? Bob was the name of Tom's father, who died when Tom was nine. This change in family dynamics caused young Tom to quickly "grow up" and become "the man of the family." Tom felt that, in order to survive, he had to take care of his mother's emotional needs. His inability to satisfy her created the "persistent judgmental stance I have toward myself in regard to women" mentioned in the preceding dream. "My emotional 'default' position is to assume responsibility for the feelings of any woman, to fix whatever is wrong, and to never quite measure up to the role. No matter what I do, I always feel, at some level, that I'm not good enough." Does this self-concept keep Tom locked up in Germany? Later dreams tie this together.

If Tom is to deal with the threat of these feelings from his past ("an impending but undefined attack") and protect himself from the cold chill ("wrap in the overcoat") of demanding moods, ego will need some help from a new inner helper, the young masculine. Remember that this is the energy that knows how to cross the borders from one state to another. This energy brings the awareness of identity (self, not father) that then allows ego to traverse the ice (frozen emotions) with skill, grace, and joy. This is the first actual contact with the unknown male in the series dreams, the first time ego and the unknown character talk. What more important gift could he provide than recognition of true identity? It seems a part of Tom's passport is developing.

We decided to include the next dream titled "Michael Jordan and the Carpet" even though the masculine character is recognized, not unknown. However, Jordan is not a personal acquaintance of the dreamer and so is literally unknown. But, as is true with anyone of such stature, reputation, and renown, Jordan could be considered an archetype, a god-like character. In addition, since Tom is Caucasian, Jordan could represent the shadow (an unconscious or unlived aspect of the dreamer's psyche) and therefore increases in importance. But finally, we include this dream because it points to the *emotional default position* Tom identified in the preceding dream.

In the dream, Jordan is visiting Tom. They are examining an oriental carpet when a phone call interrupts them. Tom is told that because his daughter is too sweet her marriage is severely threatened. Tom had an immediate hit on this personality trait as one of his chronic lifetime problems in his relationships. This automatic adaptation to being overly compliant and even self-sacrificing to others, women in particular, had seemed a necessity to young Tom, who assumed responsibility for his mother's happiness after the death of her husband. Now, sixty-four years later, if Tom wants to save the "marriage" (of his dream daughter), an inner integration of his own inner masculine and feminine, of doing and being, he needs to allow himself to be/feel real rather than sweet, a choice he was not allowed as a child.

As the dream continues, Tom tells Michael Jordan he will have to wait, as Tom must deal with this problem of too much sweetness. Jordan says "That's OK, man, I can wait." It's as if this powerful masculine force is willing to be patient as ego struggles for this inner balance.

In dream group Tom committed to staying conscious of this old behavior pattern of automatic sweetness. This proved immediately fruitful. The following week Tom reported: "The days following the dream I uncharacteristically did some powerful and clear boundary setting with an adult child of mine who was definitely crossing over into my space, inappropriately." This kind of clear, firm, unsweet boundary-setting behavior also showed up in a subsequent dream when Tom confronts a nasty female. This next dream, though technically not part of the series, is included because it deals with the transition of the mother issue.

> George Harvey's mother has died. He wants to send her remains home especially fast, so my assistant and I arrange for a plane to take the casket. My assistant, a tall, angular young woman, makes a lot of critical remarks to me. "Listen," I say, "Why are you being

such a bitch? Stop it!" She says, "Yes, I guess I am. I don't know why." I think maybe she has PMS or something.

Reflecting on this dream, Tom writes in his dream journal: "George Harvey is mild, pleasant, and too sweet. Again, I am confronted by that aspect of my personality. It has caused a great deal of pain, not only with women but also professionally. Because my mother demanded that I be forever sweet, never honest, my feelings can explode from the opposite end of the spectrum, spewing unwarranted criticism and judgment on those close by. This seesaw dynamic has clearly created a need for emotional balance, the kind necessary to skate powerfully as I did in a previous dream. I want emotional honesty without fear of being frozen into submission by my mother's icy moods. Therefore, it doesn't surprise me that the mother in this dream has to die. Disposing of her 'remains' has been my task in therapy for several years."

Because confronting a bitchy woman, in this case the volunteer, is so hard for Tom due to his "sweetness addiction," his dream group shouted approval when he stood up to her. We pointed out how quickly she fades under ego's rebuke. As often happens when emotions are high and the creative spark flies from person to person, Tom made a connection to the acronym PMS. "Post-Mother Syndrome!" he shouted.

One of the most frustrating aspects of series work is the changing faces of the repeating symbol. Suddenly the dream guide or hero is shown as needy or wounded. So it is with the following dream, in which the unknown masculine is a crippled boy needing help from ego.

> A group of children are preparing to swim. A crippled boy, about nine or ten, needs to be lifted from his chair to some apparatus that will lower him into the water. When the rope starts to slip I see he is going to fall so jump in front of him to help. He is suddenly a full-grown young man, handsome with black hair and graying temples. "Thank God somebody is here to help," he says. I do not tell him I have a bad back. It seems strong enough to handle this task.

So here we see a larger truth of this repeating character. The masculine that can easily traverse emotional states, that can truly identify ego, that can soften understanding (tile-setter) must be crippled in some way or Tom would have had access to these qualities all along. The dream suggests that ego must get involved, make conscious decisions to help. In this dream, the crippled boy, age nine or ten when the dream begins, will be unable to submerge himself into the healing waters without ego's help. Remembering the ice in a previous dream led us to wonder if some previously frozen feelings have thawed, creating an emotional pool where the crippled boy can go for healing.

Two when/then dynamics appear in this piece: When ego offers help, then the young one matures immediately. When ego embraces his own crippled way of thinking and doing (the masculine principle), then he recalls his pain from the past: "I do not tell him I have a bad back." (Psyche often shows past history as the dreamer's back.) However, when ego recalls his own wounded past, he is aware of his present power to deal with this burden: "It seems strong enough to handle this task."

The importance of the connection between ego and the wounded self from the past was extremely significant to Tom. He wrote, "I have had a tendency to vehemently deny any crippled parts of myself. Therefore I have not had awareness of what needs help. The recognition and compassionate acceptance of these kinds of limitations has been a central focus of my psychotherapy, to which I previously brought a kind of furious denial of any personal limitations."

One of the great powers of the dream is that it brings awareness beyond or beneath the intellect. I believe this awareness causes the transformation that is obvious among rigorous dream students. The experience within the dream seems to be acting out what the awake ego is determined to deny. But when we star in our own dream theaters, our frozen feelings are accessed before we can awaken and cast them aside as unimportant.

As is true of all series work, this is a work in progress. So far, all the dreams in this series have occurred within a five-month period. Weaving the dreams together creates a lovely new carpet, an understanding that will surely help the dreamer move on in a more healed way as his life continues to unfold. Tom wrote: "In reflecting on this short series, I see and feel a clear need for a force that can easily transcend various emotional states and, in particular, move swiftly beyond the exclusively serious masculine work ethic to also embrace a more feminine enjoyment of life. And this is certainly happening—in my volunteer work, in my poetry writing, and in playing jazz again.

"It has been critical for my ego to return to the dark days of my youth to find what has been hidden: my true identity. I think that really experiencing the truth that I am not my dad and no longer need to carry on his role allows me to pull up the cold, hard foundation upon which I have, in some ways, been standing more than sixty years.

"Without question, embracing the crippled part of me without fearing the pain of my past feels enormously powerful. I am anxious to see what this unknown masculine will lead me to next!"

I asked Tom to compare the processes of working each dream individually as it occurred to working with all the dreams as a series. Here is his response: "By weaving each dream together, uninterrupted in series form, I can more deeply feel the presence of an inner force determined to get me free to feel all the joy that life affords. I am nearly overwhelmed with the love that I feel from and for this unknown masculine dream character and for the dream process itself. Even at my age, it is clear that this dreaming force holds me tenderly, ever moving me home."

CHAPTER TWELVE

The Unknown Blonde Woman

Dreamer: Lynda
Recurring symbol: unknown blonde woman
Length of dream series: 7 years
Number of dreams presented: 16
Script messages addressed:
"A woman must sacrifice her authenticity to please her partner."
"You deserve abuse when you make mistakes."
Benefits to the dreamer:
Reviewed issues of former relationship and substance abuse addiction.
Acknowledged the emotional devastation that results from inauthentic sexual/relationship behavior.
Revisited grief from the past.
Identified destructive ways of thinking and doing that interfere with inner peace.
Learned to more deeply honor her feelings.
Dream approach: Symbol focus
Summary: A 40-something woman reviews her history of substance and relationship abuse, and recognizes healing that leads to authentic wholeness.

This chapter complements the preceding one because the recurring symbol is another unknown character, in this case, a blonde woman. As with the previous study, this dreamer presented most of these dreams as they occurred, to a dream group. However, Lynda did not receive full benefit from the dreams until she worked with them as a series.

A goal of this book is to provide procedures for approaching a series of dreams containing a recurring symbol. Series consisting of more than five dreams required some kind of organizational plan. Without a structure, dreamers who participated in this study were overwhelmed by the complexity of the task.

This chapter uses *symbol focus* to simplify and organize sixteen dreams containing the recurring symbol of a blonde woman. In this process, the recurring symbol is extracted from the context of the dreams, synthesized and partially separated from the overall dream drama. To understand this procedure, imagine seeing a play with only one character highlighted from scene to scene.

The symbol focus summarizes the activities of the recurring symbol in each dream. This method can be used with dream characters, animals, houses, cars, and other symbols. The dreamer examines the full dream and then extracts the symbol to become deeply familiar with it. For example, here is the full text of the first dream from "The Blonde Woman" series, followed by the symbol focus technique.

1993: *The Blonde Woman Priest*
I am in a large institutional type building (a hospital?) when I realize I have missed church through busyness and just deciding not to bother. I hurry to the chapel in the basement but as I enter, I see the service has

ended. Folding chairs are stacked against the wall and the priest—a woman with long blonde hair and a full-length black robe—is gathering up the communion accessories. She looks at me as if puzzled, smiles with welcome, and returns to her task.

Two women are close together, praying quietly. I look to the altar and suddenly am filled with spirit. A light shines brightly white and the crucifix is radiant. Tears leap to my eyes. I wonder how I could have stayed away so long. I remember why I must go frequently and regularly to worship. Then I simply stand there, filled with awe, wonder, and gratitude.

Focusing primarily on the symbol of the blonde woman provides this synthesis of Dream One: In a hospital chapel in a basement, a priest is gathering up the communion accessories. The priest is a blonde woman wearing a full-length black robe.

Obviously, the overall significance of the dream is lost in this synthesis, but only temporarily. With patience, the symbol focus process allows the dreamer to clearly see the movement of the symbol from dream to dream. In the present dream study, this approach highlights the various incarnations of the blonde woman character—alterations in her appearance, patterns formed by her behavior, attitudes and values she embodies. Most of all, it shows how the symbol transforms from the beginning to the end of the series. Keep these goals in mind as you read.

When Lynda and I tried to synthesize all sixteen series dreams, we found that five dreams would not comply with the symbol focus structure. Because dream ego and the blonde woman are interchangeable or intricately connected in each of those five dreams, the full dream must be presented. However, the symbol focus process is used with the rest of the dreams. Watch the flow to see if this approach will be useful for you.

Dream One
In a hospital chapel in a basement, a priest is gathering up the communion accessories. The priest is a blonde woman wearing a full-length black robe.

Dream Two
At a surprise birthday party in the dreamer's honor, a young, blonde, foreign woman tells dream ego, "You have no breasts."

Dream Three
A blonde woman is part of a family grieving at the edge of an open grave.

Dream Four (complete dream)
A lovely blonde woman (I both see her and am her) is kneeling on the bathroom floor over the toilet, violently ill. She is dressed in a blue hospital gown. Everything about her seems vulnerable—she is miserable and in agony. She is vomiting as a result of something she has done, probably drinking too much.

Her husband, a pompous, judgmental minister, is furious with her, lambasting her, telling her she is disgusting. He grabs his things and stomps from the house.

The blonde woman hauls herself from her knees and walks determinedly through the door and up the walk, squaring her shoulders. She taps her husband on the shoulder. When he turns, she slaps him several times with feeling and vigor. Her/my anger and outrage have a calm dignity to them, however. She will not accept verbal abuse from him even though she has made some mistakes.

Dream Five (same night, following Dream Four)
The blonde woman embraces and then disarms a male predator.

Dream Six
(included because Marilyn Monroe was
the quintessential blonde stereotype)
An aging Marilyn Monroe, simple and unadorned, peaceful and reflective, has left an island to escape from the abusive man she lived with for so long. She is ready to heal, to start over, to find herself, and to find peace.

Dream Seven (complete dream)
Clearly divided into two people, I am sitting on a bed and also watching myself lying on the floor on a mat in a dimly lit bedroom. The me on the floor has thick, straight, blonde hair.

The blonde woman on the floor is naked, legs spread, inviting a man to have intercourse, which he does with great vigor. There is an obscenity to it. She acts like she is very aroused and makes all the right movements and sounds. But the observer me knows she is acting. She may as well lie there inertly and let him use her, for all she feels. But she wants to please him, so she pretends.

He gets up to leave the room. Suddenly we two females come together. We are twins, we reflect each other. I am aware of holding and loving and comforting myself! The skin touching skin feels delightful and wholesome. I can feel myself being held and holding from both perspectives at the same time. The emotion is one of deep compassion, caring, love, and gratitude.

Then the man returns. Though we hate to lose the sweetness, we prepare to adjust ourselves to adapt to his lust.

Dream Eight
A blonde woman describes ending her relationship due to some blatantly cruel act of her mate when she was pregnant.

Dream Nine
A beautiful blonde woman on a bicycle is very upset with a woman who is on a bed flirting with some men. The blonde woman feels that the flirt should join some other women searching for the missing children.

Dream Ten (same night, following Dream Nine)
The same blonde woman from the previous dream is very simply dressed, not made-up with lots of artificial products. She is calm, strong, dignified, and clear-sighted. She is a high-school teacher.

Dream Eleven

A blonde woman has borrowed a complex airplane. Although she is not a pilot she seems to assume she can successfully complete her mission. In the cockpit she is gathering evidence about a murder.

Dream Twelve

A blonde woman is in a bathroom. Her husband is forcing her to have sex. She tries to stop him but cannot.

Dream Thirteen

A group arrives at a church commenting about a blonde woman who got off a bus and turned right. She had luxurious, beautiful, long, curly strawberry blonde hair that went to the small of her back.

Dream Fourteen (complete dream)

In a church a young, blonde, rather heavyset woman is overwhelmed and beginning to break down, collapsing under the weight of worry and stress of caring for a young boy. I put my arms around her, comforting by allowing her to express her feelings. I keep repeating, "It's okay, we're here for you, you're not alone, we'll get through this together, we will help you." I feel tremendous love and compassion as I continue to hold her.

The next two dreams, the last of the series, show the dreamer as a blonde woman.

Dream Fifteen (complete dream)

I see myself in the mirror. I am an attractive young woman in my late teens or early twenties. I have platinum blonde, shiny, straight hair that comes to mid-neck. I am occupying a new body. I have small breasts and a small ass. Though different, my body is definitely in proportion.

Dream Sixteen (complete dream)

I am looking in a mirror, combing my hair. I notice how light it is getting; the natural blondeness is showing through. I like the way it looks and know that if I let this process continue it will be quite blonde before long. I think how different I will look, but that my hair will be lovely and soft.

This simplified process makes it is easier to see the patterns contained within the series. For example, Dreams Four, Five, Eight, and Twelve all contain themes of abuse from a spouse or mate. Dream Seven continues the relationship theme, showing the blonde woman inviting intercourse with a pretense of enjoyment despite her obvious despair. Dreams Four and Five show a female victim regaining her power. Three dreams take place in a church (One, Thirteen, and Fourteen). Two dreams (Fifteen and Sixteen) show dream ego examining her blonde self in a mirror; these connect to Dream Two, which presents an observation from the blonde woman about the dreamer's body. Dreams Six and Ten show women without makeup and therefore completely authentic; this contrasts with Dream Seven, which presents a woman compromising her authenticity with sexual pretense.

So what's next? How do we continue to mine these dreams for their gems? We could choose one theme (such as the abuse dreams) and focus only on that. Or we could hunt for the when/then shifts from dream to dream or theme to theme. We could review the series by focusing on only dream ego. But first, because the initial dream of the series is often a harbinger of the dreamer's future growth and development, it usually warrants in-depth study. It often suggests the overall reason for the journey and points the way to proceed. (As is true with many studies, the first recorded dream in this series occurred years before the second series dream.)

In the first series dream, dream ego feels a strong need to reconnect with a consistent spiritual practice. ("I look to the altar and suddenly am filled with spirit. A light shines brightly white and the crucifix is radiant. Tears leap to my eyes. I wonder how I could have stayed away so long. I remember why I must go frequently and regularly to worship. Then I simply stand there, filled with awe, wonder, and gratitude.")

Our focus is on the blonde woman, so we pay close attention to her role in this beginning dream. The blonde woman appears as a priest who is dealing with items of communion. A priest is a spiritual leader, one who ministers to others. Communion is an act of becoming one with, a union or fellowship, an exchange or a form of synergy. For Christians, communion is a symbolic act connecting the human realm to the spiritual. At one level, communion is a valuable outgrowth of dreamwork—connecting the dreamer to disparate parts of himself or herself and bridging the human and spiritual domains. The dream suggests that the repeating symbol will be instrumental in spiritual healing, in creating wholeness (communion). This is particularly apparent in four dreams spanning seven years, wherein the dreamer feels herself to be in union with the blonde woman.

Dream Four

A lovely blonde woman (I both see her and am her) is kneeling on the bathroom floor over the toilet, violently ill.

Dream Seven

Clearly divided into two people, I am sitting on a bed and also watching myself lying on the floor on a mat in a dimly lit bedroom. The me on the floor has thick, straight, blonde hair.

Dream Fifteen

I see myself in the mirror. I am an attractive young woman in my late teens or early twenties. I have platinum blonde, shiny, straight hair that comes to mid-neck.

Dream Sixteen

I am looking in a mirror, combing my hair. I notice how light it is getting; the natural blondeness is showing through. I like the way it looks and know that if I let this process continue it will be quite blonde before long. I think how different I will look, but that it will be lovely and soft.

We have "reduced" the dreams by focusing on only the blonde woman. Now we shift our focus, weaving the dreamer's life story into the series. We review the dreams again, including more material but now with a heightened awareness of the recurring symbol.

The first series dream occurred in 1993, five years before Lynda joined a dream group. At that time she was dealing with a difficult divorce and the death of her beloved grandmother. This first dream suggested that it was important for Lynda to move into a deep place (basement) to meet a blonde spiritual leader intent on communion. As the series unfolded we found that blonde woman repeatedly led Lynda to dig into old boxes, long stored in the basement, below conscious awareness. Each dream activated within Lynda a sorting and tossing-out process, particularly related to her sense of herself as a woman.

To proceed with this study we decided to test the theory that dreams present views of life and of self needed to achieve health and wholeness. On that premise, we went through the dreams, reading the symbols and metaphors as "directions" that were to be followed—as instructions from psyche. This time we synthesized the metaphors from the simplified dreams to see what instructions the recurring symbol provided for Lynda. In some cases, the lesson is observed by or experienced by dream ego, in the dream. Assuming the blonde woman to be a part of Lynda, we searched for her lessons and applied the pronoun *you* to describe them. For example, in Dream Three when the blonde woman is seen grieving at a graveside, the lesson to Lynda becomes this: "You need to grieve." In some cases, the message resonated only when Lynda worked with the dream. Following this process of an overview of the flow of psyche, you will learn more about the dreamer.

Dream One: Your life task at this time is communion with self, others, and God.

Dream Two: You need to deal with issues of insufficient nurturing ("You have no breasts").

Dream Three: You need to grieve.

Dream Four: You need to see the ways in which addiction destroys you. Become aware that the fact that you have made mistakes does not mean that you deserve to be abused.

Dream Five: You need to confront and disarm abusive processes, as well as any form of abuse from others.

Dream Six: You need to see that even the most famous, exploited, abused, and self-destructive sex objects (Marilyn Monroe) can mature, heal, and become authentic.

Dream Seven: You must not only see but truly feel the degradation that comes from playing sexual games, from acts of codependency, and from pretending rather than being authentic.

Dream Eight: You must end any abusive relationship in order to protect what is potential (pregnancy) within you.

Dream Nine: You must search for the lost potential, the vulnerable feelings (the lost children) rather than engage in sexual games (flirting).

Dream Ten: You must see that the healed feminine (the one who searches for the lost children rather than playing sexual games) is authentic, beautiful, calm, strong, dignified, and clearsighted.

Dream Eleven: Complete your life's mission by taking a risk (flying the airplane) to find out what has been murdered.

Dream Twelve: Beware of being raped by a masculine energy that will not honor the needs of the feminine. Protect feelings (feminine) from destructive thoughts or forced accomplishment (masculine rapist).

Dream Thirteen: On the way to your spiritual center, notice that the blonde woman with the beautiful hair is leaving the collective way and taking the right path.

Dream Fourteen: In the spiritual place ego must support, with love and compassion, the heavy feelings (woman/feminine) that are overwhelming.

Dream Fifteen: See yourself as a youthful and vital woman whose ability to nurture (breasts) is in proportion with your past (behind/past).

Dream Sixteen: A transformational process (hair dyeing) is occurring, which leads to a lighter, softer way of thinking (the blonde hair).

Not all dream series can be reduced and dealt with in this manner. However, if yours can, you may see what the dreamer saw when she read these directives. "It's as if psyche has been providing me with a very explicit map for my recovery, for my development. I'm amazed at how totally accurate these directions are."

Having glimpsed the suggestions from psyche by tracking the blonde woman, it is time for you to meet the dreamer. Reading her story will add meat to the psychic skeleton of the synthesized dreams.

Lynda's hair is a stunning part of her petite but powerful persona. It is long and curly, bright red, and as exuberant as she is. Lynda is an extremely energetic, bright, witty, open, direct woman. It is hard to believe that, for several decades, this vibrant person used drugs and alcohol as a crutch for dealing with the grief of a difficult life.

Lynda is the youngest in a family of five children. Because her dad was in the military, the family moved often. Lynda suspects that her father took many unnecessary trips to avoid dealing with difficult family problems. Similarly unable to cope with the rearing of five children, and driven by her own inner demons, Lynda's mother began drinking heavily when Lynda was five. By the time Lynda was in junior high her mother was mixing tranquilizers with alcohol. The family moved to Taiwan, where her mother became paranoid, accusing Lynda of behaviors of which she was innocent.

The addiction dreams in the series caused Lynda to newly reflect on her former use of drugs. During her sophomore year of high school, she began smoking hash and opiates. The onset of hallucinations ended those practices, but they were replaced by binge drinking. "We were just the average family of the sixties," she quipped. "We kids were running wild while our mothers were acting out with sex and drugs!"

"Though I was raised as a good Catholic girl, I got pregnant at age eighteen. My mother escaped to Bangkok, leaving me to cope with the pregnancy without her. I stayed with an older, married sister until the baby was born and then gave the baby up for adoption. I feel as if this loss will forever haunt me. (This grief is suggested in Dream Three.)

"I suffered from depression and social binge drinking punctuated by long periods without alcohol. I had started smoking cigarettes in the eighth grade, quit for a couple of years, and began overeating. I then discovered the joys of vomiting for weight control and practiced bulimia for a year.

"Eventually I started drinking daily. For eight years I slowly accelerated the amounts. The daytime drinking led to blackouts. Finally, after realizing how alcohol had become a very toxic medication, I joined a recovery program." (This toxicity is reflected in Dream Four.)

From this brief history it is obvious that at the time of the first series dream, in 1993, Lynda needed to connect to a strong, inner, feminine spiritual force (the "priest" in Dream One) in order to begin facing her addiction to both substances and relationships. Healing addictions and creating healthy relationships (and communion with all parts of herself) became her mission in life, leading her to search for her "murdered" aspects (Dream Eleven).

Lynda's dreams showing the horrors of relationship and substance addiction are linked to those that highlight inauthentic ways of being. Psyche attempts to balance that destructive behavior with dreams showing women who do not cover their true being with "makeup."

The series indicated Lynda's need to grieve (Dream Three) and to search for lost children (Dream Nine). Although she had previously grieved the loss of her first child, she needed to revisit that experience as part of this series. In addition, Lynda was able to acknowledge the loss of her own childlike neediness. As a child of absent parents, Lynda learned to care for herself at an early age. The dreams in this study showed her that her tender qualities continued to be destroyed by a stubborn and insensitive masculine force (the abusive men in the dreams), by destructive ways of thinking about herself and living her life. In addition, the lost child dreams showed her that she had been denying her own vulnerability. As a proudly independent woman, she often preferred to feign strength rather than ask for help from others.

Lynda saw a strong link between the dreams of relationship and substance addiction and the dreams about the women pretending in order to please their men. Alcohol and other drugs are needed to assuage the pain and stress of hiding one's true feelings. Therefore, recovery is—to a great extent—based on the honest presentation of self. The dreams of women without makeup suggest Lynda's willingness to show her true self, blemishes included. She wrote, "I want to learn to be more alive, to be authentically female without playing psychological games.

Instead of being manipulative by using sex as an insurance policy, I want to be fully honest." That level of honesty is equally important in the individuation process—in achieving wholeness.

The dreams focusing on victimized women led Lynda to recognize that she had abandoned her own feelings—her own feminine principle. To satisfy the needs of the material world, of "getting the job done" and accomplishing goals, she victimized herself. She is now on guard to acknowledge and protect her emotions from being "raped" by the demands of the masculine principle. She can no longer ignore her inner reality.

Addressing the blonde hair of the recurring symbol brought to mind the many jokes about blonde bombshells, dizzy blondes, and buxom blondes as symbols of easy sexual exploitation (like Marilyn Monroe). The victimized blonde in this series clearly portrays that unhealed aspect of the feminine in our culture and within Lynda. However, the dream that depicts Marilyn Monroe (who modeled unhealthy values until they destroyed her) as aging, unadorned, and peaceful suggests that healing has begun.

Finally, Lynda was fascinated by the realization that the blonde woman symbol seemed to embrace the best and the worst, the healed and the wounded, the authentic and the stereotypic false female. "It's as if I need to see that my wholeness contains it all, the full spectrum from the divine to the most desperate aspects of my being." Indeed, only by recognizing and embracing the entire array of sub-personalities contained within us all can we hope to attain authenticity and achieve communion/wholeness.

Chapter Thirteen

Military Uniforms

Dreamer: William
Recurring symbol: air force uniforms
Length of dream series: 22 years
Number of dreams presented: 33
Script messages addressed:
"You are superior to others."
"Your father's lineage and life were valueless."
Benefits to the dreamer:
Recognized a life-long anxiety stemming from feeling separated from others.
Learned to value and embrace the vulnerable feminine (feelings and being).
Became comfortable with the authentic ways in which he is different from others.
Freed himself from the "pseudo-superiority" role created by his mother.
Summary: A 72-year-old retired U.S. Air Force Lieutenant Colonel exchanges "uniformity" for authenticity.

William volunteered to do a study for this book because two recurring symbols, vehicles and military uniforms, intrigued him. I favored the vehicle symbol since that dream symbol is common to most dreamers in our mobile world. Furthermore, every vehicle dream I've studied has been important to the dreamer, revealing something crucial about his or her way of moving through the world; drives and motivations; feelings of being stuck, stalled, or out of control. Common vehicle dreams warn symbolically of danger, of some form of a crash, or of insufficient power to proceed or succeed. Usually these dreams provide a clear view of an internal thought process or external behavior that needs monitoring. Because of my preference, William agreed to pursue the vehicles. He worked diligently with these dreams, classifying the type of vehicle, where he was headed in that vehicle, what the setting of each dream suggested, and a variety of other tracks.

Every time we met, William was eager to share the results of his work with the vehicle dreams. However, as the uniform series developed, he began to understand why these dreams had frustrated and upset him for twenty years. During our fourth formal study session, the vehicle dreams and the uniform dreams came together like a well-planned and very satisfying meal. It is this nourishment we offer you in this study.

William is a sophisticated, soft-spoken, articulate man with a ready sense of humor and a strong intellect. His hair is close-shorn and gray, and his chiseled face matches the thinness of his tall body. William served in the United States Air Force for twenty-seven years. He retired as a Lieutenant Colonel twenty-two years before this study began. Given this history, it might seem absurd to pursue a study of military uniforms. After all, if William's dreams were just examining former experiences in the Air Force, he would surely be clad in uniforms. Nevertheless, William was convinced that the uniform dreams represented far more than simply appropriate attire for the dream scene.

The first uniform dream was recorded in 1979 when William began keeping dream journals. However, he never had a way of working with his own dreams until the summer of 1999, when he attended a conference of the Association for the Study of Dreams near his hometown. There he heard a lecture on the value of serial dreams. He subsequently joined a dream group and began to acquire the skills necessary to work with his own inner material.

As the basis for this study, William retrieved more than thirty uniform dreams in his surviving journals. He also suspected that he refused to write at least that many dreams because of the unpleasant feelings attending the dreams. "I came to feel bored and hag-ridden by these nocturnal ordeals. I would see a history of previous dreams during subsequent ones. Because of the 'reality' of the dreams, I had difficulty, while awakening, determining which memory was literally true. I almost hated to go to sleep."

As William considered the symbolic meaning of a uniform, he had a vivid memory from forty-five years before. He introduced the uniform series with this recollection: "My first real awareness of the significance of wearing a uniform came in 1945 when I heard a man define his business attire as a uniform. He said that his tweed jacket, gray flannels, oxford button-down shirt, university tie, argyle socks, and white bucks were the Ivy League uniform.

"Eight years later, in Officer Candidate School, I learned the verb form of the word uniform. I had never before experienced the intensity of attention to detail as was demanded by the exactness of the USAF uniform. I had to *be uniform*, exactly the same as everyone else. How one wore one's uniform was deliberately translated into a test of fitness to earn a commission.

Precision measured survival, and I embraced it without realizing how deep the internalization went."

Like every study participant in this book, William had strong feelings about his recurring symbol, but his memory of the dreams was inaccurate. "Only by studying the dreams as a series did I realize that the uniform dreams, which were fraught with anxiety, should be more specifically designated as 'Inappropriate Uniform' dreams. By studying each dream, I picked up a recurring pattern. Basically, these recurring anxiety dreams showed me desperately searching for missing uniform items such as hats, shoes, shirts, pants, insignia, or class ring. In some dreams I had certain items, but they were incorrect for my present need. The dreams showed mismatched items from different seasons or functions, such as a summer khaki shirt with a blue winter uniform; combat flying boots with 'dress blue' office wear; garrison cap instead of parade hat; outdated and no longer authorized 'blues.'"

Collecting and typing his entire history of uniform dreams allowed William to more clearly perceive what was actually repeating within this anxiety series. "In dream after dream, I find myself working with a team of men to complete an assignment at a military installation. As I am getting ready to leave, I realize I'm not wearing the proper uniform items and cannot get them at the Base Exchange Store. I am unable to leave my room because I am 'out of uniform.' In addition to uniform problems, I have far too much baggage, which I have not begun to pack for the trip. I am supposed to leave the installation in a variety of vehicles. Finally, in almost every dream, I'm about to miss my team's departure because I am late."

As William began to organize his dreams, he noticed the following twists and turns within the theme of anxiety-producing uniform dreams. Over the years, dream variables include:

Time periods: "Some dreams took place in the historic past, others in a kind of science-fiction future, while still others showed different periods from my actual career. Because the anxiety of an insufficient or improper uniform ranges over these variations of time, it is as if psyche wants to show that the problem is the same in every time, place, and circumstance."

Geographic location: "Throughout the uniform series, I find myself in settings such as Victorian British India, eighteenth-century France, the Alaskan interior, WWII Germany, Central American cities and jungles, several air bases in the western United States, abandoned desert installations, formal campus parks, barren plateaus, Japan and China, and even Vietnamese river banks. Again, it is as if I need to see that what I'm being told is not just about 'place.' The problem of identity, presentability, uniformity is the same everywhere. The different settings are to emphasize this for me, to keep me from confusing my situation with location. It is as if my dreams want to keep me from diagnosing or dismissing the uniform problem as 'localized.' I may need to see that, regardless of where I am, I can feel inappropriate, insufficient, unprepared, and stuck."

Service branch or organization: Throughout the series, William is shown wearing uniforms from many different services: U.S. Air Force; U.S. Navy; Special Forces Army; Confederate Army; and British, French, Japanese, and Chinese armies. He even appears as a member of the Star Fleet (from the television series *Star Trek*). "I think this suggests that, no matter what role I'm playing, I feel inappropriate, not 'uniform' enough!"

At our fourth meeting, William linked the frustrating history of vehicle dreams to this uniform series. "As I studied the uniform dreams, I realized that they were tied to many of the vehicle dreams. In most of the dreams, I am desperately trying to create the appropriate uniform so that I can join the others waiting for me to depart with them. In each dream the others on my team will be traveling on a specified vehicle. Thus, it is clear that I am going to miss the boat, bus, propeller/jet aircraft, space ship, sailboat, rubber raft, limousine, and even dog sled! From this I see the obvious metaphor that, over and over again, I am missing out on opportunities to proceed with my life journey. In dream after dream, I'm anxious and immobilized, totally stuck due to my inappropriate uniform. I take this to mean that my long-conditioned thoughts and feelings render me not correctly uniform, that is, unable to fit in. Thus, I am unable to move, to join with others, to proceed in life."

At our fifth meeting, the import of this extensive dream gathering leaped into clear focus when William said, "I have long regarded myself as separate from the average, but studying this series makes me feel the pervasiveness of my separation. Over and over, I can now feel the horrible cost of this separateness in my gut, not just in my head. This is the core issue of my entire life."

This realization led us into William's family script, a rather unique and extreme one, seeming more appropriate for a British citizen than an American. From an early age, William did not wear the same uniform as other children, did not fit in, was not part of the team. "I was raised to be an aristocrat, to feel separate from, better than, different from and superior to others. Because my grandfather established the small town in which I lived, my family had nearly royal status, making me the Crown Prince. This sense of being better than but separate from others has fostered the deep sense of anxiety so clearly represented in the dream series. Despite many experiences in my awake life which told the same story as the dreams, I didn't/couldn't get the message until studying this series." William shared two memories that highlighted this message. "During my USAF career, I roomed with another officer whom I now see as my opposite. While I strove to show my superiority, Chuck was determined to play the role of the common man, the 'aw shucks' kind of guy. 'I'm just the average Joe,' he said one day. 'And you, William, are too, but you just won't admit it.' Indeed, I would not. My sense of superiority was my greatest defense. The separation caused by my 'superiority' created my greatest pain, as the dreams have finally shown me."

A second memory surfaced as William continued. "After presenting a briefing at the Commanding General's staff meeting, a senior colonel approached me saying, 'Good briefing. In fact, the briefing was too good. Why don't you just relax and be a team player with the rest of us!'" Even then, William did not suit up with the rest of the gang.

In the first recorded series dream, we meet a powerful character who must be dealt with if ego is to advance—that is, to change the pattern that keeps him isolated.

April 27, 1979:
Watching the Dark Insignia of Increasing Power
I meet Colonel Sam Thresher. He pretends to be sorry that I was passed over for promotion, but I can tell from his arrogant demeanor that he doesn't mean it. Indirectly, he tells me that if he had really wanted me to be promoted, it would have happened.

I see that Sam's "collar insignia" is morphing. No longer a colonel's eagle, in the space of a moment it changes from one to two dark stars, and finally, I introduce him as a three-star general. I say, "He is in charge of most of the nuclear weapons on this planet."

Then two nervous and upset secretaries from Sam's office interrupt us. They need to report something important to "General Sam." I cannot tolerate how rude the General is to them, so I leave to write in my dream book.

"I think of pairs in dreams as representing something emerging into consciousness," William reported. "In 1979, the feminine, the guide to my way of being and feeling (secretary), was nervously demanding attention from the arrogant masculine of superior rank whose power is increasing extraordinarily (morphing insignia). This masculine controls the ability to destroy (nuclear weapons)."

If this were my dream, I would see that an arrogant, power-inflated, potentially destructive force limits ego's ability to grow and develop ("be promoted"). Ego symbolizes that part of my psyche that is growing, changing, and developing into wholeness with all other aspects of my being. Thus, if a power-inflated way of thinking has control over that development, I am stuck, over-powered by an archetype that will not let me advance.

According to the dream, this type of masculine has no patience with feelings and being, nor with the feminine aspect that is so important to wholeness. Rude treatment of the feminine causes dream ego to leave the general and write in his dream journal. What a great way to deal with the conflict between the masculine and the feminine!

William thought this meant simply doing something meaningful. I saw more in the image, so offer it to the reader as if it were my dream experience:

When my thinking/doing process (masculine principle) has overwhelmed me, I turn to the feminine process (of feeling/being) to get relief. When my arrogant, ruling masculine, capable of great damage, is dismissive of the feelings that I need to experience, the feelings will often come through the dream. Thus, much of my dreamwork, at one level, balances thinking (masculine) with feeling and intuiting (feminine).

Many people in this culture, both men and women, arrogantly value thinking and doing far more than feeling and being. Overvaluing either process causes a devaluing of the other. This imbalance is detrimental to relationships and to the development of wholeness within individuals, families, and cultures.

Most of the series I've studied have followed a discernible pattern. The first dreams define the problem or life issue from a variety of perspectives. Then one particular dream, a "turning-point dream," breaks the pattern. The dreams that follow the turning-point dream show the many aspects of, and possible solutions to, the problem.

William's turning point occurred in a dream entitled "Victoria's Funeral." This is the first dream in which ego discovers that he is not just missing some part of a uniform, but that he is wearing one that is dramatically different from that worn by the other personnel. In the dream, William, a member of the British Army, is the only person in a white uniform. The rest of the army is clad in the ceremonial dark green (nearly black) uniforms of The Black Watch (The Royal Highland Regiment). "We are attending the funeral of Queen Victoria. I see how different I am and realize it doesn't matter. For the first time in my dreams—

and probably in my life—I experience only my enthusiastic interest for the events around me, a new sense of total presence rather
than my usual self-conscious concerns. Instead of focusing on my
uniform, I can hardly wait to see what will happen next. I'm anxious to learn about the ceremony." Dream ego's feelings, unique
and filled with wonder, show the feminine principle in all her
glory. The ability to fully experience an event/transition without
the imposition of old thought patterns that cripple or exploit is a
powerful sign of healing. As we explore the rest of the dream, we
see what has "died" in order to allow this change.

A funeral is a ritual that honors the end of something. In this
dream we see the end of the Victorian era, a highly conformist,
structured, repressed, dutiful, and proper time. An ending is also
a beginning—in this case, of the cultural, scientific, and artistic
revolution of the twentieth century. A big shift, indeed.

Thinking of this in my own terms, I realize that many
dreams help me celebrate the ending of the Victorian era.
Broadly speaking, most dreams overturn an old, repressive
authority in order to welcome a new, more creative and liberat-
ing philosophy. As in the Roaring Twenties, these pivotal dreams
invite us to live a more spontaneous, exciting life. In my view,
burying Queen Victoria translates to something like this: I am
about to experience some kind of freedom from a script that
rigidly dictates what is proper, moral, and strictly acceptable.
This will allow a multitude of possibilities excluded during the
repressed era. No longer bound by the black-and-white, either-or
thinking of the Victorian period, I will feel an inner loosening, a
granting of permission to express the passionate, the mystical, the
outrageous. In my experience, this is a valuable goal of dreamwork: to identify the scripts that imprison the dreamer. Seen in

this light, many dreams are acts of rebellion against an old system that needs to die.

Because of the dramatically different feeling depicted in the "Victoria's Funeral" dream (i.e., being comfortable with a uniform totally different from that worn by others), William was alerted to some important inner change and growth. "I'm not immobilized by being out of uniform. Though different, I feel as if I am dressed appropriately." Ego has transcended the stage of being controlled by concerns about what others are thinking and doing in order to be genuinely himself in the moment.

We examined the specific types of uniforms presented in the dream to see if that would explain the sudden sense of comfort and appropriateness. The British dream army is wearing the uniform of The Royal Highland Black Watch, a regiment historically led by William's ancestors. William is not wearing that uniform. This suggests that he no longer is identified with the old script, the former demands of the family, the duty to tradition so honored in the Victorian age. "It's as if I finally have my own identity. And that's fine."

Six months after the "Victoria's Funeral" dream, William took another look at this family script. He titled the dream "The Changing of the Guard."

> As an adult, I'm returning to my former junior high school. I'm here to evaluate the teachers. I feel uncomfortable, as if I don't belong. I wander around a PTA carnival, which is decorated in a Scottish theme.
>
> Everything is shoddy, including my costume, which was made for me by my mother, from a cheap

old beach towel. The towel is wrapped around my body to represent a Highland costume.

Embarrassed, I whip off the beach towel to find that I am wearing the real thing underneath. It is a perfectly fitting Royal Stewart Highland uniform. When I see this uniform, I realize that I am wearing a true identity under the pretend one.

Highlander is a term applied to someone from the Celtic-speaking tribes that once dominated the British Isles and remain as a form of aristocracy in the remoter regions of Scotland and Ireland. These are William's paternal ancestors. Because William's mother created this shoddy costume, the implication is that she is desecrating his paternal heritage.

William wrote this in his dream journal: "When I claim the identity that is hidden underneath my mother's shoddy creation, I find the strength and potential of my father."

Here the family script divides into two conflicted aspects: mother versus father. William explained: "My mother was from Virginia's landed aristocracy. Her father, raised on his family's plantation, fought in the Civil War, and then created pioneering empires in the American northwest. My grandfather raised my mother to be a princess. Her lifelong obsession was to memorialize her parents and their home (now a National Historic museum once featured on the television show *America's Castles*). In order to live an authentic life and be able to travel with others (the ongoing dream series issue), I must be free of this pseudo-superior burden my mother imposed on me.

"When I look beneath the persona created by my mother, I find my father's outfit and feel good in it. This provides me with a great sense of inspiration. At approximately my present age, my father began to assert his individuality, laying aside the burden of dutiful son and compliant husband. He began to travel and to devote himself to projects of his own design. In his seventies, he finally created a joyful life free from the domination of my mother." In the language of the dream, William's father put aside the uniform/costume created for him by his wife (William's mother) and began to live his own authentic life.

As we studied this dream together, William said, "Finding the genuine uniform underneath my mother's costume frees me from the debilitating attitudes and behaviors that she taught me. Within the dream, I felt that I had come to an end of a pervasive inner conflict of identity. I recognized my genuine self in this dream and liked what I saw."

A costume is the attire donned to play a certain role, supporting the theory of family and cultural scripts. William described that this way: "I realized that I can choose who I want to be, how I present myself, what uniform I will wear. I can take it off. I can put it on. I felt that this insight uniquely freed me from my previous dependence on uniformity and, paradoxically, my inability to fit in. I am not disabled by my uniformity or lack thereof. I have transcended my fixation on the details and symbols of uniformity, of an almost hysterical need to fit in (which I rarely managed) and, on the other hand, I don't need to be immobilized by feeling different from others."

The last dream presented in this series shows the uniform on a significantly different form, that of a female officer. This dream brings the issue of valuing the feminine full circle, from rude treatment in the first dream ("Two nervous and upset secretaries from Sam's office interrupt us....I cannot tolerate how rude the General is to them, so I leave to write in my dream book"), to full acceptance in this last series dream:

May 20, 2000: Resolved

I am in a conference room with one other person, a pretty, young female officer to whom I am offering an important job. She is not sure she can handle it. "Will they recognize me for what I am and not just a woman?" I work to convince her that her competence will win. Finally she says, "Of course, I accept. Now, where are you going?"

I walk around the table to congratulate her on her confidence. I answer her question by saying, "Now I'm going back and see if I can get the same offer to a job I turned down before."

She instantly understands and comes into my arms to congratulate me. She is crying in gratitude and pride. I hold her very gently, amazed by how very frail her body feels inside the uniform. I'm almost afraid she will break.

Here, as in several other studies, we are again brought to the importance of the feminine principle. In a goal-oriented, fast-paced society such as ours, the feminine principle is surely fragile, frail, and easily broken. Honoring and valuing feeling and being is difficult when they get in the way of thinking and doing. The young female officer wants to be recognized for all that she is. It is as if she is calling for validation of feelings, of intuition, of relationships, of being in the moment, of the sacred. Embracing, empathizing with, and building the confidence of this perceptual process is highly significant for William as he struggles to escape from the script of superiority that separates him from others. Human connections are made from heart to heart. The feminine is the guide for this journey; when ego gets her moving ("I work to convince her that her competence will win"), she offers a challenge of her own by asking William where he is going. "Now I'm going back and see if I can get the same offer to a job I turned down before." The suggestion from psyche is that William had previously been offered a task (authenticity? individuation?) that he must face. Now that the feeling aspect is bolstered by new confidence, ego can return to complete the job he previously rejected.

William felt that this dream provided a resolution to this entire study of uniforms and vehicles. He wrote: "The gentle power of this dream experience remains with me. With its perspective and encouragement, I have, for several months, had the confidence and courage to remember a number of strongly formative events, previously buried in my past. Though buried in the past, these experiences were still corrosively active at the unconscious level. Now, knowing that I can reenter those rooms and examine what is there, I experience freedom from a variety of compulsive behavior patterns. I believe this is the job to which the dream referred. I feel gratitude for this life-giving process, which I am now enjoying."

This study ends with the ever-present promise of more to come. William is committed to moving into rooms from the past to discover what they have to offer his growth and development. He is convinced that his discoveries will lead him to feel at peace and involved with life, regardless of the uniform he is wearing or the role he is playing. With that accomplished, he will be able to leave his room, join with the rest of the team, and travel on the various vehicles that intrigue him.

CHAPTER FOURTEEN

Incarceration

Dreamer: George
Recurring symbol: feeling incarcerated
Length of dream series: 8 years
Number of dreams presented: 7
Benefits to the dreamer:
    Recognized addictive thinking and behavior patterns from
      the past.
    Acknowledged the polarity between obsession and absti-
      nence.
    Embraced a desire to abstain from sexual addiction.
    Experienced stimulating, exhilarating feelings resulting from
      recovery.
Summary: A 55-year-old man frees himself from the prison of
sexual addiction to find peace and joy in monogamy.

George worked with four of the following seven dreams in
his dream group in 1988 and 1989, when the dreams were fresh.
Remembering the series and its importance prompted me to
invite him to participate in the study for this book. He was initially enthusiastic. After our first meeting, however, he began to
relive the depression he had experienced at the time he had had
the dreams. Thus, he wrote me a letter containing these remarks:

"Despite my enthusiasm for the dream series project, as I worked with the old dreams I got a very heavy feeling of being pulled back to the past, of being pulled under by an anchor. I suspect that the work might be valuable for other men, but putting myself back into these dreams causes me to lose the peace of the present for which I have fought during the past ten years."

This sort of reaction to reexamining series dreams is not unusual. When the series reflects a difficult piece of psychological work, the dreamer is often reticent to reenter the cauldron of simmering emotions. George was concerned that stirring this old dream pot might cause his former feelings to boil over when he would be better served by keeping the lid on.

All the participants who reworked their series for this book gained tremendous awareness and value, so I encouraged George to reconsider. I suggested that the peace he presently experienced indicated that he had already grown a great deal beyond the issue reflected by the dream series. True peace of mind results from integrating the changes called for by the dream series. When I suggested that the work he feared must have already been accomplished, he was willing to give the series study a second chance. George then participated fully in the project, writing nearly fifty pages about these dreams during the six months that we met together to reframe the original work done ten years before.

This short series has the recurring symbol of either a prison or an army environment. What we are really studying, however, is the recurring feeling of incarceration, the repeating sense of loss of freedom. Because most of the dreams depicted only male characters, George felt that the issues he was dealing with were common to the male gender. Indeed, women, also feel trapped and imprisoned, but George's particular task—moving from the life of a roving, free sexual being to the commitment of marital monogamy—is more likely to be an issue for men than for women.

The first step in any healing process is to identify the problem. The initial dream in George's series did that by setting the dream in an army environment and by reconnecting George with a buddy from his past who poignantly represented an important problem.

> *September 17, 1988: The Lower End*
> I'm in the lower end of a large army barracks with many other young men. The guys in this part of the barracks have had a hard life of deprivation.
>
> I come to the bunk of my old friend, Eddie. He's lean and pale. His eyes look hard and bitter. When we leave the barracks, Eddie starts to jog, challenging me to keep up with him. His pace is too fast for me, and I'm really not interested in the challenge.
>
> As I follow him, the road becomes the gravel alley behind my childhood home. There are deep ruts in this uphill road. He's trying to anger me into a fight.

Dream ego was not interested in the challenge offered by Eddie. However, awake George engaged with Eddie by following him back to their shared past, thirty-five years before. Eddie was a former college friend, a scrappy guy from a poor background hoping to become a successful professional dancer. Unfortunately, his promising career was derailed by alcoholism and nicotine addiction. The Eddie character's insistence upon engaging dream ego led George to see his own internal, very angry, and frustrated "addict" which needed to be acknowledged. George wrote: "Denial of discontent can only increase it. Thus, I am grateful to this piece for reconnecting me with the addict from my past who is demanding that I engage with him. I really need to see how pissed off he is and to consciously take him on!"

Why does the dream place George and Eddie in the army? George needed to admit that he felt that he was locked into a system without freedom or personal identity, descriptors of his own army experience. Though this was not a pleasant admission, it was an essential realization that helped George identify one cause of the depression that burdened him at the time of this dream.

At the time George originally worked the dreams, he attributed his discontent and feelings of loss of freedom to his recent mid-life marriage. No longer allowed the sexual freedom he had experienced for twenty-five years as a professional musician, he struggled with his new identity as monogamous husband. For George, enjoying varied sexual opportunities was one of the benefits of his troubadour lifestyle. His first marriage had been an "open" one, meaning that both he and his wife agreed that, since George was on the road, monogamy was impractical and undesirable. That marriage ended in divorce after six years.

George continued the footloose and fancy-free life until he met Jane, a woman unlike anyone he had previously known. They clicked on many levels, enjoyed an ever-deepening psychological and spiritual connection, and soon began living together. Despite the fact that Jane insisted on a monogamous commitment—completely altering George's lifestyle—George eventually surprised them both by proposing marriage. George believed he was ready to alter his former lifestyle, exchanging the desires of a philandering artist for the rewards of a committed relationship.

Reining in his previously untethered libido presented more of a challenge than George expected. Though happy in his marriage and thrilled with the benefits of truly knowing someone deeply, he soon missed "the chase" and the thrill of sexual conquest that had enlivened his former years. This dream series, which began when he was fifty years old, presented George with a great deal of focus and awareness that helped him deal with his marital transformation. Because this series consisted of only seven dreams containing the feeling of confinement and the symbols of either the army or prison, George was able to summarize the feelings of dream ego in this way: "These are the dreams of a man who feels repressed, confined, without freedom."

George had been married for two years at the time of this first series dream featuring Eddie. The honeymoon phase of his marital relationship was over and old sexual yearnings were beginning to surface. George was aware of feeling depressed, but he had not consciously begun to label these feelings. By returning him to his days as an army recruit, George's first dream reconnected him to feelings of incarceration and a loss of identity created by a social system (the army) that must strip away individuality to create an obedient force. This dream allowed George to admit that his commitment to monogamy was creating intense inner challenges similar to those he previously knew in the army. He had lost his sexual identity and was confined by a system he felt he could not—and did not want to—escape.

These following dream sentences presented another important awareness: "I'm in the lower end of a large army barracks with many other young men. The guys in this part of the barracks have had a hard life of deprivation." As is often the case, this metaphor has two very different meanings, one from the old self and one from the higher wisdom of the dream. George was familiar with a Hindu system of thought that identifies chakras, energy centers in the body said to define differing levels of consciousness. The lower chakras include the areas of relationship and sexuality. George wrote: "The *lower end* is the old, rundown part of town. It is the place of hopelessness, a place to be avoided. I think of lower standards, lower expectations, lower self-worth, and a steadily lowering likelihood of growth. These are the aspects of myself that I hope to heal within my marriage. When I think of this as a metaphor for my life I realize that, during my more sexually free times, I have often lived in a *deprived state* of solitary exile (times devoid of sexual encounters), a condition alleviated by my marriage."

In addition, George certainly felt deprived of his former sexual activity. And, paradoxically, to live only in the lower, sensual, sexual, instinctive part of the self is to be deprived of some deeper aspects of relationship with another, and of the self that operates from higher levels of consciousness. This shift in perception about the lower end reflected George's former feelings and provided a warning to the developing consciousness for which George was willing to fight. (Recall that Eddie, the addicted one, wants to engage George in a fight.)

On the same night as the first dream, George had an additional dream. In it he is a recruit looking for an acceptable place to sleep in a rough, cold barrack built on several levels. Dream ego wanders into the next building looking for someone in charge to help him find a better place to sleep. He encounters officers mingling with rich socialites and recognizes a wealthy young Jewish boy from his childhood. Dream ego feels that he is excluded from both groups, the guys in the lower end and the rich officers.

Awake reflections of this dream piece led George to see that he had never really felt included in a community of men, could never find a comfortable place (bed) among other men. From his early years, he had been far more interested in girls than in establishing relationships with the guys. He realized that his later focus upon women and his frequent obsession with sexuality had worked to create another form of bondage: an exclusion from the camaraderie with other men. George was beginning to see that his former lifestyle had provided him with sexual freedom and the ego rewards of an entertainer, but few other components of a full life.

Realizing the limitations of a yearned-for past is a major step toward integrating a newly chosen lifestyle or personality aspect. As dreams encourage us to more consciously examine the past, we often discover what has been missing. By the next dream, dream ego is fully able to feel the close friendship of other men who are with him in a place of detention.

September 23, 1988: Doin' Time

I'm in a place of detention with many other guys. I've been incarcerated for something insignificant. There is a comradely feeling among the men. I have a small portion of pot in my pocket. It's all mixed up with money so I don't want to throw it all away.

A friend tells us prisoners that we can escape if we remove our watches and pretend that we are deathly ill. We do as we are told. The guard declares that we are sick because the factory that made the watches is contaminated.

It is rare that the decision to alter behavior and surrender an old pattern for a more healthy way of being is all that is needed for change to occur. The commitment to the new self traverses different stages. At the time of this dream, George's inner progress is shown by his feeling like one of the guys, thus moving into a perception of himself as more than a musician and sexual addict. In addition, he recognized that many other men live happy and fulfilling lives while committed to monogamy. But reservation remains, as expressed in the following sentence: "I have a small portion of pot in my pocket. It's all mixed up with the money so I don't want to throw it all away." "There is still value in my addiction," George wrote. "Though very little remains, I do not want to throw it away as yet."

The image of the watches fascinated George. He recognized the truth in the metaphor that time—how we use it, how it uses us—can be toxic. As George reflected on this he realized a great deal about time as it related to his former self and to his recovery from obsessive sexual behavior.

"As an entertainer I lived in a dream-like state. The performer me was not connected to the awake me, to my nonperforming world. I nearly always lived in a state of only momentary gratification. I had no concept of time affecting the progression of events, no idea that my own efforts in the present would influence the evolution of my life. As is true for most addicts, visions of the future never formed in my mind.

"I made my sexual choices almost unconsciously, with no interest in long-term involvement. The future did not exist in these encounters. This kind of ego-centered uncommitted living created a very strong type of prison. I couldn't get what I wanted because I only knew what I didn't want. Indeed, I never really asked myself what I wanted, aside from sexual activity as frequently as I could manage it.

"There is a great saying that you can never get enough of what doesn't satisfy you. In my former life, I felt that lack of satisfaction. This resulted in depression and a profound sense of inner confinement. Eventually, my pain broke through my denial. Rather than remaining totally incarcerated, committed without my conscious consent, I had to find a way to commit myself to another way of being. Thus, at age forty-eight, I proposed marriage to someone who truly wanted to be with me for life. This was not just the beginning of a new 'time'; it was the first conscious day of this new time in my life.

"In the past, I was limited only in my sexual choices. For my sexually addicted self, my marriage created a definite kind of prison. But for my newly developing self, new values began to emerge. Whole new vistas came into view. The fog lifted and I could finally see the connection between now and the future. Time has taken on intense meaning.

"The confinement or prison created by leashing my unchecked sexual behavior is presented in the following dream. This scenario, though extreme, accurately describes denying the sexual instincts that had previously had free rein. The greatest difficulty was not in abstaining, but in convincing myself of my desire to do so. I resented losing the opportunities and activities that might lead to sexual involvement. I most resented denying myself opportunities, activities, and relationships with interesting women because they might lead to sexual involvement."

March 19, 1989: Thought Control
I'm living in a totalitarian society. The government allows no creative thought, no emotional response

and no criticism of itself. To even express feelings is a life-threatening act.

A man friend visits me frequently, giving me surreptitious messages to help me survive. He tells me what I must conceal from the authorities.

A government agent who sits at a judge's bench questions me. Behind him is a dance floor. The individuals on it are shuffling slowly and without rhythm. They remind me of zombies. Their faces show expressions of defeat and sadness. Others sit watching dully. I would like to dance but I know I must not show any interest or enthusiasm.

The interrogator asks: "If you were sitting in front of a lit fireplace on a cold night, would you start thinking? Would you be stimulated? What kinds of things would you consider?"

"Oh," I say, knowing that I must not reveal any possibility of imagination, "I wouldn't think of anything. I might enjoy the warmth." (Should I even have used the word enjoy?)

About this piece George wrote: "This was a very disturbing dream because it so powerfully portrayed the system of self-censorship (the government) I had activated to maintain my first monogamous relationship. Even though my sensual desire could not be satisfied within the confines of my marriage, and temptation abounded, I would not risk my relationship with my wife. My monogamy caused me to feel that I had to reject all my feelings, that I had to deny what stimulated me."

Proceeding on the assumption that all dreams not only lead us to recognize a truth of our present experience, but also help us move beyond what is—in this case—imprisoning us, George and I searched for value in this depressing piece. We noticed that the "friend" who provided dream ego with surreptitious messages wanted to keep him safe, to enable him to survive in this repressive situation. "He helps me survive but does not address the issue of freedom." By examining this character George was able to identify the truth of any addict: to give up the addiction is to stay safe while losing a very definite sense of aliveness and possibility. Literal death is guaranteed for an alcoholic who continues to drink despite cirrhosis of the liver, so abstinence and a limited lifestyle are the only options for survival. To choose life at this stage of recovery feels like living in a totalitarian state, without emotional or behavioral options. And so it was for George. If he chose to follow his former life patterns, his marriage would die. For now, the best that could be seen in this dream was that George was being told what he needed to know to remain safe. Although still feeling totally restrained, at least he was not at risk.

Remaining safe despite feeling victimized and repressed apparently allowed some inner progress, for the next dream—the last of the original series—brings a return of feelings as well as hope. Most recovering addicts will report that after a period of controlling their urge to activate their addictions, feelings of depression eventually dissipate, replacing the ravages of illness with the peace of health. During the nine months following George's last dream, that seems to be happening in this dream, which begins with what is foreign and exotic.

December 27, 1989: Exotic Desert Army
I am a member of the foreign legion army in an exotic desert. Because the army is composed of both men

and women, a terrific aura of eroticism exists. During a circle dance in water, it is decided who will become couples. There are many women I would like to be with, but the choice is not mine.

A tall, soft-looking blonde girl chooses me. Because she loves me I decide to be her partner. We dance a few times around the circle. But then a higher authority picks me to be with someone else.

My army engages with an enemy force of men and women. Our eventual reward will depend on how many we kill. Though it is hard to distinguish the enemy, as they are dressed in dark clothes, I kill many as we pass under a balcony.

Despite this, a spy captures us from behind. His superior officer imprisons us. I recognize him as an actor I once knew.

Just as I'm resigning myself to my captive state, our forces show up and liberate us. We are taken to a fabulous spa, an oasis, and estate. I am reinstated with higher rank and honor. The two armies of men and women mix freely on the premises. There are no weapons but it is understood that my army is in charge.

This dream demonstrated that significant transformation had taken place since the earlier dreams, and provided George with a great deal of valuable information. Consider the opening lines: "I am a member of the foreign legion army in an exotic desert. Because the army is composed of both men and women, a terrific aura of eroticism exists." Ego is in an unknown place ("foreign") of inner integration ("both men and women") which brings a return of feelings ("eroticism"). Indeed, at this stage of his recovery, George was aware of heightened feelings (the presence of the feminine), of moments of joy and hope.

> During a circle dance in water, it is decided who will become couples. There are many women I would like to be with, but the choice is not mine. A tall, soft-looking blonde girl chooses me. Because she loves me I decide to be her partner. We dance a few times around the circle. But then a higher authority picks me to be with someone else.

Although George had not joined a self-help group to support his recovery process, he was devoted to spiritual study. This helped him recognize that he had to surrender his addiction to powers greater than his ego. The dream process was one of those powers. Here the dream tells him that his ego is not able to choose his partner. George felt the truth of this in his marriage, for Jane was in no way like any of the women he had chosen during his years of sexual addiction. Yet, with her, his recovery was continuing and his life was deepening in meaning and value.

> My army engages with an enemy force of men and women. Our eventual reward will depend on how many we kill. Though it is hard to distinguish the enemy as they are dressed in dark clothes, I kill many as we pass under a balcony. Despite this, a spy captures us from behind. His superior officer imprisons us. I recognize him as an actor I once knew.

George is not yet out of woods. He is still embroiled in conflict with forces hard to distinguish because of their dark clothes. George understood this to represent the shadow or unconscious aspects of his psyche, all of those beliefs that caused him to act out sexually, that motivated his behavior while confounding his logical or conscious decision-making. True for any recovering addict, what threatens George and takes him captive is his old way of acting ("an actor I once knew").

> Just as I'm resigning myself to my captive state, our forces show up and liberate us. We are taken to a fabulous spa, an oasis, and estate. I am reinstated with higher rank and honor. The two armies of men and women mix freely on the premises. There are no weapons but it is understood that my army is in charge.

The state of captivity is over and dream ego feels as if he is of a "higher rank and honor," a vital developmental need in the battle with addiction. At this point in recovery, the part of the self that has fought a hard battle against the old ways has won and is now in charge. This step in the recovery process is essential to maintaining abstinence. Without a power shift away from the old and toward new, healthier ways of being and living, the addict is never safe from relapse.

George's next series dream occurred six months later and showed him "as part of a unit of men escaping from a Nazi armory." Though the escape is a "surreptitious act," it demands "a direct confrontation with the enemy" accomplished "by driving up to a gate and looking the guard directly in the eye." This is important because it reflects that George is no longer fearful of facing his problem. However, because George does not speak the language of the enemies, he fears capture. The only German word he knows is *danke* (thank you). At the time of this dream,

George was very grateful for his recovery as it allowed him to feel a unique and welcome peace.

The inability to further communicate with the enemy that controls and represses (the addiction) suggests the ways in which addiction often seems to defy understanding.

Further on in the dream, dream ego is confronted by the Nazi guard. He becomes "rattled, confused, and deeply frightened." He is then "unable to find the key to the truck." "The key looks like a safe-deposit box key." He must have this ignition key for his escape. George wrote: "When I am rattled, confused, and frightened I lose what guarantees my safety (key to the safe-deposit box/truck)—in this case, my escape from harmful patterns of behavior." Such keys can be found in various forms of therapy, daily spiritual study or ritual, dreamwork, physical health practices, and education. Each recovering human must find his or her own "safe-deposit box." This dream reminded George to stay on the path.

This was the last dream in the original series. Five years later George found himself back in the dream army again, feeling the doldrums of long-term recovery.

December 24, 1995: Escape from the Compound
I am a prisoner or a soldier in a huge military-like compound. I'm not of high rank but I am well known, accepted, and respected. I have been here a long time, perhaps longer than many others. It is not a terrible place to be despite the constant sameness of the military dress, conduct, and function. It is not a time of war but there is no contact with the outside world.

I work myself to the periphery of the compound as I try to escape. With the silent collaboration of my friends, I slip away. But before I acquire civilian clothes I encounter some officers who would know I am AWOL. Though I try to hide, they see me but do not challenge me. Is this tacit approval? Am I really free? I think so.

Though again suggesting imprisonment, this dream shows an important change in status for dream ego. "I'm not of high rank but I am well known, accepted, and respected." Some part of George feels as if he now knows himself well and he accepts, likes, and respects what he knows.

Despite that, monogamy can feel like the constant sameness of the military dress—a role or persona without options. George admitted that his life as a sex addict was usually exciting and adventurous despite the depression that activated when he was without a partner. Recovery can seem blissfully free of conflict (it is not a time of war) but there is no contact with the outside world. This can be stated more positively and productively with a when-then statement from the dream. When George was not in conflict about his commitment to monogamy, then there was no sexual acting out in the outside world. Alas, this felt like a loss. Perhaps that is because dream ego is not yet of high rank, evolved enough to exult in his recovery all the time.

Although this place is not so awful, dream ego is determined to move on ("I work myself to the periphery of the compound as I try to escape"). Other parts of his psyche are cooperating. ("With the silent collaboration of my friends, I slip away.") Dream ego's readiness to recapture a sense of individuality ("civilian clothes") suggests that it is time to define himself anew, without his addiction. Not surprisingly, the recovering addict about to escape the confines of his former prison feels as if he is being unfaithful to the disease process, or as if he is going AWOL. ("But before I acquire civilian clothes I encounter some officers who would know I am AWOL.") The good news is that that is not a problem. These officials, unlike the forces of the repressive totalitarian government from a previous dream, seem to support his escape. "Though I try to hide, they see me but do not challenge me. Is this tacit approval? Am I really free? I think so."

"Am I really free?" is an all-important query of the transforming self. According to this dream, the indications are positive. However, the process is not yet over, nor does it continue to be easy, as shown in the next series dream a year later.

> *November 11, 1996: The Inquisition*
> In an all-male barracks, I'm being persecuted by young, self-righteous thugs identified as born-again Christians. They are survivalists. They think I am a pervert. This judgment is rendered after I have refused to have sex with a female stranger. It is clear that I am expected to join this sleazy female but I say that I'm staying with Jane.
>
> Hearing this, the tramp looks at me with disdain, like a woman disgusted with a mama's boy. I feel like a loser.

A great paradox of healing is that the inner conflict between the old ways and the new is often heightened as the transformation process proceeds. In this dream, the call of addiction is sounding clearly, determined to survive ("survivalists"). By recognizing that the part of him that had been "born again" through recovery was feeling self-righteous and attacking (Who is more self-righteous than a newly recovered smoker or drunk?), George was able to consciously engage with the very important issue presented by this dream. Without such understanding, a "sober" addict can be hauled back to the old behavior with no idea what caused the slip.

George's "aha!" arrived by examining the accusation of being a mama's boy. George had remained faithful to Jane, his marriage, and to recovery for eight years. Now it was time for him to examine a saboteur—a negative self-judgment still supported by his born-again self—that could clearly undermine his commitment. If he thought, at some level, that maintaining his commitment to Jane was part of an old and despised identity—being a "mama's boy"—he would be able justify to himself a slip into his old sexual patterns.

George wrote in his journal: "The term 'mama's boy' holds particular power for me because, as a young boy, I often was described that way. My overprotective, fearful mother kept me from the normal and usual risk-taking of boyhood. I greatly resented this smothering, while at the same time enjoying the rewards of a close relationship with my adoring mother. For the first time, this dream allowed me to see the parallels and dissimilarities between that old, unhealthy mother/son experience and my commitment to Jane. What I must remember is that my former life as a sexual addict was no more rewarding or growth producing than being a mama's boy. It may have felt good, comfortable, but it was smothering my growth. In contrast, my psychological and spiritual growth as a recovering sexual addict is profoundly stimulating and beneficial."

This is the last of George's dreams focusing on imprisonment. Seeing all the dreams woven together, George wrote: "After finishing the work on this series, I have a tremendous feeling of completion, a sense of being caught up, current. With greater understanding and acceptance of where I am now and how I got here, I have a new feeling of fullness and confidence in my ability to make the most of the rest of my life. The self-doubt and regret that plagued me for most of my life seem to have dissolved in this process. They've been replaced by joy in the knowledge that nothing, particularly my struggle with sexual addiction, has been wasted.

"Before working on this project, I had not realized the value of tracking serial dreams. Now I know it is the best way to see my overall progress. Individual dreams bring new awareness, but we need the status reports seen by following a single dream thread. Without these dream updates on our progress we can prolong our limitations far beyond the time we have actually conquered them, just from habit, like a kid not realizing he could ride the bike without training wheels.

"Serial dreaming helped me see dream ego objectively. As I saw all the dream characters interacting with dream ego, I became more the observer and less attached to my own personal bias. This allowed me to better see what the dream wanted from me. Serial dreamwork has helped me see the larger picture. Knowing that I have an unfailing, limitless source of information and creativity flowing effortlessly through me every night, I rejoice in this connection to the inner presence, and am grateful for its unconditional nurture and support. Because of this and all the growth seen in the series, I now feel fully safe in my recovery from unproductive and limiting sexual practices. My sense of being imprisoned has been replaced by a profound feeling of expansion and freedom."

Thus, George's fears about taking the lid off his dream pot have been replaced with gratitude. This is the great overall benefit of doing serial dreamwork.

CHAPTER FIFTEEN

Big Cats Moving In

Dreamer: Francesca
Recurring symbol: lions
Length of dream series: 3 years
Number of dreams presented: 8
Script messages addressed:
>"Girls should be seen and not heard."
>"It is unsafe to be a successful, powerful woman."
>"It is better to stagnate than to take risks."
>"Nothing is more important than your role as mother and wife."

Benefits to the dreamer:
>Overcame fear of personal power.
>Learned to assert herself and speak out.
>Balanced nurturing role by developing strong leadership qualities.

Summary: A 65-year-old woman expands her limited role as mother to assume leadership in her community.

Fascinated by her three-year intrigue with dream animals, Francesca enthusiastically volunteered to provide a case study for this book. Her dream images of wild cats, frog babies, a squealing pig, a weasel, various dogs, a donkey, an elephant, and a carved owl evoked strong emotion. A veritable zoo charged across Francesca's dream screen, but big cats became the recurring symbol upon which we chose to focus.

Dreamers often become very emotional and energetically enlivened when studying their animal dreams. About this Francesca wrote: "There is no better heart/soul connection for me than the image of an animal. I am somehow more easily able to pass through the biases of my ego when dealing with animal dreams. My intellect tends to confuse and trick me. Animals, on the other hand, are simply and magnificently who they are. I can be objective while studying their qualities, habits, and mythology and relate those to aspects of myself."

Symbols from the animal kingdom provide an opportunity to examine aspects of human nature that are often ignored or unrecognized. Perhaps animal dreams carry such intense interest and feeling because our Western societies are so dominated by the intellect. Devoted as we are to our ability to reason, to control ourselves and our environment through thought and technology, many dreamers look to animals to provide a contrasting view of the more earthy, primitive, and instinctive inclinations that so-called civilized people tend to ignore.

Animals bring the honesty, spontaneity, and uncomplicated presence that often are absent from human behavior. Animals do not feign friendship nor rehearse verbal responses. In short, animals do not pretend to be what they are not. It's true that they posture for power and dance for sexual favors, as do people, but presumably animals do not rationalize their behavior nor deny their reality. What you see is what you get, like it or not. These are clearly shadow aspects of the highly orchestrated mores and expectations of modern cultures.

On the other hand, the instincts that motivate animals do not allow choice. Swallows must return to Capistrano. Monarch butterflies come home to Pacific Grove, and gray whales travel a specified north/south water route every year. Therefore, animals can represent our instinct to respond to script, to react as we have been taught, even our compliance with ancient cultural responses. This kind of unconscious human reaction, which feels like safety, keeps us locked into incessantly repeating patterns.

Considering the possibilities for both freedom and constraint suggested by animal symbols, Francesca and I donned our safari outfits and hiked into her study of wild cats. The very first dream provided an unexpected slant by presenting the first lion as a pet. Be aware, as you read this dream, that metaphorically hair often represents not only persona but belief systems, the intellect—that which grows out of our thinking place.

Dream One (July 4, 1993):
Change, Hair, and the Lion
I'm in a bank where a teller hands me a great deal of change, which I must sort into wrappers.

In a beauty shop where my hair is "being worked on," I notice my pet lion has gotten loose. He is scaring the others in the shop. Clearly the people need to be protected, so I take the lion to my station wagon.

I'm sweeping my newly purchased house. A man tells me that this is an excellent property.

This dream contains a directive, a concern, and a promise: Francesca needs to adequately contain the change she has been acquiring (sorting coins/change into wrappers). Perhaps this is accomplished by the alteration of her thinking processes ("my hair is 'being worked on'"). As her beliefs change, she thinks she must deal with protecting others from a powerful force (lion). That accomplished, she can take ownership of an entirely new way of living (newly purchased house), which is valued by an unknown masculine.

Let's first consider the issue of change. Every dream that supplies a new perception or awareness brings some level of change. For a certain period of time, each change may go unnoticed, but eventually the accumulated changes need to be organized. Just as dealing with several hundred pennies is easier when they are contained in paper jackets, altered beliefs and perceptions are more manageable when contained within a format. This major kind of reorganization of an individual psyche could be called an *inner paradigm shift*. Such internal alteration inevitably results in external changes that may not be easily embraced by familiars. If this kind of change creates unexpected ways of being with others, the transforming one may suddenly be considered wild and unruly or dangerous, as powerful or unpredictable as a pet lion.

What about this *pet-ness?* In order for a wild creature to become a pet it must be tamed. Taming a wild creature can be accomplished by feeding it and gaining its trust. In a sense, people tame each other (and furry creatures) with friendship. So, to tame is to mold to one's desire or to become familiar and comfortable with, to accept and befriend. Except for one dream, all the big cats that populated Francesca's dreams were involved with human dream characters. They were never imaged as hanging out on the veldt in their natural prides. Given that, it seemed likely that psyche was presenting Francesca with a representation of a large, wild power that has been altered and made compatible and comfortable within the human realm.

This dream series began when Francesca was in her mid-sixties. She enjoyed a very satisfying life as a mother of five grown children and as a grandmother and wife. All of her material needs were abundantly met. Her active participation in spiritual study and in dreamwork during the previous twenty years had broadened Francesca's concept of herself and of her interests. However, change was called for in Francesca's awake life. She recalls that at the time of this first series dream she was in a great deal of discomfort, emotional as well as physical. "Lower back pain plagued my sleep patterns, Morton's neuroma (nerve trauma that created a sensation similar to walking on shards of glass) had all but extinguished my morning walks. As I search my journal I see that the dreams preceding the first lion dream show distressing images of blocked creative energy, stagnation, life-lessness, being held back by woundedness. I felt bound up, con-tracted by my physical ailments and emotional lethargy. I was not a happy camper. I can now see my body problems as a metaphor for the inner experience of blocked energy and stag-nation that I was feeling at that time. The lower back pain and Morton's neuroma kept me focused on the pain and my inabil-ity to go places, get around easily, explore new things. It sapped my energy. All of my creative juices seemed to be reduced to a trickle because of these 'infirmities.'

"Then I went to your workshop, Kathleen. You had over-come all kinds of problems and were doing the creative work that you love. I was impressed with your vitality. I figured that if you could do it, so could I. That is when I had the first lion dream and that is when the changes began." And, as seen in the follow-ing dreams, a paradigm shift began to unfold.

The next dream in the series shows powerful creatures, still contained but roaming freely, watched over by a fearless masculine energy.

Dream Two (January 19, 1994):
In the Land of the Beasts

I'm in a natural habitat where wild animals roam freely. A male caretaker tells me about the tigers as they walk by. He is clearly fearless in their presence but I am cautious and somewhat frightened.

I'm walking around a compound that contains peaceful and contented lions. I see a sleeping lioness who is so long I think she will never end. Another lioness, a mother, is down, resting. I am astonished that I can walk safely among these great beasts. Nonetheless, I am a bit frightened because they are so powerful.

After accumulating all of her lion dreams, Francesca realized that dream ego is fearful throughout the series. Considering lions as a representation of extreme power led us to examine connections between fear and power. Clearly, it is healthy to be fearful of a powerful source that is destructive. But Francesca realized that the dream lions are never characterized as actually dangerous. So what is suggested by dream ego's fearful response?

In general, it seems that people are as frightened of their power as of their weaknesses. Embracing one's unique talents invariably creates change and a new level of responsibility. Clinging to the mundane saves us from going beyond our safe routines into what is unfamiliar. Some people grappling with this feeling of stagnation tell me they hear internalized phrases such as, "Better to be safe than sorry" and "If it (this safe life) was good enough for my parents, it is good enough for me." This old scripting puts a twist on an old aphorism: "Nothing ventured, nothing LOST!"

As Francesca and I addressed this dynamic in her life, we discovered strong contrasts between the teachings of her mother and her father. Francesca recognized that from her father, a traditional Italian, she learned that women are neither valuable nor powerful. Her father was a strict, dominating man who often controlled people with anger. To express a unique point of view or to disagree with her father created a very risky situation. Any show of personal power made Francesca vulnerable to her father's scorn and punishment. To be a good girl, she needed to seem powerless. To be powerless was to be safe. Making daddy angry (by revealing her personal will) created a very risky situation.

Our parents' rules remain safely protected as long as they are unconscious and unchallenged. Breaking the script by learning that it is untrue (women are valuable and powerful) is a major threat to the status quo, even after the biological father is dead. Thus, it was inevitable that Francesca felt threatened by the suggestion of an inner aspect as powerful as a lion. The need to control this power would be paramount to survival.

Conversely, the primary message Francesca received from her mother was this: "You are a wonderful, creative person and you can do anything you want to do." This belief certainly created an inner environment where a lion would feel at home! Thus, throughout the series (and her life), Francesca dealt with fear of overstepping her father's admonition while honoring her mother's perspective.

Francesca's mother's second major belief was her high regard for family and relationships. In the "Land of the Beasts" dream, Francesca becomes aware that a great power is asleep ("I see a sleeping lioness who is so long I think she will never end"). In addition, it may be time to relax the primary mothering instinct ("another lioness, a mother, is down, resting"). For many women in mid-life, refocusing maternal energy frees a great deal of unlived personal power. Francesca recognized the need to separate herself from the details of the daily lives of her children and grandchildren in order to experience her own power in a new and vital way.

The changes of recurring symbols from dream to dream indicate the dreamer's perceptual changes as well as her growth and development. The dreams of those consciously engaged with their series dreams are likely to show more transformation than those of passive dream students. This is because the awake ego changes as the dreams are studied. These alterations are then reflected within the series. Francesca was very committed to her inner journey as these dreams occurred and thus the modifications from dream to dream are significant. From first dream to second, the powerful, instinctive energy has been released from its cage and is able to roam about freely under the watchful eye of a knowing masculine. Nonetheless, the need for dream ego to control the powerful force continues in the following piece, the third in the series.

Dream Three (February 22, 1994):
The Gorgeous Wild Cats

I'm unsuccessfully trying to control my pet lion by feeding it a hot dog.

I'm walking on a tree-lined residential street with sidewalks. Beautiful male lions lie on the grassy area between the curb and the sidewalk. All of the lions are leashed and each has a handler.

Francesca identified hot dogs as a favorite food of the young. Perhaps ego, still frightened by the huge cat power that wants attention, thinks that it is possible to control this force by minimizing it, by feeding it a substance that placates the immature. Consider this unfortunate belief that too often feeds modern youth: "It is important to appear average, even stupid, to be accepted by peers." That notion is reflected in old movie scripts containing a scene with mama telling eligible daughter to keep her intelligence a secret in order to attract a husband. That was a strong cultural teaching when Francesca was a teen in the 1940s. This ploy is ineffective, says the dream, as the lion will not be controlled by junk food, which fills up an empty space but does not really nourish. In other words, remaining within the confines of cultural or familial dictates will quash legitimate personal power and development.

Whether ego likes it or not, the lion energy is proliferating, becoming more commonplace in the collective ("tree-lined residential street with sidewalks"). About this Francesca wrote: "I took comfort in the dream fact that these beautiful beasts were at home in the neighborhood. This suggested that I could relax and release my fear of this powerful lion force. I have, for many years, felt my power to teach and help others within my own family but I think this dream is suggesting that it may be safe for me to show my power beyond the structure of my family. The dream says that what I have feared can be handled through training and that it does not have to be locked away."

As Francesca grew more comfortable with the lions, her need to protect the powerful energy became evident, as in the following piece.

Dream Four (August 27, 1994): The Lion
Two young neighbor boys are playing catch in my backyard. They have gained access to my yard through a gate constructed by my neighbor without my consent. This upsets me because my pet lion is there and I do not know how he will react to the boys.

When I charge over to my neighbor to confront him, my lion comes lumbering after me. He has some kind of rope or yarn in his teeth. I am astonished when my neighbor calmly approaches this huge beast and pulls the object loose from his mouth.

I find other gates going to the neighboring yards on either side. Like it or not, the lion can easily pass back and forth.

Dream ego still wants to keep her powerful, intuitive, mysterious power separate from others, from the collective, but that is not going to happen. Indeed, the dream suggests that it is important that the lion's space be invaded. This allows the neighbor to extract what is caught in the place of self-expression ("pulls the object loose from his mouth").

Removing an implied obstruction from the lion's mouth may help a powerful force to speak, nourish itself, hang onto, or even to play. Any of these possibilities are important for the lion—and for developing Francesca's personal power.

"Speaking up, speaking out, speaking clearly had been a problem for me through my childhood and into my adult years. The quiet, shy face that I presented to the world was the *controlled me* but not my *authentic self*. I longed to break free—to express my own ideas, to reveal myself."

"Two young neighbor boys are playing catch in my backyard." The newly developing masculine is playing catch, building the skills of giving and taking, throwing and receiving. In all of the dreams thus far, an unknown masculine energy has been present and helpful. Francesca saw this as significant because "in order to break free from the script I have internalized (women are neither valuable nor powerful), I must rebuild, reinvent a masculine energy within myself that is not angry, critical, and wounded (her internal father). The helpful male trainers and handlers in the dream series are showing me that I possess all of the qualities necessary to achieve that goal."

Dream Five (March 6, 1995):
The Lions, the Bear, and the Cave
I'm walking along a road where many lions roam about. I wonder why no one is paying any attention to them.

I find myself trapped in an underground cave containing several lions. I climb onto the top of a pinnacle to escape from a huge bear. Though I am frightened, I am just out of his reach.

The lions in this dream are not pets and they are not contained. They are roaming, uncaged, unleashed, uncontrolled by human intervention. Something has shifted here, for dream ego has no fear of or need to handle the lions. The threat in this dream comes from a bear in the underground cave.

I like the when-then approach to this piece. When ego is finally fearless in the presence of an uncontrolled power, then a new threat emerges from the unconscious (underground cave). This is very often the case in human development. As we peel away the layers that protect and hide the authentic self, conquered fears are often replaced by emerging ones.

To better understand Francesca's new fear, we examined the hibernating behavior of bears as they go deep within the earth, withdrawing from the activities of survival and mating. (Bear symbols often appear in the dreams of people who need time to communicate deeply with themselves.) This feels very similar to a human taking a retreat, creating time to contemplate and to feel deeply, without the intrusion of everyday life. Busyness can be a defense, keeping unconscious any feelings that may lead to positive action. Creating time for human "hibernation" allows repressed regrets and desires, unfinished business and future development to become conscious. Introspection is needed in order to hear the desires of the deeper self. Experiencing these deep feelings may pop off the top of Pandora's box, threatening the status quo. Dream ego wants to stay just out of range of this possibility: "Though I am frightened, I am just out of his reach."

About this dream Francesca wrote, "Five weeks before this dream I attended a weekend workshop on recurring dreams. Because I was blown away by seeing the importance of recurring symbols for all the participants, I committed to pursuing more formal dream training. Thus, I joined a biweekly dream group that opened up a whole new world for me. As my commitment to the dream developed, I began to yearn for the opportunity to facilitate dream groups." Aha! The yearnings of Francesca's deeper, more powerful self become conscious in this statement.

It's interesting that the lions in this dream inhabit the same cave as the bear. This suggests that Francesca's recurring symbol, her source of power, needs to cohabit with the introverted, deeply resting energy. Such a blend provides a brilliant balance of doing energy (lion) and being energy (bear in cave).

It seems that Francesca's growing enthusiasm about her inner world created a stronger connection to her own power, her internal lion, for the next dream says that she has been given her own lion.

> *Dream Six (March 17, 1995):*
> *Caring for the Wild Animals*
> Wild animals, including lions and tigers, have been distributed to various families in my neighborhood. I have been given a lion.
>
> Later I see the wild animals scattered around the yards as I drive through my altered neighborhood. I stop in front of a house where a large cat, a lion or a tiger, is sitting on the front lawn. I become nervous when the unknown animal approaches my car because it may be a threat. I consider rolling up the car window so I can feel safe.

Here we see that wild animals are not just lying around on the lawns but they are distributed to individual families. Francesca's neighborhood, the collective environment, has been altered indeed! As she watches others living on the "wild side," expressing their power and living their dreams, Francesca's own process (car) is approached by a similar source of power. Again dream ego's fear pops up. Better put some separation (window) between ego and lion power!

This dream shows that the instincts or power (lions) not only are free and uncontrolled, but can be found more commonly than one might imagine; they are "distributed to various families." Perhaps that is because Francesca is becoming aware that personal power, independence, intuition, instinctive knowing are more common and more accepted than she thought in the past. It is certainly true that as we move into a new way of being, we find that others have preceded us and that the place we once thought we inhabited alone is not so isolated after all. As we find others whose perceptions support the changes we have embraced, we are much more comfortable letting our newness off the leash. Additionally, the culture that taught Francesca to be a quiet, good girl has changed significantly since the 1940s, now encouraging women to act powerfully. Still, caution remains an issue in this dream sentence: "I consider rolling up the car window so I can feel safe."

Dream four showed the lion in Francesca's backyard, but in the following piece that powerful, instinctive force is moving inside and multiplying.

> *Dream Seven (November 22, 1995):*
> *The Lions, Dark, and Light*
> I am at home in my living room area when I see a large animal slip into the house. I am frightened by this female lion, so I go into the bedroom, hoping she will leave. As I close the double doors, a large paw tries to push the door open and enter the room. I try to hold the door shut.
>
> Later, several cubs have invaded the house. They look more like big fluffy kittens than lion cubs. I realize that a big, dark lion is also in the room. When I open the sliding doors, the lion leaps out and falls on its side. Due to its stillness I think it is injured. I see a deep gash along its neck and shoulder area.

> The mother lion enters, searching for her cubs.
> She joins the other animal and lies adjacent to him,
> touching his nose with her own. I am touched by her
> devotion and vigil over the mortally wounded creature.

This is the first intrusion of the wild power, the instinctive, the independent nature, into the intimate areas of Francesca's life, her bedroom. She has been able to deal with it outside the inner sanctum, but now its invasion into her most private place demands attention. Indeed, an entire family of wild beasts has intruded ego's private space. Along with the mature energy comes the playfulness, the rambunctiousness, the uncontained exploration and mess of a litter of cubs! The part of the self that likes a controlled environment is likely to be antagonistic to spontaneity and the joyful, messy activities of kittens or cubs.

The dream also says that while the newness is breaking in, an oldness is dying. The wounded one, the dark masculine, is dying and being honored as it does so. About this Francesca wrote: "When I move back into the dying lion in this dream I feel a deep sadness. When I think of the old wounded lion, I think of how my father showed his woundedness through his anger, criticism, and general frustration with the world and his life. I can almost feel his rage at the rigid societal demands of his time. He had been taught to get ahead by displacing someone else, in a job, in sports, and even in his family. This took an enormous toll on my father, cutting him off from his feelings, from compassion for himself and for others. He was left with a toxic personality and a loveless, though productive, life." Francesca must have access to healthy masculine power if she is to take her talents into the collective, so the death of the lion—the transformation of the wounded father/masculine—is imperative.

It is good to ritualize the death of the old, the wounded, that which no longer serves. To be with, to honor, the dying is to prepare for the living. About this Francesca wrote: "The nurturing female lion in this dream has given birth to new possibilities and brought them into my home. There she lies in respectful vigil, ushering out the old ways of being that caused so much damage to my own soul and potential. This change brings with it not only a great deal of hope but also of responsibility. No wonder dream ego is fearful!"

As is often the case, ego fights against what is trying to break into her most intimate way of being. Happily, ego is not in charge. For the greater good of growth and overall development, the old will die and the new young energy will move in. When it does, according to the next dream, it brings a great deal of creativity and public exposure.

Dream Eight (April 15, 1996)

My daughter and I are at home preparing for a school dance. We are joined by my daughter's friend, who writes and sings songs. This is quite amazing since the girl is only eight or ten years old. Because she is wonderfully talented, she will perform at the dance.

I'm helping the songwriter prepare for the dance. Outside, a large pen holds her pet lion. When I take a pan of water to the animal, she presents herself to me. I restrain her so she will not escape the safety of her enclosure, which is really a very wide field.

The girl's performance was very well received.

When Francesca brings in the creative feminine that is singing its own tune, she finds that the power she has been courting all these years has a very large field in which to roam! This dream presents a great sense of expansion. This is the last dream in the series so far, and what a great ending dream it is, offering hope for continued growth.

Nearly fifty animal dreams, including the eight lion dreams, reflected Francesca's struggle to accept her own intuitive, instinctive, natural personal power; to sing her own song; and to prance with pride in a wide field. Francesca now facilitates dream groups, takes on various active leadership roles in her church, conducts seminars on women's issues, and teaches special art classes to young students.

I asked Francesca to comment on the value of working with these dreams as a series. She responded: "Writing about my parental script delivered to me the keys to the kingdom by recognizing my father's patriarchal Old World messages: 'Girls don't count.' 'You have nothing valuable to say.' 'Keep quiet and do as you are told.' The final dream in the series delivered the antithesis to this script. The young girl owns the pet lion and keeps her safe in an expansive place. She writes and sings her own songs and is well received when she performs. This girl does count and clearly expresses her authentic self.

"When I facilitate dream groups I use my own voice and draw from my own experience. I am well received. I have the guidance of my pet lion to thank for that!"

Francesca's personal growth, enhanced by dreamwork, has enabled her to enter more fully into life outside her family while still being true to herself. As with all of us, accepting and making a home for her true personal power serves the greater good, the broader community. "Viva la lioness!"

CHAPTER SIXTEEN

Bookstores

Dreamer: Dennis

Recurring symbols: bookstores (main symbol); homosexuals (secondary symbol)

Length of dream series: 25 years

Number of dreams presented: 56

Script messages addressed:

"Only sissies are sensitive."

"Real men don't show feelings."

"Thinking is safe. Feeling is dangerous."

Benefits to the dreamer:

Acknowledged and overcame repression of the feminine.

Balanced intellect with feeling and being.

Strengthened inner nurturing (mother) force.

Acknowledged spiritual value of life.

Found acceptance and safety in vulnerability.

Dream approaches: Identifying and studying a theme within a theme.

Summary: A 56-year-old man is fulfilled when he learns to identify and accept his feminine principle.

At the beginning of this project, I used the Internet to find men who were willing to study a recurring symbol. Dennis, an Irish-American, enthusiastically responded from his home in Malaysia. His is the only study in this book conducted entirely via the Internet. I had concerns about attempting a series study electronically. In-depth dream study requires the dreamer to expose significant life experience. I wondered if the trust needed for such exposure could be formed with a total stranger living half a world away. Dennis banished my concerns by writing that he thought it would be easier to bare his soul without being influenced by my physical presence. So, we logged on and the study began.

In some ways, this mode was more efficient than face-to-face interviews. Online, the tendency to ramble is diminished. The written word can be saved, whereas millions of spoken gems suffer the fate of most dreams, flying off into the ether, never to be thought again. Dennis and I could both tend to the tasks of the study when we chose, often letting questions simmer for several days before responding.

Dennis was always immediately responsive, never complaining about the more than two hundred hours he spent on his end. He gathered his series dreams, wrote associations, remembered times from his past triggered by either the dreams or my questions about them, identified his emotions (past and present), and learned to look objectively at the many dreams in his study. To work with his dreams, Dennis learned many new ways to consider his abundant material. He was a willing student, clearly attached to his dreams. He was determined to understand his recurring symbol (a bookstore) and the overall intent of the series. We studied a total of thirty-one dreams from the fifty-six in his bookstore series. The foundation of the series is represented here by the first five dreams, which spanned twenty-one years.

Then we will focus on four dreams that created a "miniseries" within the "maxiseries."

The dreams for this study contain several similarities to the studies of Darian and Griffin Rose. In each case the first dream of the series occurred when the dreamer was in his or her early twenties. In all three, the dreams that we studied spanned twenty-five years. There were ten-year dream gaps from the early seventies to the nineties, when all three dreamers began recording multiple dreams per year. I wondered about these similarities. By the 1990s, had the collective environment altered sufficiently to support individual dreamwork? Or does it take a quarter century for us to pay attention to our internal, repetitious messenger? Perhaps we need to reach a certain level of maturity before we can process an ongoing dream series. Regardless, it seems that psyche is either immensely patient or very determined, or both.

Dennis described his repeating symbol, bookstores, as among his favorite places. "I could easily spend hours just hanging out in a bookstore, old and musty or modern and classy. So many possibilities are found on the shelves! My excitement rises as I cross the threshold of a bookstore, usually heading for the health, psychology, and personal development sections."

We compared bookstores to libraries, since both provide similar services for the public. But we realized that borrowing a book from a library is a short-term arrangement, whereas purchasing a book implies permanence and the responsibility suggested by owning something. Psychologically, when we speak of owning a trait or characteristic, we are admitting to or identifying with it. Thus, a bookstore indicated a more serious intent for learning and for embracing change.

Dennis said that when he was a child, books were his primary nourishment, his best friends. I relate to that and value books as important friends and teachers. I can keep this "friend" forever on my shelf, visiting with it now and then, or introduce it to someone in need. As I open a new book, I am aware that I may be entering dangerous territory, for what I read has the potential to alter my worldview and, therefore, my values, goals, and, ultimately, my life.

This dangerous possibility was highlighted in the first dream of this study, which occurred in 1971. In it, some students begin a "revolution in a bookstore." Dream ego wants to remove his "girlfriend and her cat" from the scene of the revolution. Though she wants to participate in the revolution, Dennis convinces her to leave by saying that "his brother, a policeman, will deal with the riot." (We would discover that this particular brother, Gerald, greatly impacted the part of the miniseries on which we chose to focus.)

Dreams often reflect the dreamer's social environment. Though America was definitely in a state of revolt in the late 1960s and early 1970s. Dennis—living in Mexico at the time—was not affected by the uproar in his native land. He was, however, experiencing a revolution in his inner world, as he had entered therapy at that time. Therapy is, for most, a process that creates revolutions against the status quo—the original family scripts, the unconscious attitudes and behaviors that limit, frustrate, and destroy happiness and freedom of choice.

This first series dream was a reaction against the rigors of therapy, which Dennis described as "difficult and distressing." He wrote, "I didn't really enjoy therapy. It was painful to have my illusions slowly torn from me, piece by piece. I had a lot of difficulty coming to terms with my feelings. I felt guilty when my wife consistently complained that I was cold and unfeeling, that I was always reading instead of doing what she wanted or expected." Seen in that light, the bookstore may be a place of intellectual refuge from feeling, from experiencing the heart, from relating intimately. This would clarify the reason that the girlfriend (the feeling component, the feminine principle) and her cat (often a symbol of the feminine and of intuition) wanted to participate in the revolution. Wanting to be expressed, the repressed parts of the self often call for revolution, in one form or another. However, in this case, dream ego influences the feminine to disengage from the overthrow of the old system by stating that the brother/police officer is in charge of squelching the revolution.

Dream police often identify an internalized rule-keeper committed to maintaining the status quo and cultural attitudes. As is often true at the beginning of a transformational process, ego aligns with the big cop and wins this round, protecting himself from the feelings and awareness he fears.

In the second dream of the series (a year after the first), Dennis finds himself in a risky place:

> I'm on a cliff that changes into a bookshelf. After arranging several books, I turn to go down, and fall. It is about a five-hundred-foot fall, but I land unhurt, although badly shaken by the experience. Not too long after, I am once again in the same position and about to fall when the bookstore owner helps me. I find myself strapped to the ladder of a fire engine being slowly lowered to the Earth.

There are two interesting elements here. Cliffs, ledges, edges, and other representations of high, tight places, may suggest that the dreamer is in a precarious place in his life or his psychological or spiritual development; this metaphor often speaks to being at the edge of one's abilities, consciousness, or comfort zone—

the limit of the ego, so to speak. Another step will take one beyond safe boundaries into the unknown.

Second, a symbol that transforms within the dream suggests that psyche is identifying a bridge or connection that is best seen when one thing becomes another. In this case, the bookshelf, that which holds new ideas, seems to be compared to a place of potential risk or the edge of Dennis's knowing or capability. This connects to the threat of revolution in the first series dream. The dream continues with a plunge: "After arranging several books, I turn to go down, and fall. It is about a five-hundred-foot fall, but I land unhurt, although badly shaken by the experience." Perhaps when dream ego realizes that neither injury nor death result from going over the edge, the frightening experience can be repeated. This leads to additional help: "Not too long after, I am once again in the same position and about to fall when the bookstore owner helps me. I find myself strapped to the ladder of a fire engine being slowly lowered to the Earth."

It is the job of the dream, in part, to alter our thinking and our perceptions. Every dream has the potential to restructure inner reality. In this dream, after rearranging several ideas (books), dream ego plummets. Plunges into the depths or the unknown? In either case, this would be an important step for soulwork, for dreamwork. Because Dennis was overly devoted to his intellect, does the dream encourage him to descend from his lofty position? Or, is he not strong enough to keep his grip as his ideas are rearranged?

When reflecting on this dream, Dennis wrote, "I repeatedly needed rescuing from the lofty, intellectual place because I did not know how to get down under my own power. The one who owns the place of revolution (the bookstore owner) must help me because I cannot seem to figure it out on my own."

The presence and action of the bookstore owner, the one who has permanent access to all the potential learning, shows an important element of dreamwork. Although dream ego is unaware of ways to get down from the lofty place, another part of his psyche has the knowledge and ability to get the help he needs. Being aware of help from the unconscious can be very motivating and reassuring to a confused person yearning for growth and change. At the time of this dream, the conscious Dennis was unable to take the plunge into the lower levels (his emotions), but he did have within himself the ability to move down safely (the owner and the ladder of a fire engine).

At this point in the study, the bookstore appears to be a paradoxical symbol. That is, it has two seemingly opposite meanings or values. The bookstore is the exciting place where new ideas can be bought. In addition, the bookstore contains what the dreamer loves and has used for comfort most of his life. Unfortunately, when comfort becomes escape, growth is exchanged for immobility. Then the bookstore becomes a place of refuge from feelings and from experiencing the now of human existence. Many repeating dream symbols have this paradoxical complexity. Therefore, whether the symbol represents the positive or negative aspect must be determined within the context of each dream. In the case of Dennis's bookstore, we will see that it is more positive (helpful to wholeness and health) than negative (interfering with growth).

Nine years later Dennis dreamed the following:

> In a bookstore I'm trying to get my mother to help me with something, but she is so busy gossiping that I can't get the advice I need from her. I feel very frustrated and angry with her. A sales clerk says that I am too young to be a father.

This dream deals with the need for attention from the nurturing part of the psyche (mother). In order for the dreamer to sustain any new concept, project, or personal growth, an inner maternal force must be attentive. Just as a farmer tends new seeds, the mother watches, values, and supports change as her offspring grows.

Dennis described his biological mother as a person incapable of nurturing. "She never seemed interested in what I needed. That remains true to this day." Rectifying this kind of deficiency is one of the great values of dreamwork and other kinds of therapy. When an external parent was inadequate or destructive, we must consciously create a better model. Our dreams will show us the condition of these inner characters. At the beginning of his series, Dennis needs help from the nurturing aspect that is unable to support him. Perhaps that is one of the reasons he was not able to deal with his feelings. The hurt or frightened child runs to the mother for support and understanding; the child needs to express his feelings, to be heard. If the mother is unable or unwilling to receive the pain of the child and teach him to cope with it, he may learn to deny and avoid his feelings altogether. This limits development, as suggested by the next dream sentence.

The sales clerk says that dream ego is too young to be a father. Dennis, age thirty-eight at the time, was not biologically too young to reproduce. But psyche is suggesting a lack of ego maturity to support a newly developing self. Had Dennis understood this at the time of the dream, he could have nurtured his own development. However, this dream was unheeded.

Over its first nine years, Dennis's series showed the following:

A revolution needs to happen in the learning place that provides comfort and transformation. The feminine feeling aspect and her instinctive nature (the cat) support this change, but dream ego is opposed. Dream ego needs to come down from the lofty, intellectual place of emotional detachment. He does have help from inner masculine (store owner), but the nurturing energy is inattentive. Dream ego is not yet mature enough for the birthing of the new.

Dennis had been journaling dreams for thirty years but did little more than form general impressions about their meaning, until a very disturbing dream caught his attention. The dream showed an unending flow of weeds coming from his mouth. He understood this to mean that his inner garden needed a lot of work and he committed to working with his dreams seriously.

A dozen years later the next fascinating series dream revealed more problems between dream ego and the feminine. At the time of the following dream, Dennis had just begun tending his dreams (mothering his own inner process). Despite this, another female dream character, his wife, lets him down.

My wife and I are in a restaurant overlooking an airfield. Planes take off and conduct carefully synchronized and beautifully executed training maneuvers near the ground. I am stunned and excited. I want my wife to watch but she is disinterested. This infuriates me so that I throw vitamins at her and leave.

To relieve my frustration and anger, I write a story about a group of GIs opening bookstores in poor areas of the city.

When the story is finished I look at all the pages I have written and discover that some are nearly illegible. The ink has leaked through the thin blue airmail paper I've been writing on. I awake feeling very anxious.

When the dreamer's feeling aspect (the wife) is not interested in what excites dream ego (the airplanes—flights of fancy, matters of the spirit including dreamwork), he turns to a process of clarification and self-expression to alleviate his frustration. He writes about those who follow orders to maintain collective safety (the GIs). They want to open up possibilities for learning (bookstores) in the impoverished parts of the self (poor areas of the city). Like police officers, GIs may represent the parts of Dennis (and all of us) that are compliant to the cultural script. In this dream, twenty-one years after dream ego's refusal to participate in the revolution, the psychic keepers of the collective order have become more disenchanted with the status quo and more supportive of change.

However, the story is not yet set (the writing is lost). In his journal Dennis wrote: "I feel sad that the pages that I write are nearly illegible. This is also a feeling that I sometimes get when I am unable to understand my dreams." What a beautiful metaphor illustrating the transitory nature of dreamwork and of consciousness! First, it seems we must be confronted by psyche over and over again. Then, when we do tend to the issue being raised, we cannot hang onto it for long. Our understanding seems to fade away like words on airmail paper.

Because what excites and pleases dream ego (the planes) is in the sky (the domain of the spirit), I suspected Dennis might be opening up to the spiritual domain in general. When I first suggested this, Dennis gently negated that notion, saying that he had always been a staunch materialist with no time or interest in the religious or spiritual.

In this piece, dream ego, the dream character that is most like the awake self, seems to have made a shift. By taking his dreams seriously, Dennis has embraced the rebellion he initially spurned more than two decades before. The choice-making part of the psyche, dream ego reflecting awake ego, has committed to the unfolding of his inner world but, as yet, has no support from the feeling or feminine aspect.

It seems paradoxical that neither the mother from the previous dream nor the spouse from this last one are supporting dream ego's attempts to move, grow, develop. Why would the feminine be so uncooperative? It is often true that the unlived part of the self (in this case the dreamer's feeling aspect) is unable to support changes when the conscious self begins to yearn for them. The rejected aspect needs to have breath blown into it before it can take form and partner with the ego. In this dream, the unlived feminine apparently needs strengthening ("I throw vitamins at her and leave"). In Dennis's case, his feelings had been repressed for so long that they could not yet come to the fore. Dennis recognized that, without connection to profound feelings, life is without meaning or value—as the next dream, three months later (twenty-one years after the first bookstore dream), illustrates.

November 1992: Why Are You Here?

The three women keep asking me the same question: "Why are you here?" I hear this question over and over. It upsets me a great deal. I suddenly realize that I have no reason for being here. Upset, I leave to search for the Good Deal Bookstore. I wander around and around in a Chinese maze/temple. I keep finding it (the bookstore) but losing it again and again. The bookstore has lots of books on homosexuality. I just notice them and move on. I continue to ask myself why I am here. I think it is too costly to leave.

Because I feel nothing here, I make the decision to leave. Despite my fears I am very relieved.

The most vital part of the dream is a question repeatedly asked of dream ego by three women identified by Dennis as his present wife, his former wife, and an important former lover. "Why are you here? I hear this question over and over. It upsets me a great deal." When repeatedly questioned by the feminine, dream ego finally realizes that he has "no reason for being here" and he leaves in search of a "Good Deal Bookstore." He wanders around and around in a "Chinese maze/temple." He writes, "I keep finding it (the bookstore) but losing it again and again." This echoes the fleeting quality of the lost writing in a previous dream. It suggests the feeling of losing awareness or consciousness as soon as it is found.

And now comes a very important aspect of this overall series and the introduction to the miniseries. "The bookstore has lots of books on homosexuality. I just notice them and move on."

This is the first of Dennis's four dreams presenting the word *homosexual*. After six months of working together, I asked Dennis to summarize what he was finding most valuable in this dream study. He said the homosexual dreams intrigued him the most. These dreams became significant as a sub-series imbedded within the broader series.

As he defined the word *homosexual* and associated to it, Dennis identified the feminine aspects that are sometimes obvious in gay men. He thought about his gay acquaintances and realized that they often talked blatantly about their feelings without the discomfort, guilt, and shame Dennis experienced from this kind of exposure. Therefore, this symbol came to represent feminine qualities available to men that Dennis wanted to integrate in his own being.

Contemplating the feeling level of his life led Dennis to the most important part of the study. He uncovered many disturbing memories of being ridiculed, shamed, and blamed for any expression of sensitivity. Just as his mother and his wife in the preceding dreams did not support him, his feelings had been neither understood nor supported throughout his early life. His father and older brother (the policeman) often chastised, criticized, or punished him for being too sensitive. Dennis's mother observed the ridiculing behavior without intervening or defending his emotional expression. As shown in a previous dream, his mother could not, or would not, tend to his feelings. Thus, Dennis's habit of taking refuge in his intellect began as a child and continued into adult life. Separation from feelings provided Dennis a sense of safety, but it also isolated him in a barren emotional environment, closed off from the rich possibilities of human experience. The first homosexual dream suggested to Dennis that separation from the feminine, feeling level creates a terrible void. If one cannot feel, what is the point or value in life, in being here at all? Without access to and expression of the emotions that make us human, why are we here?

As is often true in important dreams, this one shows that the needs of the evolving self are in conflict with the familiar, patterned way of being. Though he realizes the futility of staying in this unfeeling place, dream ego feels that the cost of leaving is too great. ("I continue to ask myself why I am here. I think it is too costly to leave.") Just as there is a cost to revolution, moving into conscious feelings may demand quite a toll. We are sure to discover issues and parts of the self that need attention and adjustment. These alterations can be costly. Familiars who know us one way often feel alienated when we commit to another, more expanded script and sense of self. It is very risky to go over our edges and plunge into the depths of the psyche. Once we learn the benefits of doing so, we can more easily align with the forces for transformation.

The "Why Are You Here?" dream ends with a vital decision: "Because I feel nothing here I make the decision to leave. Despite my fears, I am very relieved." This vital decision lays the foundation for a new way of being that will eventually manifest in the awake world. Determined to leave behind the barren and emotionless, dream ego looks more closely at what is happening in the realm of feeling, of the feminine within the masculine.

The next dream, which came almost exactly a year after the first homosexual dream, shows some changes are taking place.

November 21, 1995:
People Think I Am a Homosexual
I am really shocked when the clerk at the bookstore suggests that I am a homosexual. Another guy there — a big guy — seems to think the same thing. He confronts me after I have made my second or third trip to the bookstore that day to order books. "What about the pictures you cut out?" the guy belligerently asks me. I'm confused because I didn't know anything was wrong with those pictures.

I see that I have interrupted his workout. His shirt is not buttoned up and he is sweating. I can see the workout equipment in the next room. In his office cupboard I get a glimpse of police uniforms and caps.

After I leave the bookstore, I worry that he will follow me down the dark street.

Here we see a common counter-response to growth and development. In dream ego's repetitive pursuit for knowledge, nourishment, and self-awareness ("returning over and over to the bookstore") he has interrupted the big rule-keeper ("big guy with police uniforms") as it is working out, maintaining its strength. The cop energy is irritated by dream ego's pursuits and focus (photos). The sense is that the actions of ego have interrupted the agenda and control of the status quo. In an attempt to regain power, there is often a show of strength from the old ways that pursue us in the unenlightened place ("follow me down the dark street"). As our struggle for authenticity continues, we must bravely face those internal and external forces that would hinder our progress. Despite fears, we continue on the road to individuation. Dreamwork is not for wimps!

It is helpful to recognize that dream images precede conscious awareness and attitude or behavioral changes. In the first dream in the miniseries, Dennis simply notices the books on homosexuality; he is beginning to acknowledge the feeling realm within himself. In the second homosexual dream, he is shocked to be accused of his feeling side, of what he has neglected for most of his life. His denial continues in the following dream when he lies about his willingness to take the journey to forbidden feeling place.

> *June 6, 1996: That's Not My Bus*
> An Indian man and I are walking on the streets of San Francisco, looking for a bookstore. In front of Woolworth's, a homosexual from Thailand, who says he remembers taking a bus to Phuket, propositions my attractive Indian friend. I lie by saying that I have never taken that bus.

At this time, dream ego was not yet ready to own his feminine aspect—his feelings, awareness, intuition, and sensitivity. Thus, he lies about taking the same journey as the homosexual man when, in fact, he had frequently taken a bus to Phuket, a beach resort near Malaysia. Dennis described Phuket as a sunny, fun place to go to rest and relax, to get in touch with his body and feelings. It is a beach area next to the sea, so Dennis thought it was also a way of being close to the unconscious. Denying participation in a forbidden way of being (traveling the same way as the homosexual) protects Dennis from the punishment he expects when breaking free of his familial and cultural script.

As each dream moves us forward, we eventually see more and more gaps in the old script. Like a flower breaking through a crack in the sidewalk, our new growth—rising from the dark depths of the psyche—seeks the light. This promise of new life must be preceded by the ending of the old. A dream character's death is often a harbinger of this ending. Such a dynamic is profoundly presented in Dennis's final homosexual dream.

July 24, 1996: A Crime in the Park
I wake up in the park where a crime has been committed. Someone named Gordon has been murdered. Both the corpse and I are dressed in black. I know I should do something but I lie on my stomach—tired, paralyzed, watching people to see if they suspect me.

Dream ego becomes conscious ("I wake up") in a place of growth (park) where something has died. When someone has been murdered in a dream, it is wise to ask if this is a good thing to the overall growth of the dreamer. Both dream ego and the corpse are dressed in black; Dennis thought this represented the old dark, depressed script or ways of being resulting from repressed feelings. If so, the demise of such a force would be advantageous to growth and authenticity.

When Dennis associated to the name Gordon, he remembered a man from his past. This person had treated Dennis in a very judgmental and discounting fashion. This description and Dennis's recollections of and feelings about Gordon very much reminded Dennis of his policeman brother, connecting this dead character to that which maintains the script. The death, then, suggested an ending of the controlling script. This death of the old is vitally necessary to allow the authentic self to develop.

When dream ego becomes aware of the corpse, he feels guilty concern ("I'm watching people to see if they suspect me"). Disobeying the familial or cultural script usually creates an expectation of punishment. There is almost always a sense of guilt or shame when the growing part of the self extends beyond the established rules and regulations of conditioning.

The dream continues:

> Some young people come looking around and pick up things on the ground (keys? change?) but nobody says anything to me. Then finally I get up and discover that my room is close by and that I do have the energy to get there.

When the young energy (the developing sense of self) finds the *keys* to *change*, dream ego is energized, the paralysis is broken, and he proceeds to his home. We are usually relaxed and without facade at home, so this can be seen as going to his place of authenticity. The dream continues, showing that transformation is afoot.

> I live over a bookstore/library, which is much larger on the outside than on the inside. It is a big modern library on the outside, a small wooden bookstore/gift

shop on the inside. It is undergoing repairs of a broken skylight.

Dream ego seems to be in an incongruent state ("much larger on
the outside than on the inside"), about which Dennis said this:
"From the outside, I appear to be much more impressive than I
feel internally because of the remaining constrictions of *wooden*
attitudes and feelings." Despite this, there is a sense of expansion
and lightening up, just as one feels lighter and has more accessi-
bility to one's true spirit (sky from the skylight) when a repressive
old script dies.

However, the path home, to authenticity, is never easy or
direct. The next piece of the dream shows dream ego dealing
with the judgments of the conservative elements of society, represented by Bob Dole.

In a bookstore, the clerk comments on the book I am
checking out. He says that Bob Dole has proclaimed
that the book is about homosexuality and that the
homosexual men are portrayed as playing any role
they choose to play. I'm angry about this and want to
argue with Dole.

Dennis wrote: "I have come to realize that it is important
and right for men to play a wide variety of roles within relationships. And, when relating to myself, I want to have access to
many parts, feelings, and possibilities of ways of being. I do not
want to be confined to the narrow, wooden roles defined by my
family." The anger felt by dream ego heralds a sense of identity
with his *homosexual* or feeling aspect. His need to defend his
sensitivity shows a great transformation from the first dream, in

which dream ego disavows the rebellion in the bookstore. Dennis seems to have completely changed allegiance by this dream.

Though dream ego is making progress, he still has some hurdles to overcome as he tries to continue upstairs to his home. The dream continues:

> This is difficult because the stairs are littered with junk and people. I am also angry about this.

In his journal Dennis wrote: "I am trying to get to higher levels of consciousness but things and people still block my way."

We discussed that higher states of consciousness are thought to contain less ego-dominated thinking, allowing connection to a more evolved or spiritual self and process. By this time, Dennis was able to acknowledge a yearning for a spiritual connection within himself, which he had previously denied during our work together. As we discussed the ways in which that connection might be made, he wrote the following: "Funny thing is, I keep thinking of how my ex-policeman brother is going to take it when he hears about my spiritual pursuits, as he eventually will. Oh well, I guess I wasn't born to please him, although I have certainly spent a lot of my life trying to do just that. There has been a very strong anti-spiritual/religious prejudice in my family that I must continue to work on overcoming. My mother is the only family member who is religious/spiritual and my brother and I have made fun of her religious beliefs for years. It's tough for me to admit that she might be on to something after all. I am working on it.

"Fortunately, because I believe in dreams and what they have revealed to me, I think I might eventually see my way to surrendering my ego's views but it isn't going to be easy! I still find it a little difficult to believe that spiritual development is going on in me. But from what few glimpses I have had of it in my dreams, I am convinced that it is going on almost in spite of what my ego wants. I am beginning to realize that my ego is relatively powerless and I find that to be an extremely irritating and humbling experience. (I am almost crying as I write this.) I invested a lot of energy in building and defending that damned ego for many, many years and here it turns out to be pretty much useless because higher and much stronger powers are at work here. I don't know whether to laugh for joy or weep from feeling helpless!"

It appears that the revolution called for in the first dream of this series was leading Dennis to acknowledge his feelings not only at a psychological level but at the spiritual level as well. As Dennis worked through the dreams presented here, and more than forty others in this series, he was able to identify what was authentically true for him, as opposed to what had been scripted by his family. He clearly recognized that his unconscious allegiance to his father's and brother's idea of who he, Dennis, should be, had forced him to abandon his true feelings and aspirations.

Dennis had a lot to say when asked to comment on the overall value of this thirteen-month study. "I feel like the revolution is still going on," he began. "The old system is certainly toppling!"

Dennis proceeded to describe many profound changes in both his attitude and his behavior. "I can see from our work that I learned well from my family and my society to repress my feelings, my thoughts, and my true self. I now know that I am a highly sensitive person who feels strongly about a number of things. I realize that I expended a great deal of energy during my life trying to be what I thought everyone wanted me to be: an unfeeling, nominally thinking, sexually obsessed, materialistic, macho male. My feelings threatened me tremendously. Expressing any type of sensitivity was too great a threat. As a result, I was an aggressive, angry, leering man who knew nothing of self-nurturing and very little of how to nurture others.

"In the past months I have noticed a significant increase in my concerns for others, for the less advantaged, the abused, and forgotten members of society. It is now easy for me to identify with others. I am vociferous in my concerns about such matters, writing many letters to my local newspaper expressing compassion for the disenfranchised and calling for societal attention and reformation. (Dennis as Revolutionary!) This is a politically risky action, as I am in this country on a visa. However, I have come to realize that the world is a much safer place than I once thought. Contrary to what I learned as a child, I can say things that are not necessarily pleasing and not be attacked! I now feel much more secure in life and can therefore live life much more fully.

"Most of the time I am happy with the way I am now. I am able to think much more clearly, to know much sooner what my real feelings and thoughts are so that I can act more intelligently. I have a great deal more energy and am spending my time more valuably. Before this study, I wasted my days with the distractions of compulsive reading, drinking, and useless conversations. Now, instead of wasting time, I want to use it very consciously. In addition, I have lost twenty-eight pounds during the thirteen months of this study. I feel. I acknowledge my feelings. And I feel better about myself than I have in years."

As I read Dennis's summation I heard and felt the echo of many of the dreams we had worked together. I was thrilled to see the kind of self-nurturing that had resulted as Dennis dove deeply into his dream life. Obviously, his inner mother had been activated.

Dennis's transformation affected more than his inner being. "My relationship with my wife has changed for the better. She likes the authentic, vulnerable, and present me much more than the man I was, and wasn't, just a year ago."

And these final words from Dennis: "I continue to work on my dreams each and every day. This dreamwork is extremely important and it is the work I always come back to when I need grounding. It has become the center of my very existence. The days when I cannot understand at least part of a dream are the days in which I do not feel happy. Fortunately, these days are very few now."

I had not anticipated the profound changes that had occurred with either Dennis or Darian. Both had relinquished long-cherished addictions as the needs of psyche and soul were met, without a therapist or even a support group. The only intervention was that created by an intense relationship between dream and dreamer. By listening to and interacting with messages sent by psyche for, in each case, more than twenty-five years, both lives have been profoundly impacted. As I write this I am feeling truly awed by the power of dreamwork to self-regulate, to bring desperately needed balance, to fill in the holes through which life had leaked out and been wasted.

CHAPTER SEVENTEEN

House Problems

Dreamer: Marla
Recurring symbol: house from a former time
Length of dream series: 10 months
Number of dreams presented: 8
Script messages addressed:
"You don't deserve to satisfy your own needs."
"Women have little value."
"Because you are stupid and incompetent, you must not express yourself."
Benefits to the dreamer:
Overcame fear of transformation to embrace new, vital masculine energy.
Learned to assert herself in her marriage and in the world.
Found and expresses her unique and authentic voice.
Expanded and altered her sense of self.
Summary: A middle-aged woman transforms fearful and unhealthy ways of thinking and being by embracing and exercising her authentic personal power.

During the six years of writing this book I have wondered whether undertaking a long study of a recurring symbol might be too complex a task for most dreamers to accomplish on their own.

Marla, the last dreamer to participate in this research, allayed my fears. She did all the work presented in this chapter with no more help than you have received by reading this book. Although Marla has done dreamwork for only a year, she is deeply involved in a training program to become a professional dreamworker. Her motivation to understand and live her dreams is very high, her normal learning style is analytical, and her determination is dogged. If you have only a portion of those qualities, I hope that reading this chapter will encourage you to undertake your own series work. Marla studied a recurring symbol of a particular house from her past. Before examining her personal material, let us consider the symbol of houses in general.

Dream houses present themselves in conditions that would challenge any architect: dilapidated; lacking doors, roofs, and walls; filled with rats and garbage; too big for the foundation or too small for the lot. In our dream theaters we see splendid glass structures stretching to the heavens and neat, quaint fairytale cottages nestled in the forest. Whether a log cabin in a town, a tenement in the slums, a mansion by the ocean, a shack on the Nebraska plain, a doghouse, or a mobile home, house images usually stir up the emotional pot. The bubbling feelings may erupt from the anticipation of developing potential or, paradoxically, the dread of physical disaster.

These extreme responses arise because a house is the place in which we live. Therefore, dream houses may reflect or predict the dreamer's psychological or physical condition. Images of new construction may thrill and entice while a crumbling dream house may lead the dreamer to a medical doctor or a psychotherapist. Consider the relevance of the very common symbol of overflowing toilets or stopped-up sinks. If a dream house represents literal physical distress, does this metaphor suggest a blockage in the alimentary canal or an emotional block that needs attention to ensure a smooth flow in life? Examining the full content of the dream usually provides the clues necessary to identify the dream as literal or symbolic. (Chapter 18 contains a pertinent example of this type of examination.)

Rooms or areas within dream houses can represent distinct aspects of the dreamer's psyche (or personality) because houses have areas designated for specific activities. Accordingly, each dream room represents a different aspect of life, either external or internal. A problem in the kitchen of the dream house may signify a need for attention to physical nourishment (diet), to nurturing (food as comfort/mother), to the entire alchemical process of transformation (food is transformed when processed in the kitchen). A remodeled dream bedroom may reflect or suggest the changes that are needed or already have taken place in the areas of intimacy/relationship (sex), self-care (sleep/recuperation), or personal space. The bathroom is a place of cleansing, releasing, changing (clothes), and privacy. Symbolically, backed-up or overflowing toilets, a very common dream symbol, may suggest problems with either emotional release (urine/water) or accumulated toxic feelings or beliefs (feces). The living room often depicts the dreamer's social or public life. Backyards, front and side yards, patios, and porches suggest external conditions.

Harry presented three fascinating house dreams to his dream group. He was intrigued by the unusual architecture depicted in each dream, featuring attractive houses in various states of construction and finally, in the third dream, fully completed. The emotional charge of these dreams was extraordinary, leading the group members to wonder about what kind of inner building was reflected by the powerful, creative dream images. What was the significance of cathedral ceilings in all three houses? Would the dreams encourage Harry to construct something new in his life? In fact, that is what happened. Soon after sharing the series, Harry decided to pursue a degree in the ministry, resulting in the development of a profound level of spirituality (cathedral ceilings) and a new career as a minister.

Dreams that return me to houses from my past have taught me a great deal. At the beginning of my conscious dream life (when I began recording and working with my dreams), these dream houses were always in distressing condition. As my own healing progressed, the dream houses improved as well, supplying potent imagery to illustrate my progress in each area (room) of my life. Similarly, Marla—the dreamer featured in this chapter—discovered that the condition of her recurring dream house diagnosed the areas of her life that needed cleaning, shifting, repairing, or reorganizing.

Marla's dream house, in a desert area of California, had been her waking-life home as a young full-time wife and mother. Although she enjoyed these roles, she suffered from feelings of inadequacy and low self-esteem fueled by nearly incessant self-criticism. Marla's husband, Ralph, was a successful businessman and a leader in community and political affairs. In part because her husband was significantly older than she, Marla felt comparatively incompetent and powerless, deferring to his authority in nearly all decisions. She felt unworthy of expressing personal desires, and abandoned her wants to serve others.

During the years that she lived in the desert house, Marla experienced disabling panic attacks, depression, and irritable bowel syndrome. Her lack of self-confidence caused her to feel painfully shy in social situations. She had no friends. She was unable to communicate her feelings, and as a result her marital relationship lacked depth, intimacy, and authenticity.

Marla's study consists of eight dreams spanning ten months. All eight dreams are presented with the interpretations provided solely by Marla. I only elaborate upon her writing to further explain life circumstances or dream theory as the series proceeds. As a model for your own study, we will comment on Marla's process, and what helped and hindered her work. You will notice that Marla chose to identify her dream self as *dream ego*. At the start of her work she found that using that term made it easier for her to better see the wholeness of the dream. She was better able to objectify and then admit to the actions or characteristics that are truly her own. At the end of the study, Marla describes the changes she experienced by working with these recurring dreams of houses. The first dream begins to disclose some unresolved problems.

May 7, 2000: Return to Desert House
I have returned to our (former) house in the desert with friends from my (present) spiritual group. I see that the living room and kitchen are both unclean and messy. The furniture is not properly arranged.

With the help of the spiritually supportive feminine ("friends from my spiritual group") dream ego is revisiting a former state of consciousness, way of living, and feeling (desert house). Dream ego is able to see what is messy, what needs to be cleaned up. Both the social area (living room) and the place of nourishment (kitchen) need cleaning and organizing. That which supports dream ego (furniture) needs to be rearranged and harmonized.

I meet a sharply dressed young female tax accountant-attorney who has corrected Ralph's taxes. I am pleased about that. When the government reports what Ralph owes, the woman defends Ralph with the correct amount. She is very certain of her calculations. I'm impressed that she takes the time to be helpful to us.

Unexpected, powerful assistance is present in this old place—a competent, accurately calculating, protecting, and defending way of being (female tax accountant/attorney). This feminine advocate knows the correct amount (tax bill) to pay the governing part of the psyche. The governing part of the psyche is usually the voice of "should" and "have-to," which prompts and controls behavior. This could be called the cultural script within each of us, which often exacts an excessive fee until we can activate our feeling component (feminine) *to account for and defend us*. The dream says that the payment must be made by dream ego's masculine energy (husband). Marla easily identified the masculine as the way she must assert herself and act in the outer world.

The dream continues by examining the external aspects of her old way of being.

Ralph and I are out on the front lawn, lamenting the condition of the landscaping. The grass has died, the trees, bushes, and flowers, untended, have disappeared. However, I'm encouraged because some scraggly trees are sprouting new, green branches.

Accompanied by her thinking abilities (husband), dream ego laments the loss of what should have been growing (lawn) and improving the environment (landscaping). Indeed, Marla regrets that her own personal growth has been ignored. However, the dream offers hope by showing the new growth that is emerging from what was old and under-watered. This accurately reflects the very active steps Marla has taken in recent years to support her development, including dreamwork. Now the dream gets juicy, and threatening.

> Several big, long, gooey black snakes come to climb on me. I don't like them. I try to chase them away, but they are adamant about climbing all over me. Running away, I pull them off, and then see a small, dark red snake coming toward me. I try to shove it away, but this makes it angry. Although I don't want it to climb on me, I realize this is inevitable. I lie very still hoping it will just crawl over me without biting me. The snake goes right for my neck and bites me there. I feel a sting on my neck.

Marla understands snakes to represent change or transformation, since they shed their skins as they grow. Thus, in this dream, not yet conscious (black) elements of change (snakes) approach Marla in the area of growth (lawn). Dream ego tries to resist these changes, yet surrenders to the inevitable, as the powerful force injects her neck.

The location of the bite is important. Psyche is very specific about the areas that need tending or, in this case, transforming. The neck is what supports Marla's way of thinking, perceiving, and communicating (the organs of perception, speech, and thinking). Certainly, very little in human life can be altered without involvement from those areas, both metaphorically and literally. In addition, the neck connects the head (thinking) to feeling or instinct (body). Marla recognizes her discomfort with emotions. She prefers to think about a problem rather than feel it. Wholeness demands that we use both ways of knowing. Thus, the snake draws our attention to the neck, the bridge between the two.

Marla wrote this summary of her first dream: "This dream takes me back to a former unhealthy way of living and thinking about myself (desert house) that resulted in my lack of self-expression. Because I was unable to speak up, I lived an inauthentic lifestyle that, in turn, manifested in both physical and psychological illness. My psyche is providing me with energies (dream characters, including snakes) that will lead me to wholeness. Although I'm resisting change (the snake bite), I know it is inevitable."

Before substantive change can occur, one must have the ability to self-nurture. The second series dream shows the state of that ability.

July 3, 2000: Dusty Desert House
We've returned to the desert house. There's a thick layer of dust on everything, especially the bedside tables. Before we go to bed I have to get the dust off the nightstands. I'm disgusted by the thickness of the dust and am glad we don't have to stay long.

Dream ego is revisiting the place where she was (and still is) unbalanced, out of touch with herself, and nonassertive. There is a layer of obscurity (dust) on that which supports illumination/enlightenment in the area of integration (bedside tables). Dream ego needs to integrate her masculine energy ("we have to go to bed") but must first dispose of the dust—whatever covers her own assertiveness, action, accomplishment, and courage.

Dream ego removes some of the obscurity, but dislikes the process and doesn't want to spend much time at it.

A visitor surprises the dreamer at this point:

> I see Mother sitting in the living room. I know she has been dead for some years, so I don't really look at her.

Dream ego sees that her ability for self-nurturing (Mother) still exists, though she acknowledges that it has long been dormant ("dead for some years"). "This part of me has been dead for so long that I can't bear to look at it," Marla wrote. Indeed, facing the deadened condition of a necessary part of the self is never easy.

> I ask her who is with her from the other realm, and she responds, "Oh, you mean up in Seattle?"

Dream Marla probes more deeply by asking what other parts of herself have been lying dormant (who is with Mother in the other realm). The dream surprises Marla by responding with a place, not a person. This illogical brilliance of the dream led Marla to a very important realization. Her associations to Seattle, that place or way of being, took her to a rare time when she had been fully independent. In her early twenties, Marla planned and executed a trip to Seattle, where she traveled alone. When ego asks who/what else is dormant (in the other realm) along with her ability to self-nurture, she learns it is her underdeveloped abilities to execute a plan, be courageous, assert herself, move forward, and act adventurously. This information, though clear, was unsettling to Marla, for consciously embracing those attributes would demand a great transformation. Happily, the snakes in the first dream have already injected her! In waking life

Marla was actively pursuing transformation through her dream-work and in other ways as well.

The next series dream shows growth and also introduces an unsavory character, a shadow aspect of Marla she did not welcome.

July 28, 2000: Desert House on Stilts
I'm at our former house in the desert. The lawn is very green and my dog Jenny is playfully tearing around in circles. I tell her to be careful, but I'm enjoying watching her run around like a young dog again.

Perhaps because Marla was consciously working with her dreams as they occurred, we see growth in the desert (green lawn). In addition, spontaneous instinct (dog) plays joyfully, has plenty of space, and is moving in a way that expresses wholeness ("running in circles"). The snakebite on the neck has begun to take effect, as evidenced by this transformation. Always the last to embrace change, dream ego is cautious about the exuberant movement, but is happy to witness it.

Inside, there seem to be many houseguests, including Wildon, who is lying on the sofa. He has been in trouble for child molesting. There are other unsavory party types in the living room.

Internally (inside the house), dream ego finds several personality aspects that are no longer acceptable to her. One is Wildon (a defense attorney in waking life)—a former *defensive* way of acting that abuses and exploits growing potential (child molesting). About this, Marla wrote: "My belief in my unworthiness results in continual self-criticism. Thus I attack my own potential (molest my inner child) when I ignore my own needs and wants. I then judge myself too harshly to be able to freely express myself." This dynamic is seen in the most public aspect of dream ego's life (living room) where we find unacceptable, social ways of acting (unsavory party types). Now the dream introduces a star quality.

> At the party is a rock star who has bought a jewel for $18,000. It is set in a white and metal cuff-type bracelet that he wears on his wrist and hand. The rock star really likes this thing and is showing it off, but I know he has been overcharged because the jewel is not genuine.

Marla wrote: "An aspect of myself that performs in the world (rock star) has bought and values something that is not genuine. This is reflected in my beliefs that women have little or no value, that therefore I am stupid, incompetent, and must remain quiet to feel safe. This falseness has put a restrictive covering ("metal cuff-type bracelet on wrist and hand") on my ability to work and create (hands). I know this self is not genuine, and that it exists at a great cost to expressing myself truly."

Next psyche shows a broader view of this old way of living in the desert.

> I go outside the house, which is way up on stilts. I remember that when I lived here before I was always afraid I'd fall off the edge of the surrounding walkway.

Dream ego looks at this unhealed state of consciousness objectively (from the outside), and sees that it is precariously balanced on very thin supports ("up on stilts"). She realizes that when she lived in this way of being she was in fear of losing her balance, knowing she was on the edge ("always afraid I would fall off the edge"). "Feeling unworthy to express myself has kept me from experiencing the security of my spiritual center. When I feel free to be me, no part of me is unbalanced, on the edge or feeling vulnerable."

Here is Marla's summary of Dream Three: "The dream shows growth in my instinctive (dog) ability to be more spontaneous and to move toward wholeness. That's the good news. However, some defensive/protective behaviors and attitudes stifle my potential. I must recognize the ways I do not act genuine in public because they cost me dearly. The house on stilts is a powerful image, allowing me to feel unbalanced in this old, limited, way of living. I'm ready to relinquish that insecurity."

The next series dream shows what is approaching the desert house and dream ego's reaction.

December 24, 2000: Desert House Shadow Men
I'm at the house in the desert. All the windows are open and unlocked. Evening is coming and I'm frightened by the men I see creeping across the lawn. So I go around the house shutting and locking everything.

This fourth dream in the series occurred seven months after the first dream. Progress is evident in the openness of the house ("doors and windows open, unlocked"). In addition, unknown ways of thinking and acting are approaching from the area of recent growth (men creeping across the lawn). Dream ego is apprehensive about these changes. That old homeostatic self likes things locked up and secure. It is almost always wary of a transformation, as in the fear of the snakes in Dream Two.

> Just as I try to lock the front door, a black man tries to push his way in. I attempt to make him go away but he really wants to come in. I let him come into the house.

Again the masculine enters this study, as a previously unrecognized way of thinking and doing (the black man) tries to enter the place where Marla feels so inadequate. Though dream ego resists this newcomer, some part of her recognizes the value of integrating what is unknown and allows him to join her. The dream continues:

> He is upset that I tried to keep him out and wants to know the reason.

I have heard hundreds of dreams containing either image or verbiage illustrating the upset, anger, or rage of the part of the self that has not been able to manifest—generally referred to as the shadow and, in this case, seen as the black man. (In the dreams of Caucasians, dark-skinned characters may represent what is rejected, unrecognized, or denied.) Ego and the shadow character engage:

> I point to the yard where the other men are approaching the house as evening falls. I tell him I can't have all these people coming into the house at once, and he responds, "Oh yeah, I see what you mean," and goes around helping me lock up.

Ego explains that the other masculine energies that are pressing for integration ("other men approaching the house as evening falls") are too much for her. Apparently this is acceptable for the present time, as what has already come in helps to secure the environment as unconsciousness (night) approaches.

Here is Marla's summary: "The dream shows help from the unconscious to integrate new ways of thinking and doing (the approaching men/masculine) in the place of inadequacy and unworthiness. I am assured that I am in the process of accepting one form of new energy into conscious awareness, and that more is approaching." This Christmas Eve dream was a great gift for the old year. The new year brought significant change in the next dream.

January 24, 2001: Big Addition to Desert House
I'm running in my bare feet on the dry dirt outside the desert house. I'm so happy that I have no foot pain. I think it has disappeared due to the warm, dry weather. I want to stay here even though it will upset my fam ily. I consider calling them and telling them I am not coming back home. I want to stay where I am free from pain.

Now, eight months after the series began, in the place where she had been unhealthy in the past, Marla discovers that she can energetically bare her soul ("run outside, barefoot") and that she is happily pain-free. The pain is gone because of a less emotional climate (warm, dry weather). Marla writes: "I am less emotionally volatile because I am willing to recognize and validate my feelings. I'm learning to communicate them as they arise, rather than stuffing them down inside. In the past my emotions would boil over from being held in too long. This was a painful way of walking through the world."

Ego wants to remain in this painless place, but feels it will upset the family energies that shaped her and to which she is still attached ("I want to stay here…it will upset my family"). Family expectations (family script) can be as "taxing" as the government (cultural script) in Dream One. To achieve the growth and healing that is Marla's goal, it is imperative that some aspects of her family script be abandoned. Further, for Marla and most of the other studies in this book, it is essential that a more appropriate, supportive script be chosen once the negative one has been recognized. The dream continues by showing more growth.

> Several new rooms and a swimming pool have been added to the house, which has been redecorated with expensive, colorful furniture and many amenities. There is even one room that serves as a classroom for children. Their teacher is here now.

Here we get the first evidence of profound inner change in the expansion of the desert house (several new rooms) including contained, calming, and enjoyable emotional experiences (swimming pool). That which supports ego (furniture) is of higher quality and interest ("expensive, colorful furniture"). In this case, the furniture reflects the new, more valuable, supportive thoughts and beliefs about her self. There is also a formal area for continuing the education of the new potential ("classroom for children, teacher"). The dream continues:

> A couple of the former owners are here as well. The house has changed hands several times since we owned it. I like the colorful expansion of the old house and think about trying to buy it.

The desert house, the old, unhealthy way of being, has gone through many transitions ("house has changed hands several times"). Dream ego is enjoying the energetic expansion and wants to own it. This is a good sign, for owning a psychological aspect connotes complete acceptance of and commitment to it. However, more clarification is necessary.

> Ralph and I want to swim in the indoor pool, but I am concerned that the water is too cloudy. I go to check out the pool and find that the water has been clearing. I am able to see most of the bottom, except for the deep right corner. I feel that will soon clear up and then we can swim.

Despite Marla's resistance to the new masculine form (the black man) in the previous dream, she is now nearly ready to unite emotionally with her masculine energy in a smooth, enjoyable way (swim). She is concerned because she cannot see this entire process clearly ("the water is cloudy"). We often want to observe from a safe distance what cannot yet be seen/known before we make a commitment to a change. However, clarity is approaching.

Marla summarized this dream: "The dream shows positive emotional changes in my self-image, and that I am learning and growing. The dream suggests that I am nearly emotionally ready for the integration of masculine energy, and am even looking forward to it." Images of growth and development, such as the new rooms and the clearing water in this dream, are common to most recurring dream series. The evolution of the house/self continues in the next series dream.

> *February 4, 2001: Desert House-Castle-School*
> I take some friends to see my old house in Desert Hot
> Springs. Because of the addition of several turrets, it
> looks like a modern castle. The house has been
> expanded to twice its size. I'm telling my friends what
> a great house it is, and that the large living room has
> fabulous views.

As in three of Marla's other series dreams, ego is using helpful,
supportive internal energies (friends) to look at a former state of
consciousness where she was unbalanced, inauthentic, and
unhealthy. Dream ego sees that her former state of consciousness has greatly expanded, and has become a fortified stronghold
(turrets, castle), with growth in the social arena (large living
room) and a broad perspective (fabulous views).

Once again, the expanded house blends into a learning
place:

> The house seems to be a school for young children.
> The inside is filled with children, teachers, and
> school furniture.

In the previous dream, one room of the house had become a
classroom. Now the entire desert house is a school where young,
growing, learning energies can be educated and supported.

> I am disappointed that the wood flooring is scuffed
> and faded. It is covered with bird droppings. The floor
> needs to be refinished.

Again attention is focused on the symbol of floors—what Marla
stands on, or her understanding. Marla wrote: "The scuffed floor

covered with bird droppings reflects an under-standing of myself
that is still in need of refurbishing. I need to remove the waste
from a spirit (bird) that has been cooped up inside instead of flying freely; I can truly feel the spirit that needs the freedom of self-
expression. I still need to refurbish my self-concept (floor,
foundation) so that it can shine in the glow of full self-expression."

> The living room is still large, with great views, but it
> is filled with cheap green lawn chairs. I find the fur-
> nishings distasteful, but comment to my friends that it
> is nice that everything is so green.

Dream ego is concerned about the casual quality of what supports social or public activities (lawn chairs). There is growth
here (green) but not sufficient sturdiness or value (cheap) to
please dream ego. Marla thought this reflected some growth in
her willingness to become more social, to be comfortable in the
social arena. "However, the dream suggests that I am not supporting myself adequately enough—i.e., with a positive, self-con-
fident attitude." That makes sense because the dream says
alterations in Marla's beliefs are not complete—floors must still
be refinished. However, growth is obvious in the next sentence:

> When we leave the house I remark that the new own-
> ers have expanded it to twice its size.

It is important to remember that tremendous improvement has
occurred in a place that formerly was psychologically and physically unhealthy. In the meantime, transformation is ablaze in the
neighborhood:

I look down the street and see that the house of my
former neighbor, Dr. Moore, is on fire.

As fire is the ultimate transformational process, it would seem
that great change is underway, this time in the area of the physical body (doctor). One of the many benefits of dreamwork, made
possible by the connection between psyche and soma, is physical healing—a major, continuing concern for Marla.

Considering the snakes in previous dreams and the connection between snakes and healing (a snake is wrapped around
the caduceus, the symbol of healing), it is not surprising that the
next dream in the series shows more snakes in the desert home.
As often happens in series dreams, there is a connection between
these two dreams: When profound transformation occurs in the
home of the inner doctor, then even more healing is possible.
This clears the way for the snakes. As before, dream ego does not
welcome the snake with enthusiasm.

February 23, 2001: Poisonous Snake
in Desert Hot Springs House

I'm back in the desert house. A large brown-spotted
poisonous snake has entered the living room. Ralph
and I shoo it out through the sliding glass door, but it
comes back in through the open slider in the bedroom.

The bedroom carpet is dusty and debris is scattered over the floor. Construction workers have tracked
in dirt and left their debris. A brand-new heating and air
conditioning system is being installed in the garage.

The snake goes into the master bath and tries to
hide in a corner under some paper. Ralph just wants
to grab it and take it outside. He grasps the snake and

struggles with it as it tries to bite him. We take it outside and let it go. We see another, smaller snake in
our driveway. I'm unhappy that there are all these
snakes around our house. Ralph returns to the bathroom to wash his back and chest where the snake had
been trying to bite him. There is some venom on
him, but he is able to wash it off his skin.

This dream repeats several themes: snakes and ego's resistance to
them, dirty floors that need tending, transformation of the masculine, and new construction. Marla summarized the dream this
way: "The dream shows that I'm avoiding change in the place
where my masculine energy is integrated (bedroom). I'm still not
ready to change my ways of acting, asserting, thinking, accomplishing. Because the floors are a mess, I still need to clean up
my understanding of some basic concepts. What I stand on
needs to be cleared. Some improvements are being made in the
regulation of my emotions with the installment of new heating
and cooling systems."

Throughout this series, connection with and development
of the masculine principle has been paramount for Marla. The
next dream introduces a conflict that hinders this endeavor.

March 30, 2001: Wild Driver at the Desert House
I'm standing in front of the desert house. Ralph is
tearing down the hill, driving the Suburban as though
it were a bicycle. I watch him slide out around the
curves and worry that he will crash. I yell at him to
slow down, but he doesn't.

Dream ego observes that her doing and accomplishing energy (husband) is feeling pressured, moving forward rapidly, has the ability to transport a large number of people (Suburban), and is successfully negotiating difficult terrain (curves).

Now the dream introduces a typical conflict, not only from the perspective of dream ego ("I yell at him to slow down, but he doesn't"), but also from a force from the past.

> My brother sees Ralph driving toward us in the Suburban. My sister Annie is in the passenger seat. My brother is also concerned about Ralph's speed, so he grabs the front of the truck and pulls it down to the pavement. Ralph and my little sister fall to the ground on their heads. I fear they are dead, but they get up and seem to be okay.

In this dream, we are introduced to two members of Marla's family. "My sister, though younger than I, is wise beyond her years." By contrast, Marla said that her brother was abusive, relentlessly tormenting, and critical of her in her youth. Because of this Marla sees her brother as her inner critic—her "I can't do that" attitude that often stops her from acting and accomplishing (reminiscent of the child-molesting lawyer in a previous dream).

Transforming the power of inner abusers is a vital part of the individuation process. In this dream, we see that a formerly abusive way of thinking (brother) wants to slow or stop the process that is moving so rapidly. In this the ego and the abusive brother are in agreement. However, ego's wisdom (sister) and driving energy (husband) are together and survive the crash initiated by the brother.

More surprising information about the masculine follows:

The front part of the house opens into the yard, where there are two large beds. Ralph and I sleep in one. Ralph pees in his sleep. He gets up and smiles as though nothing has happened. His body has become youthful and muscular.

Dream ego's masculine (thinking) element eliminates emotional toxins (pee) through dreamwork (while sleeping). As a result, the ability to accomplish (masculine) is renewed and strong (youthful and muscular). Alas, a mess remains:

I enter the bedroom where Ralph and I slept when we lived here. Trash and paper are scattered about and tangled in the old TV cables coming out from the wall. The bedroom carpet needs to be vacuumed. Fleas jump out of the carpet and onto my ankles.

Marla is clearly developing new and healthy ways of thinking and doing ("His body has become youthful and muscular"), but cleanup is still necessary in the place of integration (bedroom). This reflects the very common experience of learning something new but not integrating the learning into everyday life. The dream shows irritating things (fleas) are rising from the unclean understanding (carpet), attaching to Marla's ability to move (legs) to drain the life force. Information is tangled in old lines of communication ("old pieces of paper tangled in old TV cables").

I pick up a card written by a seriously ill woman named Janee. I vaguely recall a woman I befriended when she was seriously ill and incapacitated. I wonder if she survived.

We are left with this vital question: Has the unhealed self survived? What is the condition of the feminine (ways of being, feeling, and relating) that was ill?

Marla summarized: "The dream tells me I can move forward rapidly. My masculine, driving, accomplishing energy has been renewed and strengthened through the cleansing process of dreamwork. There is still some cleaning up I need to do in the area of integration with masculine energy. I need to know the condition of the unhealed part of myself."

Since this theme repeats within the series, I asked Marla to write what she now knows about her masculine principle, how it has functioned, and what needs to happen within her to achieve what she wants for herself. This is her response: "For me, this masculine principle, now activated, brings self-assertion and much needed self-expression. Without those abilities I turn inward, berating myself with self-criticism and hopelessness (brother). Now I can use my masculine energy to more easily say and get what I want and need. Finally, I often feel that I can act confidently in the outer world, expressing myself joyfully and spontaneously without fear of judgment."

It appears that this study has provided Marla with an entirely new foundation upon which she can stand. Metaphorically, those littered, dirty, cluttered floors/carpets in the dream series have been cleared and cleaned. Now Marla can launch herself from a firm, clear understanding of her own value and power. These images, woven together, suggest that Janee (the sick feminine) has indeed survived and healed.

To assist you in using this chapter as a model for your own work, I asked Marla to review and describe her experiences while doing this study. Marla wrote: "I approached the series dreams with an unwavering conviction that all dreams come to us to promote our healing and wholeness. This provided me with the confidence and will power to cope with the demands of the transformational process of the series.

"Practically speaking, dedicating myself to the study of the dream put me in a kind of hothouse of self-examination and development. The knowledge that most dreams are symbolic in nature allowed me to be objective in my analysis, distancing me from the fearful emotions produced by potent dream images such as snakes biting me. I allowed myself to engage with the dream images, to let them occupy my mind throughout the day, to dialogue with them, and to express them through art. These processes brought me insights and power. Putting my faith in the ability of the dream to be my healing agent infused me with excitement and the energy to make the necessary commitments to change.

"My progress lapsed at times when I reverted to old patterns of holding back, not expressing my feelings or being authentic. When my old script reactivated, I lost the courage needed to integrate the new patterns of behavior that are healthy for me. Instead of holding steady to what the dreams were asking of me, I found it hard in my outer life to put into action what I had been learning from my inner life. But the dreams kept telling me what I needed to know, and the repetition of their healing messages gave me the desire and the strength to carry into outer life the changes I needed to make."

Two days after I received this process summary from Marla, I was surprised by another series dream, hot off the dream press. It seems the best possible way to complete this chapter.

July 25, 2001: Day Breaks at Desert House
Ralph and I have returned to the desert house for a vacation. We are in bed, engaging in foreplay. The

bedspread is heavy and I want to push it off the bed. I discover the reason it's so heavy—there is a large book wrapped up in it that falls out as I push the bedspread off onto the floor. Ralph has been reading it.

Our two grown daughters have returned with us to the desert and burst into our bedroom. It's 7 A.M. And the light is streaming in through all the windows; all the blinds are up. We put on our sunglasses because it is so bright. I remark how great it is to wake up at sunrise and watch the dawning of the new day. The girls are excitedly discussing all the wonderful things they might like to do today.

We all go into the living room, where Ralph is telling our new dog, a curly-coated brown and white water retriever, to sit. I pet the dog's curly coat and realize it will not shed much. The new dog is sweet, but does not react as quickly as our last dog.

Marla wrote: "The dream shows that I have made a great deal of progress in the area of integration (bedroom). My masculine abilities (thinking, asserting, and doing) and my feminine abilities (feeling) are engaged in foreplay. I have finally been able to remove the heavy covering that was encumbering my integrative process (quilt). It is heavy because my masculine (husband) has been engaged in a difficult learning process.

"I am excited that the blinds are up, and the light of consciousness is streaming in. Since it is the dawning of a new day, I truly am looking forward to the new possibilities that await me as a more complete, whole person. Perhaps this is why we are all in the living room. It's good to know that I have new, more contained instinctual ability (dog) that can keep me in touch with my feelings. This dog does not shed (irritate others) because it is less emotionally reactive."

There is no mention of dirty floors in this piece. According to psyche, Marla's inner understanding is cleared, providing her with a new foundation of self-worth in this expanded place from the past. Making this series a reality in the world will depend on Marla's continued willingness to capture, record, work with, and honor her recurring symbols and serial dreams.

CHAPTER EIGHTEEN

Cancer: The Internal Threat

Dreamer: Barbara
Recurring symbol: cancer
Length of dream series: 4 years
Number of dreams presented: 27
Script messages addressed:
"Girls should live risk-free, protected lives."
"Wives should be financially dependent."
Benefits to the dreamer:
Acknowledged the importance of "processing" emotional material.
Overcame inability to express herself in important situations.
Acknowledged emotional damage resulting from the ridicule of others.
Realized the connection between low self-esteem and creative productivity.
Balanced the dynamic between dependence and active empowerment.

Summary: A 42-year-old woman examines the "cancerous" thoughts and attitudes that limit her self-esteem and diminish her creative potential.

Early one morning I received a long-distance call from a client I will call Frank. A dream had so distressed him that he felt unable to attend his scheduled business meetings until he had a sense of the dream's message. Here is what Frank reported. "In the dream I was told that, due to a brain tumor, I had less than a year to live. I awoke fearing that my frequent headaches are a symptom of that diagnosis. Should I take this dream literally or symbolically?"

That was the most important question Frank could ask with this type of dream content. To answer it, however, we needed more data. I asked Frank how the message was given in the dream. Had he heard a disembodied voice make an announcement or was the statement made within a dream drama?

As is often the case, Frank said there was much more to the dream. By pulling out the frightening sentence and ignoring the rest of the dream, Frank had committed a very common mistake of novice dream students.

"Here's the dream as I wrote it," Frank said.

> I'm being driven by a wild taxi driver, careening through the streets of Mexico City. I'm sure we are going to crash at every circular intersection. I tell the cabby to slow down. He tells me I should worry about my own problems, such as the tumor in my brain. He laughs as he says that I have only a year to live.

"The dream so scared me that I awoke with my heart pounding out of my chest."

"And how do you feel about this dream now?" I asked.

"Well, I'm more calm. Just by reading the dream again, I can see several questions to ask about the symbology that did not occur to me in my panic. For instance, why am I being driven by a wild man who thinks it's funny that I will die in a year from a brain tumor?" By considering the wholeness of the dream, Frank had gone beyond his first fear response to see that psyche had much information to impart.

As we worked with the dream, Frank was able to thoroughly identify with his own wild, taxi driver energy. "This destructive, manic behavior is what my cardiologist describes as Type A personality. He calls it the 'inner killer' for someone with my heart condition. This part of my personality is an unrelenting, driving, and driven force that won't let me relax. If that is what the taxi driver represents, it enjoys seeing me in pain."

As his dreamwork progressed, Frank connected just as powerfully to the other symbols in the dream. By the end of our phone session, he was confident that the brain tumor was symbolic of the processes and beliefs that fueled his hyperactivity, resulting in life-threatening stress. He fully embraced the dream message that lethal thinking (the tumor was in the brain) threatened his peace of mind and his physical health. So impacted was he by the dream that he joined a meditation group, began therapy, and committed to daily yoga exercises. Within six weeks his frequent headaches disappeared.

Despite the many connections that Frank made to the symbols and metaphors in his cabby dream, I continued to hold it in my awareness and advised him to do so as well. To dismiss such a dream as strictly symbolic would be irresponsible. Five years after reporting this dream, a robust and grateful Frank is convinced that his crazed taxi driver reflected an inner dynamic that could have become fatal had he ignored the dream.

Though the warning provided by Frank's dream was not about an actual brain tumor, research reveals that sometimes dreams accurately reflect actual physical problems. Patricia Garfield writes about many such dreams in her book, *The Healing Power of Dreams*. Marc Barasch shares how his dreams led to the diagnosis of thyroid cancer in his book, *Healing Dreams*. Jeremy Taylor reports a stunning lifesaving dream in *Where People Fly and Water Runs Uphill*. A dream group member had such a strong feeling about the validity of her dream, which symbolically suggested uterine cancer, that she cancelled a European trip to pursue medical intervention. Several doctors told her she was asymptomatic but her unease continued. She remained convinced that the dream was a literal warning. After additional tests, cancer was indeed detected. There seems no doubt that her life was saved by her feelings about the dream.

Because of the importance of dreams about illness, I was thrilled when Barbara said she wanted to study a dream series with cancer as the repeating symbol. Barbara began recording these dreams when, at thirty-seven years old, she joined a dream group. She soon recognized a repeating dream theme of cancer. This series spanned six years and included twenty-seven dreams.

When the series began, Barbara was fairly sure the material was symbolic, but one particular dream motivated her to have a general physical examination. Because the exam results convinced her that she was physically healthy, Barbara was quite comfortable examining her cancer dreams metaphorically. When she began to see the pattern of meaning emerging through the series, her concerns for the literalness of the dream message disappeared altogether. As you will see, examining the metaphors suggested by parts of the body and the functions they perform provided Barbara with valuable insight and focus for psycho-spiritual healing.

Of the twenty-seven dreams in the series, eleven identified a specific type of cancer. Five dreams designated cancer of the stomach. The other parts of the body named as cancerous were face or head, ear, lung, breast, liver, and blood. Each of these types occurred in only one dream. The other sixteen dreams identified people in treatment for undefined forms of the disease.

Barbara defined cancer as a destructive, hidden, life-threatening condition that destroys healthy tissue from the inside. The condition can exist for a long time before making itself felt. It destroys the life force and blocks the natural flow of energy. The longer the disease progresses, the more life force is destroyed. Once discovered, the problem must be treated. The treatment, often painful and traumatic, can produce side effects more distressing than the presenting symptoms.

As we studied the dreams, Barbara and I began to see that the various forms of cancer identified places where her energy was blocked, either metaphorically or literally. The dreams also uncovered the psychological or spiritual beliefs that maintained the blockages. When we examined who had what type of cancer, we began to see the parts of her personality that needed healing. Eventually, a pattern of threatening cultural and familial beliefs came into focus, allowing us to see what was impeding the life force of this woman entering her middle years.

Since stomach cancer was the prevalent symbol, Barbara and I first focused on understanding it metaphorically. Because the stomach processes what is taken in, what is bitten off and swallowed, we considered the damage done by swallowing negative beliefs. The phrase "to swallow feelings" prompted us to think about the damage caused by suppressing emotions. In addition, we pondered the need to process food and what happens to the physical body when that process is stopped or blocked. Constipation is, at best, uncomfortable. If it remains unresolved, the resulting toxicity can be as deadly as cancer.

Since the stomach is the organ that processes food, we considered that a process is an action that moves things along to their allotted space, destination, or customer. An unhampered process allows the necessary flow to occur. When a flow is blocked, trouble occurs. Ponder the consequences to a factory that does not process invoices, a chef who does not process orders, or a parent who does not process the warning signs of a troubled child. Human beings need to process, or deal with, psychological, physical, or spiritual experiences. Events that are not processed—that is, examined, understood, integrated, or released—may be repressed or denied. These forgotten situations often fester, unrecognized, creating both physical and behavioral pain and dysfunction. Often a dream directs the dreamer to focus on a forgotten time or an incident that needs to be recalled and dealt with, processed, to facilitate healing.

The first dream in the series identified the loss of contact with an important aspect of herself. Because the "lost self" has cancer, the dream focused on the healing necessary for Barbara's development.

October 17, 1990: Mary Has Cancer
A woman I once knew is giving a talk. Judy and Ruth remind me that I used to admire this talented teacher. I have lost contact with her and don't really know her anymore. I notice she is being treated for cancer.

At the time of this dream, Barbara was a thirty-seven-year-old artist needing and wanting to develop career options to financially supplement her artistic endeavors. This first cancer dream occurred shortly after she had been hired for her first part-time university teaching position. She was terrified of speaking in public and was frequently embarrassed by an inability to express herself in important circumstances. "It is as if my throat contracts. I know the words I want to say but either my voice shakes, changes tone, and squeaks, or I just cannot get out the words. It's like they literally get stuck in my throat. I clearly have to deal with this if I am to be a successful teacher." Thus, the first dream presents an admired teacher who is able to express herself verbally ("give a talk") but who has cancer. Psyche dramatically presents an image of what threatens Barbara if she is to develop effective teaching skills.

The dream offers some hope by suggesting that Barbara once knew and admired this teacher. Dreams of a formerly known and admired person often indicate the existence of a valuable part of the self, often forgotten. (Surely, everyone was able to express honest emotion at the first bellowing stages of infancy!) Even though the awake self (or dream ego) may be unaware, psyche seems to be offering assurance that what Barbara wants and needs is available within.

The second dream in the series showed an eight-year-old black girl who had "stomach cancer caused by a weird energy from the past."

We wondered if something had happened when Barbara was eight years old that had not been processed and was now interfering with her natural life flow. Barbara could not recall a particular traumatic incident suffered at age eight, but she did describe that as a time of significant socialization in elementary school. It is common for eight-year-old girls to develop cliques, exclusionary groups that can cause considerable harm to the uninvited and unwelcome. Because she was severely pigeon-toed,

Barbara had suffered rejection and vicious teasing. This form of social ridicule continued throughout Barbara's schooling, making her feel unaccepted and, perhaps, damaging her ability to freely express herself. It is hard to speak up, to stand out and be noticed, when fearful of ridicule. Perhaps at age eight Barbara first suppressed experiences or feelings ("weird energy from the past") too painful to acknowledge. Examining the black girl gave Barbara the opportunity to work with this old, unprocessed material.

A month after the first stomach cancer dream, Barbara dreamed of "wanting to contact the little black girl and get more information about stomach cancer." Then, a year later, dream ego seems to know a bit more and wants to help the stomach cancer patient identified as Lois:

> *April 29, 1992: Lois Needs a Healing*
> Lois says that her stomach cancer is affecting her reproduction. I suggest that hypnotherapy and other forms of process work might help, but Lois rejects this.

Barbara described her friend Lois as "someone who suffers from low self-esteem, is emotionally repressed, settles for less, and believes she has no power to change. She allows fear to stop her creative process." Barbara found no pleasure in owning this characterization, though she admitted that all the descriptors of Lois were true of her, as well.

The blending of stomach cancer and reproduction fascinated us. The dream said that the aspect of Barbara that suffers from low self-esteem (Lois) has not processed past trauma (stomach cancer) and is still unwilling to do so ("I suggest that hypnotherapy and other forms of process work might help but Lois rejects this"). Barbara's description of Lois allowing fear to stop her creative process in the awake world led us to see the connection between stomach cancer and reproduction. In this case, fear of not being good enough, acceptable, blocks Barbara's ability to express herself verbally. In addition, this belief blocks her ability to create satisfying careers, to support herself, to be re-productive.

A dream that occurred two years later shed some light on an aspect of Barbara's family script that was interfering with her productivity:

> *April 11, 1994: Grandmother's Dirty Apartment*
> I am telling Donald that my maternal grandmother died of cancer. I am unsure if she had stomach or prostate cancer. Donald says the prostate is a connec-tor. I notice grime and dirt on the table. I tell Donald my grandmother would not have allowed that, as she was a neatnik.

The presence of grandparents in dreams provides the opportu-nity to examine the less conscious aspects of the family script. What kind of metaphoric dirt or grime might psyche want to reveal in the place of the grandmother? And why did the grand-mother have stomach or prostate cancer? Barbara and I discov-ered the answers to these questions contained within some beliefs that hindered Barbara's ability to support herself.

Barbara was raised in an affluent Jewish home. Her material needs were abundantly met and she always felt loved and safe. She was taught, by word and example, that girls should live risk-free, protected lives. From both her mother and maternal grand-mother, Barbara learned that women should not be required to earn a living. It was the husband's duty to provide. This cultural belief diminishes the need of a young girl to develop her own survival skills and her ability to succeed in the outer world.

Linking the grandmother's stomach cancer to the prostate, a male organ, led us to examine the concept of the masculine principle. In the Jungian theory of archetypes, every individual possesses both masculine and feminine functioning. Masculine functioning is seen as the directive, goal-oriented, outward ways of doing. Feminine functioning is thought to carry the tasks of relationship, of feeling, of inner needs, of being. For Barbara to mature and take her rightful place in the world of art and commerce, she would have to develop these aspects of her personality threatened by the grandmother's metaphoric dirt: the belief that women should be financially dependent. Seeing that her grandmother's masculine functioning (prostrate) was cancerous was particularly potent since Barbara adored her maternal grandmother. She was loath to see this shadow element of her upbringing. Psyche often presents a dream that alters the family myth so that the dreamer may more realistically identify the dysfunctional or no longer useful patterns of the family script.

Donald, the dream character being told about the grandmother, is a very successful man who has created several meaningful and unique careers in Barbara's geographic area. It makes sense, then, that this kind of powerful masculine energy needs to see the metaphoric dirt and grime that hampers Barbara.

The loss of the masculine is an emotional one, as shown in a powerful dream that presented the masculine as dwarfed:

April 23, 1991: Lung Cancer and the Dwarf
I'm in a hospital bed in a large room with other patients. A woman in another bed has lung cancer and is hoping to get rid of it. I ask questions about her

> cancer but she doesn't want to discuss it. She is read-
> ing a Swedish book that I read a long time ago. It is
> about male dwarfs.

This woman is not speaking or processing. She is suffering from lung cancer, which Barbara associated to unexpressed or unrecognized grief. Therefore, the one with blocked grief (lung cancer) is learning about the foreign (Swedish) masculine who has not grown to full stature (dwarfed).

Why would Barbara need to see that some part of her was not processing grief? If you have had a dream or vision that has not manifested, you may be able to relate to this. To know that you have talent and ability but insufficient drive (masculine energy) to carry your gifts into the world can produce a painful, existential grief. Seeing her masculine as dwarfed and feeling the grief of that motivated Barbara to further examine her family script and to go beyond it.

At this point in the study, we decided to focus on the masculine principle as seen through the male dream characters. Five dreams identified men with cancer. In the order given by the dreams, these characters were:

1. A man with yellow skin who wants to commit suicide in the ocean. He is helped to accomplish this by a minister. We often think of yellow representing without courage. To commit suicide is to consciously choose death. Thus, the cowardly masculine is choosing his own demise. His decision is being supported by a spiritual masculine, the one who ministers to the collective. At the time of this dream Barbara was a student in two healing programs training her to "minister to" the collective.

That the cowardly masculine was willing to die seemed a very positive indication of growth.

2. My uncle is putting snuff, a carcinogen, on his lip. Barbara connected this image to her difficulty with verbal expression (which comes through the lips) and also to the stomach cancer dreams (the lips being the gateway to the digestive tract). Barbara described this particular uncle as "a man who suffers from chronic depression." A depressed, inactive masculine energy is certainly not helpful to self expression or to productivity. Barbara's family script, which directed her to be dependent, suppressed (depressed) her ability and desire to be self-sufficient, and clearly interfered with activating the masculine principle.

3. A man is attending a dream workshop to become more aware of his unconscious processes. He says that he has dreamed he has cancer and wonders what he should do now. The masculine wanting to become aware of his unconscious processes connects to Barbara's need to be aware of what she has taken in that remains unprocessed, unconscious, and threatening.

4. Bob says he has cancer and wonders what to do about it. Barbara described Bob as a successful businessman whose business had remained unchanged for twenty years. Though Barbara considered his life humdrum and boring, she did admire his work ethic. Bob seems to represent a shadow side of Barbara: her unlived masculine that is committed to professional success. Like the speaking ability of the teacher in the first series dream, this important character trait—a positive work ethic—is in danger from cancer.

5. In her dream, Barbara's friend dreams he has stomach cancer. Barbara reported that this particular friend tends to repress his feelings, rarely expressing his emotions. This repeats the metaphor of stomach cancer representing unprocessed or repressed psychological material.

The masculine principle played a paramount part in this recurring dream study. From the prostate cancer of the grandmother through the material presented in the other synthesized dreams, Barbara learned what threatened her ability to accomplish what she really wanted. The study of this cancer series led Barbara to process a great deal of unrecognized historical and psychological material, thus clarifying the preponderance of the stomach cancer dreams. Nearly every night she was processing rich, inner material and cleaning out the toxic beliefs that imprisoned her sense of self and her potential. Her dreamwork became the psychic surgery necessary for Barbara to rid herself of the beliefs and attitudes that metaphorically threatened her life.

Barbara successfully completed her part-time university teaching job and is now on staff as a teacher in a healing center in her community. She has established two successful and creative careers in the healing field. To avoid a "relapse," Barbara is particularly alert to threats and blockages to self-expression and to that vital productive force, her masculine principle. These series dreams, wherein cancer is the symbolic threat to life, have been particularly helpful in identifying and ridding Barbara of the inner blocks before they destroy her ability to develop, to live fully.

PART THREE
Studying Your Own Series

CHAPTER NINETEEN

Tracking Your Recurring Symbol

Studying a recurring symbol proved to be a life-altering experience for the dreamers whose series are presented in this book. However, like all explorers into the unknown, we trudged down many dead ends and often felt inexorably lost. As you undertake your own trek, you will discover ways to carve your path. This chapter offers you a variety of implements and routes, but you must trust your own knowing to provide what you need. When frustrated, ask your dreams for help!

The first step is choosing the recurring symbol you want to examine. An animate or inanimate object, a known or unknown person, a place, a time in history, a color, an archetype (e.g., the mother or the shadow) are grist for the mill. Litters of kittens, the sound of a whistle blowing, the approaching storm, the little red wagon—all of these recurring symbols want something from or for you. Pursuing a recurring feeling that travels from dream to dream may be very illuminating. You might choose to study a recurring process, such as dreams showing your inability to crest the top of the hill, extricate yourself from the mud, or avoid falling over the edge of a cliff. If you follow the recurring symbol dreams, they will lead you on an intriguing journey. This chapter provides a general map to make the trip less confusing.

If the recurring symbol you select is stored in your memory from dreams past, the first part of the journey will be backward, "journal-tripping." Whether your search takes you through only one journal or many, this part of the process is imperative. If you have decades of journals to peruse, do so with a sense of revisiting your past. Check out a couple of dreams that surround the recurring symbol dream, but don't get waylaid by wanting to read everything that strikes your fancy (unless you are a very patient person with oodles of time). Consider that you are exercising both your masculine principle (by pursuing the goal of finding the dreams) and the feminine principle (by embracing and enjoying the dreams along the way).

Once you've located the dreams, make copies and organize them chronologically. All of the dreamers in this study typed dreams that they originally had journaled in longhand. Devote a separate sheet to each dream, so that you can play with them like puzzle pieces, moving them around as you proceed. As you find, read, and type the dreams, you will begin to notice some interesting patterns (all the little red wagons are rusty; you are always in the same old car when you go over the cliff; the kittens are always dirty or sleeping). Begin keeping track of such discoveries. Notice the dates of the dreams—sometimes the dates form a pattern of their own.

At some point, you may want to spread out all the dreams, looking for patterns—similar colors and shapes—that appear to fit together. Sitting on the floor surrounded by your "puzzle pieces," shifting your eyes from piece to piece may snap something into focus. Let your mind wander—look with soft eyes. Hum a tune as your eyes fall on this and that in the dream. Relax your body and your mind. You will be amazed at what springs into focus with this gentle play. This is a valuable way to engage your right brain at the beginning of the process. Another way is to read five or six dreams at a sitting, drawing a doodle on each sheet after each reading. One series student kept his dreams on his phone desk. When he was forced to spend many minutes on hold during business calls, he read parts of his recurring dreams, doodling absentmindedly. One day he realized that most of his doodles repeated a similar theme, which helped further his understanding of the series.

Shifting to your left brain, write a short autobiography corresponding to the history of the dreams. Some series dreamers had journals and diaries to support this process. However, if you are unable to recall or reconstruct the details of your waking life at the time of the dreams, don't despair. When an ongoing series spans many years and even decades, it is more important to see the flow of psyche than connect to the details of daily life. I have learned that a long series (one not related to posttraumatic stress) usually shows what our wholeness would like for or from us, as we evolve. This suggests that a series is more developmental in intent than reflective of the specifics of daily living. As demonstrated by the series presented in this book, awake-life circumstances are broadly connected to the dreams. In general, dreams that do not fall into the recurring symbol category are more likely to deal with the dreamer's daily concerns, while an ongoing series is more concerned with the overview of the dreamer's psycho-spiritual development. Therefore, do not relinquish your series study if you have little recall of the life circumstances that surrounded your dreams. But if you do have a daily diary for the period during which the dreams occurred, use it to discover patterns of feelings or circumstances that are repeating—it will surely be of help in unlocking the meaning of your recurring symbol.

During your autobiographical writing it is easy to be seduced by a desire for perfection, attempting to create a memoir worthy of publication. Beware of that, for you can easily be trapped by unnecessary work that ultimately detracts from the dreamwork. To avoid this difficulty, several dreamers created charts, aligning pertinent autobiographical facts with the recurring dreams. This circumvents the need for polished prose. Charts makes it easier to see patterns of events, which may create an awareness of when-then: "When I was in the middle of my divorce, then my recurring symbol occurred fifteen times. After the divorce, the symbol was absent for nine months." By searching for the ways in which the recurring symbol wrangled with a major life transition, the dreamer may get a strong sense of the symbol's value in times of crisis. It is possible that the recurring symbol shows up only in crisis. If so, this is extremely valuable information.

Following are the steps in studying a recurring symbol that were helpful to the dreamers whose series are presented in this book.

Step 1: Choose the symbol.

Step 2: Find the dreams containing the symbol. Then type or copy each dream onto its own page. Be sure the dreams are dated (to the best of your ability) and titled.

Step 3: Construct a simple autobiography spanning the time of the series dreams.

Step 4: Decide which dreams you will study. If a series contains more than twenty dreams, Step 4 is necessary and sometimes difficult. Unless you are extremely motivated, have excellent professional help, or are an extraordinary dream fanatic, you may be unable to handle the in-depth study of dozens of dreams. Of the studies in this book, two contained more than sixty dreams each, two others more than fifty. There was no manageable way to study them all. We had to make the important choice of which dreams to study in depth. Using charts that presented an overview of all the dreams, the dreamers compared the dreams to their autobiographical data. This allowed us to narrow the field to one we would be likely to cover. In general, we concentrated on the first five dreams, skipped to the middle of the series and chose five more, looked for the turning point dream, and studied the dreams that surrounded them. Each study was different, forcing us to rely on intuition as much as intellect to determine which dreams most warranted attention. In all four cases, as we worked the agreed-upon dreams, the dreamer felt a need to include one or more additional pieces, because they fit patterns similar to those in the series dreams.

It is important to consider why the initial dream interested the dreamer enough to be written in concrete form. Though the first series dream often expresses a psychological or spiritual goal too obtuse for the dreamer to grasp until years later, this dream sets the stage for the entire series. Thus, establishing a strong connection to the first dream was extremely fruitful as we approached each study.

In six of the studies in this book, the first series dream was an isolated event, with the next recorded series dream not occurring until ten to twenty-five years later. In these cases, the second dream thus became the first dream of part two of the series. We found it very useful to study each dream that appeared after a long absence of series material.

Step 5: Categorize and Contain: In a series with more than twenty dreams, it may be useful to develop series subcategories. I learned a great deal about this while studying the Victor Biento series. From 1983 until 1992, I worked dozens of dreams as they occurred, either alone or with colleagues. Then, when I began the kind of research presented in this book, I scoured all of my dream journals and diaries, discovering a surprising number of Victor dreams I did not recall. As I began the work that eventually evolved into my first book, all of these unheeded dreams needed to be understood. I tapped all of my dream resources to deal with more than one hundred dreams in this series. Once I had worked the dreams, I retitled most of them to better reflect the content, which I now understood more clearly. This helped me see that the dreams fell into categories, which I noted after the title: health issues, unresolved high school trauma, relationship dreams, process dreams, family dynamics, and so on. I then spent three days examining each of the dreams, spread around me on the floor, to see what I could see. I organized the categorized dreams chronologically, comparing the topic to autobiographical data. Next I examined all the dreams in one category to see what was continuing, decade after decade, and what was shifting or changing. The speculation about the cause and effect of the healing (what was changing), or lack thereof (what stayed the same), provided me with the motivation to alter behavior and beliefs which continues to affect me to this day.

When I realized that the work I was doing was evolving into a book destined for publication, I wanted to study every dream in the series. It is not likely that you will need to be so dedicated (or demented). Thus, as was true with most of the long series in this book, you may wish to choose just one category to examine in depth. You can always pick up another strand in the future, but to begin with, you must choose a process that can be successful.

Step 6: Focus. If you have more than five dreams in your series, you may need to choose a particular focus for working with the dreams. This is a difficult decision that demands patience and determination. The material must lead you. As you become more familiar with the dreams by following the preceding steps, you will engage with the material more intuitively than intellectually. You will discover patterns, in some form, that will pique your curiosity. Follow your interest—or your irritation! For example, Dennis submitted fifty-eight dreams presenting the bookstore symbol. We studied the first ten dreams and then felt overwhelmed by the abundance of material until we found the theme within the theme—the word *homosexual*, which recurred in four of the middle dreams. Baffled and intrigued by this word, Dennis decided to concentrate on this motif, releasing the rest of the bookstore dreams for another time.

As the patterns emerge and your interest develops, you may choose to focus on various aspects of the individual dreams. For instance, you could highlight the recurring symbol, examining whether and how it changes throughout the series. (This procedure was used in the study titled "The Unknown Blonde Woman" in chapter 12.) Sometimes the dream suggests what causes the change. If not, here is where your autobiography may be valuable. When a significant change occurs with the recurring dream symbol ("the previously crippled children are walking and playing without crutches"), check to see what happened in the awake world to cause such a shift ("I had decided to take a vacation, and play, every year whether my husband liked that or not"). It may be easier to get the overall picture if you chart the symbol, either with words or with drawings.

You can zero in on dream ego, discovering what the *I* in the dream feels, does, notices, or reacts to from dream to dream. Is it obvious what dream ego looks like or what clothing he or she wears? Does that change throughout the series? How does dream ego relate to the recurring symbol? If a major change occurs ("for the first time I actually see the horse and touch it"), check your autobiography for indications of cause and effect. These kinds of questions will encourage you to see the movement, the changes, and the growth (or lack thereof) as the series progresses.

Some of the series dreamers searched their material for what remained constant. For example, when "the car is always stuck in the mud"), the dreamer approached this dynamic by examining the dreams for further clues. Often the when-then approach is helpful here. In one case, the dreamer discovered this: "When I refuse to speak my truth in the dream, then the car gets stuck in the mud." Aha!

Step 7: Choose a particular focus to lead you through the dreams of one night. How should you proceed when the recurring symbol is buried in a mountain of dream material from one night? This was a particularly perplexing question for Darian as we studied her river series (chapter 6). Her dream writing blended into comments and associations, often hiding the dream from view. We had to rewrite each of her journal entries so that the dream could be seen pure—but never simple. Many of her dreams contained multiple scenes. A difficult decision had to be made about how much of the dream material to incorporate into the study. For example, is it necessary to study all five parts of a long dream when the recurring symbol appears in only one scene? We found that by first working with the scene containing the recurring symbol we could then determine whether the other scenes needed to be included or released.

Step 8: Enhancing the recurring symbol through art. Drawing, painting, sculpting, and creating collages of your series dreams are powerful ways to bring them to life. Artists can learn a great deal about what is unfolding within them by painting or sculpting an image over and over again; in a similar way, the psyche uses recurring symbols to reflect our inner development. In both cases, a creative process reveals subtle (or dramatic) changes that occur as the artist and dreamer engage with a symbol.

Step 9: Ritualizing. Your recurring symbol has come to help you change your beliefs about yourself and to rectify erroneous teachings from your past. A loving source within you repeatedly guides you to better physical and mental health. For some dreamers, studying a recurring symbol changed the very direction of their lives. Having worked with my own series dreams and those featured in this book, I suspect that our destiny may emerge from our recurring symbols. But none of these rewards will be granted unless our awake selves actively engage with our sirens in the night. We can hear the wailing, see the flashing, and even record the event but until we consciously embrace what must be seen, we will not fully benefit from the series dreams.

Once we commit our curiosity, talent, time, and detective skills to an in-depth study—even when we see the patterns which release the "aha!"—we are still not finished. For me, one form of connection has emerged from the hundreds of facsimiles of eagles given to me by loving friends and clients. Each gift has supported, in concrete form, what psyche presented to me in May 1981 with a dream that changed the direction and goal of my life. Though the dream itself probably lasted only fifteen seconds, its force was like the nearby Loma Prieta earthquake: No aspect of my life was untouched after this one psychic image altered my perception of reality forever.

It was a simple image of an eagle inexorably caught in a spectacular spider's web. The grief that image created haunted me until I committed whatever it took to freeing the eagle.

Embracing that dream led to the discovery of the Victor Biento series, and ultimately to my career as a dream professional and writer. Destiny? I think so. But that is another book.

As you engage with your recurring symbol, be aware that it intends to alter your life. And once you've embraced it, show your symbol the respect it deserves by ritualizing it in a variety of ways. As Francesca has done with her lions, collect figurines of your symbol. Griffin Rose made buttons reading "Dead Rights Activist" to honor the ancestors and their gifts. The ultimate honoring of a symbol was manifested by Darian's release from addiction as she moved toward her dream river. George's commitment to monogamy has resulted in a powerfully rewarding relationship with his wife. Similar gifts and more were granted me by the repeating dream themes that have provided the background symphony for the evolution of my life. I sincerely wish the same for you.

Reading this entire chapter may leave you feeling somewhat overwhelmed. Don't let that sabotage your desire to study a recurring symbol. Go beyond that, one step at a time. Six people volunteered to participate in studies for this book, but abandoned their studies before completion; however, all of them found value from engaging to the degree they were able.

As in all long journeys, each step is what matters. Start with excitement and proceed with faith, for any time spent with the recurring symbols from your dreams is guaranteed to be of value.

CHAPTER TWENTY

Unwritten but Not Lost

People are so fascinated by recurring symbols that even dreamers who have never journaled a dream nor read a dream book are conscious of repeating symbols. In restaurants, banks, service stations, on airplanes, or during business meetings, individuals who hear that I am a professional dreamworker launch into a recitation of their favorite (or most unnerving) dream series. The most bizarre experience of this type occurred as I lay on a gurney in an ER room in Albuquerque, New Mexico. "OK, you're good to go, but before I sign your discharge papers you have to interpret my recurring dreams about smoking cigarettes." I was sorry to disappoint the enthusiastic young doctor with the bothersome fact that no one can immediately interpret a repeating symbol or explain the purpose of a dream series. As the participants of this book discovered, patience, perseverance, effort, and commitment are required in order to fully understand a recurring symbol.

All of the dreamers discussed in this book learned that their memories of recurring symbol dreams were faulty. All were unaware of the inaccuracy of their recall until they examined the recorded dreams. An unwritten series is not likely to provide a strong foundation from which to launch an in-depth study;

however, even unwritten recurring symbols prove useful to some people. Here are some examples.

Before they married, Sarah and her fiancé agreed that they did not want the responsibility of parenthood. Instead, they chose to develop their careers and to travel. Two years into the marriage Sarah began dreaming of her own pregnancy. As she recalls the unwritten series, each month she dreamed of the pregnancy as it would have developed in "real" time. Every month she saw and felt her dream-self expanding with the growth of a fetus. By the ninth or tenth month Sarah "gave birth" to a beautiful baby boy. The feelings of joy were so intense that she began "lobbying" for a baby in waking life. Her husband soon agreed and within five years two wonderful boys were born to the couple. Sarah now believes that the dreams reflected her deep, unconscious desire for motherhood—a desire so strong that it transcended the decisions of her awake ego. She and her husband are profoundly grateful for the dream series that motivated them to become parents.

During a plane trip a middle-aged woman told me of her unwritten dream series concerning contact lenses. As she recalled the dreams, the lenses would become hopelessly lost, either popping from her eyes or washing down the sink during application. She said she had been having these dreams for at least twenty years. She always awoke frustrated and, in recent years, depressed. She was beginning to fear these dreams. I asked Jane some questions that may help you as you contemplate an unrecorded series of your own.

"Can you guess when the series began, when you had the first of these dreams?" She remembered telling a college roommate about the first dream she recalled, and pinpointed her age at the time as twenty-one.

"Do you recall anything particularly significant that happened about the same time?" Yes, indeed. That was about the time of the breakup of her first significant romantic relationship.

"And do you remember the last time you had this type of dream?" She did, and beat me to my next question: "It was last February, just after a terrible argument with my best friend." There is no way to prove whether the lost contact lens dreams always occur when Jane has suffered a loss of contact with another person or even a part of herself, but the possibility of the connection inspired her to commit to writing her recurring dreams in the future.

I was told about a similar series by a man who reported that his dream contact lenses were always changing shape. Unlike Jane's dream contacts, the lenses were never lost and he rather enjoyed the dreams. Remembering Jane's contact series, I suggested that the lenses might be psyche's way of showing contact with others or with parts of himself. He laughed as this notion connected to a frequent observation from his wife: "She says she is always shocked when I choose new friends because my taste in people consistently changes." He liked the notion that his contact lens dreams occurred when his awake-life contacts changed shape. Would the written series prove this theory? Alas, there is no way to know.

At a dinner party, a sixty-something engineer told about a series of dreams that had frequently haunted him throughout his very stable, thirty-year marriage. To his wife's chagrin, he proceeded to tell me about the common dream theme of the unfaithful spouse. Both husband and wife rushed to assure me that the dreams could not have been literal. I asked them if they had noticed any behavior patterns or similarities that might have been present at the time of these dreams. Neither was aware enough of the dreams to offer a suggestion. I encouraged the husband to record his next unfaithful wife dreams, share them with his wife, and then chat with me about them the next time we connected.

When I saw the couple at a social gathering about six months later, they eagerly shared the results of their research. Hubby had had the dream twice since our conversation. Each dream occurred following a similar frustrating conversation with his wife: He had wanted her to act as mediator between him and his oldest son, the child from whom he had always felt emotionally distant. "As usual, I told my husband to solve the problem himself. I'm not his therapist!" Because of these two similar dream experiences, the couple felt they had solved the mystery of the unfaithful wife series. They concluded that this dream theme surfaced when the husband felt emotionally abandoned by his "unfaithful" wife.

An artist related a similar dream series about her husband having affairs and leaving her bereft. She suspects that the dreams haunt her when she has abandoned her art for too long. "I'm sure my husband represents my masculine process, my productivity. These dreams always make me feel so wretched that I return to my studio immediately."

Many adults recall recurring symbol dreams from childhood. Usually the emotions are as intense as the details are sketchy. A middle-aged man in one of my dream groups shared his theory about a recurring symbol that first appeared in his childhood dreams. Raised on a cattle ranch in Wyoming, Jake rode horses from age four and has never been bitten by nor thrown from a horse. However, his early dreams depict him happily riding a horse that suddenly turns vicious, bites him in the leg, and throws him to the ground. Forty years later he still is occasionally plagued by this nightmare. At first he suspected it might reflect the physical distress created by a leg cramp; close observation of his next few horse dreams disproved this theory. Jake's dream group suggested that the dreams might occur when he feels emotionally thrown by some awake situation. That seemed plausible but did not provide the "aha!" we seek in dreamwork. The series finally became clear when Jake did a little archeological work—digging back into his past history to discover significant life circumstances at the time that the dreams began. Jake recalled being comforted by his paternal grandmother when the first dream woke him, crying. When he was nine years old, Jake's grandmother had moved in to care for his family after his mother "deserted the family." Now very interested in this series, Jake began recording the horse dreams, which occurred quite frequently.

Keeping track of awake-life experiences at the times of these dreams, Jake discovered that they occurred whenever he felt betrayed by either a co-worker or a personal friend. "It's as if I am riding along having a great old time and am then amazed when my friend (the horse) turns and bites me. I am thrown, emotionally ('aha!'), as I was so thoroughly thrown when my mother suddenly disappeared." This is an example of daily life being reflected by recurring dreams as they pull an association from childhood. Recurring childhood dreams often reflect a repeating feeling connected to a past difficulty or trauma.

A very important question to ask about any dream is, "Why is this dream surfacing now?" With a recurring symbol dream the question might be "Why is this dream symbol appearing again at this time?" If the dream is related to a childhood trauma, it may well be a warning that a threatening situation (or feeling) is again presenting itself. At such times, the dreamer's waking behavior may regress to coping mechanisms used in childhood. In Jake's case, he usually withdrew into depression after his biting horse dreams, just as he had when his mother abandoned him and his family. The recurrence of the dream and the accompanying familiar depression convinced Jake to seek psychotherapy to help resolve his firmly entrenched resentment and fear of abandonment.

Like recurring dreams that are recorded, an unwritten series may well change to reflect inner growth. A woman told me of a series of being stuck in the mud up to her neck. The unwritten dreams changed gradually after she began spiritual counseling. Her recall of the series was that the mud became thinner in each subsequent dream, until it finally transformed into fine sand from which she could easily extricate herself. The chances are good that, in the future, the mud will thicken if the dreamer becomes mired in a situation she has not consciously recognized as dangerous.

Here are some ways to "research" a recurring symbol even if the dreams are not written:

Can you guess (or, in the case of childhood dreams, find out from parents or siblings) when the series began, when you had the first of these dreams? Do you recall anything particularly significant that happened about the same time?

Do you remember the last time you had this type of dream and the life circumstances of that time?

Can you think of any behavior patterns or other awake-life similarities that might have been present at the time of these dreams?

If you can't recall any connections to the dreams' occurrences in the past, can you imagine why the dream symbol is surfacing again now?

It might be useful for you to write what you do recall of the recurring series in preparation for the appearance of the next dream in the series. This creates a foundation for the kind of work and growth experienced by the dreamers featured in this book. It is never too late to start this work. As you have learned from the studies presented here, psyche is as patient as she is persistent!

CHAPTER TWENTY-ONE

Common Recurring Dream Themes

Dream researchers have identified approximately twenty recurring dream themes that are common enough to be thought of as "universal" dreams. Some of these themes trouble and even traumatize people for years. For instance, some dreamers feel truly victimized—even in awake life—by the "evil" characters in their chase/attack dreams. Following a night of difficult dreams, a "dream hangover" may negatively affect the mental attitude and awake activities of sensitive souls. Some people come away from the most distressing of these dreams feeling hopeless and helpless at best, or pursued by a malevolent force at worst. But seeing these dreams more completely will help even the most beleaguered dreamer to recognize them as benevolent and potentially healing.

This chapter includes the fourteen recurring themes most frequently presented by my clients and radio audience. Rather than present common theories about the meaning of these recurring themes, I offer questions that have proven useful to these dreamers. They may also help you to work with these themes, bringing your own personal spin to the symbols and metaphors. Questioning opens up possibilities that theorizing shuts down. An inquisitive approach is the best path to your own knowing.

To discover the meanings of your universal recurring themes, record your dreams along with comments about your waking-life experiences, thoughts, and feelings around the time of the dream. Recurring dream themes tend to come up at times when the dreamer is experiencing similar life situations and inner circumstances. When the recurring dream evokes feelings of distress, think of it as you would a trusted friend or therapist reminding you that you are in a familiar hole. Awareness will provide the ladder you need in order to rise to the light. Therefore, with each theme I include samples of "dream ladders" from my client files.

Recurring themes are usually symbolic and metaphoric, not literal or precognitive. However, certain categories—such as vehicle-out-of-control dreams—may provide warnings about actual mechanical problems not consciously noticed by the dreamer. However, the message is probably symbolic if the theme is familiar—that is, if you awake thinking: "Oh, that dream again!" With that awareness, pay special attention to details as you write your dream.

All or Some of Your Teeth Are Falling Out

- What is the feeling tone within the dream? For example, does dream ego feel upset, excited, happy, neutral?
- How did you feel when you woke? Some dreamers feel grateful or relieved at the conclusion of this type of dream. This "feeling residue" is usually important.
- What are teeth? Define teeth so that someone unfamiliar with the word would fully understand what teeth are, look like, and do.

- What are the functions of teeth? What are all the things that they do? In what ways are teeth valuable?
- When do human teeth fall out naturally?
- What happens to humans and other animals without teeth?
- Have you had a personal experience of losing teeth traumatically? Does this inform your dream?
- Teeth play a role in taking in nourishment. Does this suggest anything to you about your theme?
- Teeth affect appearance. Is that a factor in your dream?
- Teeth help to bite through and hold on. Is that important in your dream or in your life?
- Teeth or the lack thereof affect our ability to speak clearly. Do your dreams suggest something about the ways in which you are or are not expressing yourself?
- Precisely which teeth are involved: incisor, molars, or wisdom teeth?

A forty-two-year-old man was ecstatic when he dreamed that his baby teeth were falling out. This man, who was still living with his parents, felt reassured by the dream that he was finally growing up and would someday be able to live independently.

A third-year university student repeatedly dreamed that her molar teeth were falling out. After careful recording, she discovered that the dream was usually triggered by circumstances that left her feeling that she had "bitten off more than she could chew," thus the loss of the molars, the teeth used for chewing. The dreams encouraged her to make decisions that would alleviate her sense of being overwhelmed.

Naked in Public

The obvious and classic metaphor of being naked in public suggests exposure and vulnerability. But look more closely at your specific dreams, answering the following questions for deeper understanding.

- What part of your body is naked? What does that suggest?
- What is the mood of the dream? Are you upset, embarrassed, shy, neutral?
- Do other people in the dream notice, or care, that you are naked? Why is that significant?
- What is the setting of the dream? Why is that important? For instance, to be naked in an office might point to feeling "exposed" professionally.
- In awake life, when are you naked? (Because we are naked when we change clothes, being naked could represent a time of transition between the various roles we play.)

Don't assume that naked dreams indicate an emotional problem. A very shy middle-aged woman was delighted when she dreamed of being joyfully naked at a cocktail party. In the dream she sat on a counter wearing nothing but red high-heeled shoes, sipping a martini, telling a humorous story to others. The dreamer felt that, after several years of therapy, she was finally comfortable enough within herself to be totally natural (naked) in a social situation.

A caller to my radio show reported dreams in which he was totally naked while wandering around his parents' home during family parties. He was always looking for a place to hide from the others. He decided that the dream reflected his feeling that he lacked a suitable lifestyle or role in life (clothing) because he had chosen to be an itinerant musician rather than joining his siblings in the socially acceptable and profitable family business.

Driving or Riding in a Car/Vehicle Which Goes Out of Control

- What is a car? What does it do? Is a car important to you? Why or why not?
- What type of vehicle is in your dream? Van? Sports car? Hot-rod? Question the type of energy the vehicle represents and the specific type of function it performs. Note the specifics if the vehicle is a truck: a semi-trailer rig is very different from a pickup—each suggests different types of work, perhaps.
- Is the car familiar, your present vehicle or a model that belonged to your parents?
- If it is a vehicle from the past, you may be looking at an old process or a former way of getting where you want to go.
- If it was a car you drove as a teenager, the dream may be alerting you to a less mature way of doing things and the problems that creates.
- What is suggested if the car is from a successful period in your past? Ask yourself what this particular car meant to you and who you were during the time you drove it.
- Who is the driver? If you are a passenger, where are you sitting?
- Can you alter the threatening situation or do you feel powerless?

- In what way is the car out of control? The brakes don't work? Can't steer? Not enough power to get over a hill? Plunging over a cliff? Each of these possibilities suggests specific metaphoric meaning.

One man discovered that his recurring dream car was always the ancient VW Bug he drove in college. He described this particular vehicle this way: "It was as slow and laid-back as my friends and I. We were nearly always loaded or stoned in this car." The dreamer finally realized that this dream car—which stalled in traffic, scaring him badly—warned that his attitude and behavior were too laid-back, stoned, or loaded—too unconscious to be able to proceed safely in the flow of life.

From the time he began to drive, a nineteen-year-old male dreamed of cresting a steep hill and realizing, as he began the descent down the other side, that his brakes didn't work. None of the dreams proved to be precognitive, but they evoked panic and left the dreamer concerned for his physical safety. Shortly after his forty-first birthday, the recurring dream shifted. The ascent part of the dream was the same, but as he sped down the hill, he applied the brakes and they worked perfectly. He felt that he had finally overcome his fear that disaster (brakes failing) would follow success (cresting the hill).

Dreams of plunging over cliffs so terrified Sally that she always awoke before her seemingly inevitable death. After reading about the positive benefits of overcoming fear within a dream, thus allowing the dream to continue, Sally determined that she would let this common dream play out. She wrote her resolve in her dream journal several times before her next over-the-cliff dream. As the dream car headed for the guardrail, Sally recalled her decision and did not awaken in fright. The car flew over the edge and went into free-fall before hitting the water, plunging Sally into darkness. To her surprise, Sally then found herself in a boat, floating peacefully. After pondering the dream for several weeks, Sally realized that the plunge over the cliff represented her fear of death itself. For about six months prior to the altered dream, Sally had begun working with dying patients in a hospice. This work and her spiritual studies had dramatically altered Sally's fear of death. This dream series helped her to experience the transformation into peace that reflected her newly developed beliefs of life after death.

It's Final Exam Time
but You Have Not Yet Attended Class

For many it is obvious that the exam theme highlights something that has not been learned due to the dreamer's inattentiveness. It is possible that the dreamer has not been attending to some important aspect of growth and development. By probing the dream further, you can determine how this metaphor applies to you. Consider these questions:

- What is the subject identified in the dream? Failing a biology test suggests something very different from being unprepared for an economics test.
- What is the environment for the test? A high school test suggests something more basic than a graduate school exam. One client discovered that his high school exam dreams usually related to relationship issues, because his teen years had been consumed by the developmental period of socialization.

- Is yours a college exam? Most university students are preparing for careers, so being unprepared for a college test may relate to professional problems—fears of being unprepared on the job.

Dreams of being unprepared for a graduate school test always warned one dreamer that she was not spiritually ready for a challenge that was about to surface (graduate school relating to the highest level of learning). In one instance, the dream preceded a meeting with her estranged father, a man she was not yet ready to forgive for childhood abuse. Because of her understanding of the dream, she postponed her reunion until she felt sufficiently prepared by counseling sessions with a spiritual advisor.

One dreamer described her recurring test theme this way: "It is the last day of class and it is time for the final exam. I don't even know what the subject of the class is or where it meets. After several years of studying this dream, I realized it is about not living up to a commitment I have made to myself. Because of this, I am unable to pass a test and move on to what is next. The last time I had the dream I had failed to honor a promise to send slides of my art to a gallery owner. As a result of the emotional pressure from my dream I followed up and my work is now being shown in that gallery."

Returning to Your Childhood Home

- During what ages did you live in this home? Often a particular home from a specific time in your life suggests a specific developmental stage.
- What of significance happened here?

- Do you always revisit the same room in the house? (Chapter 17 provides ideas about the importance of specific rooms in house dreams.)
- Did the room in your dream actually exist in your childhood home? If not, what does that suggest?
- Is the yard or a particular perspective of the outside of the house significant in your dreams?
- What is the condition of the home?
- If the dream house is not the same as when you lived in it, how has it changed? Pay careful attention to the changes and write a comparison analysis to clarify the transformations that have occurred. Does this suggest ways in which you have changed?
- How does it feel to be in the dream house?
- Are others with you?

A colleague reported that her dreams of childhood homes "tell her where she is coming from" in a certain situation—in other words, how some aspect of her script may be activated at the time of the dream.

A female dreamer reported the following: "I'm looking at the whole neighborhood and notice that a dysfunctional family no longer lives there. In other dreams a whole new section of the neighborhood has been urbanized and is very beautiful." This might suggest a when-then dynamic: When a dysfunctional way of living is removed, then a beautiful way of being with others (urban) is possible.

Another woman dreamed that it was hard to find her home because she didn't recognize familiar landmarks. She thinks this means that her attitudes and ways of being have changed so dramatically that she is no longer oriented as she was in the past.

Being Chased by Something or Someone Who Will Victimize You

If you look carefully at the details of the dream, you will surely discover important information that will serve you well.

- Identify and describe the threat—a gang is different from a tiger, a stranger is different from someone familiar.
- What age are you in the dream?
- What is the locale of the dream?
- If you are feeling threatened inside a house, is the house familiar? Is it your present home or a home from another period of time? What does that suggest?
- What do you do in response to the threat?
- If you always act and feel the same way, what is the dream suggesting about your way of dealing with threat or fear?
- Question dream ego's assumption that what is chasing you is threatening or "bad." This category of dream may highlight something that needs to catch you or something that needs to break into you (your house).

One of the most important dream series I have heard revolved around the theme of men trying to break into the dreamer's waking-life house. Over a three-year period, this thirty-something woman presented nine dreams with this theme. Bobbie was a painfully shy and timid woman suffering from many physical illnesses. She lived on welfare and, despite a master's degree, had never held a job long enough to feel professionally successful. Bobbie complained about the dreams and worried that they were precognitive. Finally, after a great deal of

therapy and a considerable amount of inner growth, this amazing dream presented itself:

> I awake in the morning sun to smell bacon frying and
> coffee brewing. I'm terrified because I know the rapist
> must have broken in while I was asleep. I find a fire
> burning cheerfully in the living room and hear chop-
> ping sounds outside. The table is set with flowers and
> plates. Filled with fear, I look out the window to see
> the rapist chopping wood for the fireplace. I think I
> must call the police but cannot find the phone. I
> awake shaking.

Bobbie's group pointed out that there was no evidence within
the dream that anything was amiss or that any threat existed. In
"dream fact," the opposite was true. Many of her needs were
clearly being met in the dream. The masculine that had broken
in was serving her well. But Bobbie so thoroughly identified with
dream ego that she was unable to connect to the positive aspects
of the dream.

However, Bobbie's therapist helped her see the value of this
symbolic dream. Much of Bobbie's therapy had been focused on
uncovering the elements of her past script that discouraged success and personal empowerment. She seemed incapable of staying focused and directed. This suggested, from one perspective,
a need to develop a positive inner masculine, without which her
life would continue to spin in cycles of illness, poverty, and failure. It was time for Bobbie to welcome a supportive inner
masculine into her psyche instead of fearing all the benefits such
a force would bring. Bobbie had a great deal of work to do, but
the dream heralded the change that was coming. Over the next

three years, she overcame her fears of personal power and developed the discipline to create a successful, unique personal business. And eventually, her chronic physical ailments dissipated.

Chase dreams often alert us to our way of dealing with fear, fleeing, and hiding rather than confronting and embracing. I had a long series of terrifying dreams of being chased up a winding flight of stairs. I could hear the pounding steps and the labored breathing of my pursuer. Deciding to end this nightly tyranny, I committed to a dream confrontation. The next time this dream occurred I controlled my fear, stopped running, and awaited the monster who was tormenting me. A man in a hat charged up the stairs, nearly bumping into me. This handsome man lit up when he saw me and said, "At last! I have a gift for you!" He handed me an elegantly wrapped present and the dream ended, forever. The real gift of the dream was the benefit that resulted from controlling my fear, a lesson that is important every day of my life.

In general, these questions open up this kind of dream:

What am I running from in my life?

What am I afraid will catch up with me?

By using my imagination, how can I alter this dream?

Losing a Purse or Wallet

This theme has several common twists, each important. For most dreamers, security (money) and identity (driver's license or other identification cards) are represented by wallet and purse symbols. (Chapter 10 contains a dream about a lost purse.) In addition, if dream ego is worried about lost credit cards, question your ability to give credit (praise) to yourself or others. As always, begin with definitions:

- What is a purse?
- Is this purse or wallet familiar to you? Does it take you back to a former time in your history (an old purse you no longer have)? What does that suggest?
- What does your purse or wallet normally contain?
- Why do you value the purse or wallet?
- What are you most concerned about losing?
- What are the circumstances of the loss?
- Was it stolen? By whom?
- Did you misplace it? Where and when?
- Did you forget it? What does that suggest?

A thirty-six-year-old man repeatedly dreamed of losing his wallet to a pickpocket. He defined this type of thief as someone who steals from an inside pocket while pretending a different kind of activity (bumping or falling into the victim). The dreamer soon recognized a need to beware of the woman he had been dating who "gets inside of me (emotionally) and rips me off!"

A woman with advanced cancer dreamed of her purse floating over the water and spilling into the ocean. For her, the dream meant that her sense of self was returning to the source of life, the great collective unconscious, and that the dream predicted her death. She died within six months.

Some years after suffering a traumatic professional rejection, a middle-aged woman dreamed that she lost her purse in a theater. She went back to find it and discovered that she had been sitting on the purse, thereby stuffing it into the plush theater seat. The dream led her to recognize that, in a place of performance, she had stuffed her identity due to the previous professional trauma and that she was sitting on what she valued most. However, the dream assured her that she was not truly lost.

Another middle-aged woman had a series about lost or forgotten purses during an intense time of spiritual transformation. She understood the dreams to accurately reflect a loss of identity and her fears about material security as she proceeded on her spiritual path, a journey requiring a shift in perception of self as well as beliefs about security beyond the material realm.

Unable to Find Your Parked Car

This theme has similarities to the car-out-of-control dreams. It is useful to begin with the basic questions, as your definitions will probably alter from dream to dream.

- What is a car?
- What value does your car have for you? What does it help you do? What does an inability to find these "values" mean to you?
- Is the dream car your present vehicle? If it is a car from the past, what does losing a process, motivation, or drive from another time suggest?
- If the dream car is not your personal vehicle but you can identify it, what unowned drive might you be seeking? For instance, a very responsible mother, nurse, wife, and primary caregiver of her elderly mother repeatedly dreamed about searching for her lost red sports car. Sue had never owned such a vehicle. She defined this dream car as providing "freedom and joyful exhilaration for one person! It is the kind of car that frequently breaks the law!" Allowing herself time away from her complex life full of responsibilities felt so much like breaking a law that Sue could never find the energy to have fun.

- Where was the vehicle left? What was dream ego doing before returning to the car? A twenty-six-year-old woman discovered the meaning of her dreams about lost cars when she realized that she often parked the car in order to see a movie. This suggested that she lost her personal power when entertained by collective projections and beliefs. This dream warned her to think for herself.

A young college student concluded that his lost car dreams appeared when he could not find the energy to get going, the motivation to move on a project. Another twenty-year-old thought her lost car dreams suggested a loss of focus after vacation. "It is like I have no sense of direction after taking a break."

Arriving Too Late to Catch the Plane, Bus, Boat

Besides the obvious warnings of timing and missed opportunities, check out the following questions:

- Where are you trying to go? What is your destination? Geographic places may represent states of mind, values, or even goals.
- What has caused you to be late? Losing a child on the way to the airport suggests something very different from being unable to pack your bags. (The baggage theme is presented in the Military Uniforms chapter.)
- Who is traveling with you? Are the others responsible for the delay?
- Is it possible that you will be served by missing the boat?

A woman client consistently dreamed of missing a luxury yacht for an elegant cruise. Though the rest of her group thought this a tragedy, the dreamer was always relieved. In her dreams she missed the cruises because she was volunteering at a shelter for abused women. She decided the dream yacht reflected the values of her wealthy, conservative parents. Since those values were not fulfilling, missing the boat was a good thing. As a result of this dream series, she pursued work that served those less fortunate than she.

An air flight is different from a train trip. Trains run on tracks, so many high achievers perceive missing the train as not being on track. This can be a good thing or a bad thing. If the dreamer has freely chosen the goals he or she wishes to pursue, this common theme is a warning to attend to his or her aspirations. If, as is often true, the dreamer has been trained to follow in the footsteps of a parent, for instance, and does so unconsciously or reluctantly, missing the train may provide an alternative to a prescribed but undesirable script.

Unable to Properly Operate the Phone

As always, check your dreams for the valuable details they contain. One dreamer discerned that the uncooperative phone in his dream was his mother's office phone. This led him to an important realization: "When I talk to others in the brisk, dismissive manner used by my mother, I cannot make the connections that I want."

If your dream calls for help in an emergency go unanswered, ask these questions:

- Do I need help in some aspect of my life?
- Is a helping part of me unresponsive to some important needs I have?
- Why can't I get through to the dream number I'm calling?

The following scenarios are common, but each contains a unique metaphor. Not having the right number may suggest a lack of resources to cope with a problem. Being unable to correctly dial the hospital number suggested to one woman that she did not know the best order to proceed in resolving her physical illness. A male caller realized that his dream phone disintegrated as he dialed 911 for help, just as in waking life his resolve always broke down before he dove into the problem-solving aspect of difficult issues. Dreams of being unable to find a phone during emergency situations led a recovering addict to realize that he was not able to find the correct tools of his recovery program to support his sobriety.

- Are you using a rotary dial or a touch-tone phone? If the phone is from the past, consider what old ways of operating are not serving you.
- Do you confuse 411 with 911? One caller realized that, in therapy and with close friends, he defends himself from change by asking for vague information (411) instead of clearly stating his true need for help (911).

Searching for a Toilet

This common dream has many variations. Examine the dreams for the specific symbols and metaphors they contain.

- What is a toilet? What is it for? Why do you need or want it in your dream?
- What is the problem?
- Where are you searching?
- What interferes with your success?
- If your search is for a public toilet, are you having difficulty finding relief or letting go in some collective arena? Look again at the dream. What kind of public place is presented in the dream—a work place, theater, ballpark, convention center, church? Obviously, each environment suggests a different area of your inner or outer life. A thirty-five-year-old woman who had never been to a professional football game was baffled by her fruitless search for public restrooms at a football stadium. The meaning became clear when a member of her dream group commented that football is a violent game of power and cunning. The dreamer immediately recognized that description as true to her very competitive corporation, a place where she could not find the emotional (urination) relief she desperately needed. The real value presented by this recurring dream was seeing that her daily distress resulted from the extremely competitive game-playing that seemed necessary to succeed in her firm. As a sensitive, artistic woman, she could not survive—play by the rules—in this corporation and soon left for more suitable employment.
- If your toilet dreams contain the disgusting aspects of overflowing sewage, what is not flowing appropriately in your life?

- If the lines of people waiting to use the toilet are too long, where do too many people hinder your ability to get the relief you need? Where does "too muchness" exist in your living or thinking processes? One male dreamer realized that his dreams of waiting in line referred to allowing the needs of others to precede his ability to get the relief he needed. A woman connected her overflowing toilet dreams to a compulsive form of "stinking thinking" which threatened her recovery from substance abuse.

- Are you unable to "let go" in a toilet because there is no privacy? There are many variations on this theme: The exposed toilet is in the middle of a restaurant, or a corporate board room, or on a chest in the dreamer's parents' bedroom. Dream toilets appear on the median of a freeway, a cliff alongside a highway, or in the middle of a strawberry field being picked by farm laborers. Sometimes the toilet is appropriately in a bathroom but all the walls are made of glass, allowing a clear view to neighbors. Each of these scenes provides rich metaphors to describe what is interfering with the dreamer getting relief or letting go.

When the dream toilet is in your own home, consider what personal or relational issues are backed up, plugged, or not flowing. These common toilet dreams are usually easy to understand when the details are examined. They tend to be extremely valuable for both mental and physical health, so do not toss them away as simple frustration dreams.

Unable to Perform Your Job Satisfactorily

It is a mistake to discard this type of dream by labeling it as an "unimportant anxiety dream." Although most people experience anxieties that are job-related, if you give your dream an opportunity to speak to you metaphorically instead of limiting it to the literal realm, you will be richly rewarded. Consider these questions:

- What does the dream identify as the problem in the work environment? If you cannot find your desk, for instance, are you unable to locate your personal "station" in life?
- If certain people are causing the problem in the dream, what do these personality types represent? For instance, a problematic dream "boss" can represent a part of yourself or someone else who is bossing you or is "in charge" in some way. A woman repeatedly dreamed that her scolding male boss "morphed" into her father. She realized that unresolved fear of her father caused her to feel unnecessarily anxious about her manager, a truly supportive person. This "anxiety" dream brought her great relief.

Job-related anxiety dreams generally are not literal. This becomes particularly clear when the dreams present jobs from the past. Years after retirement, teachers dream of being unprepared to teach or unable to control students within the classroom. Retired doctors dream about botched operations, nurses about losing patients, accountants cannot find files, policemen fire guns that are not loaded, and so forth. Our dreams use symbols and feelings that are both familiar and evocative. For instance, a retired physician dreamed of unsuccessful operations after futile attempts to communicate with her cantankerous husband. Do not assume that a dream about a former job stems from a need to relive the past. Search for your important "aha!" awareness by asking valuable questions such as these:

- What is causing the anxiety in the dream? What metaphor does that suggest? My dreams of dysfunctional equipment at my radio station led me to see the faulty aspects of my own equipment (skills and procedures) for broadcasting (teaching in the collective).
- Is the environment of the dream accurate to the awake-life situation? If not, what is different and what does that suggest? One man repeatedly dreamed that he was unable to find the tools he needed in his job as garage mechanic. He frantically searched through empty cabinets, hunting for what he needed to do his job. When he realized that the dream cabinets were from the kitchen of his childhood home, he realized that he was unable to repair what was broken because his parents had not provided him with tools (self-confidence, self-love) that nourish and support. In this case, the cars that needed repairing represented his own frequently ailing body as well as his way of moving in the world.

Too Old to Be Pregnant or to Have a Young Lover

This theme is not on the usual list of universal themes, but it is one I hear quite often, perhaps because the majority of my clients are women over the age of forty. It is unfortunate when dreamers disregard these dreams as simple reflections of literal reality. Since that interpretation does not supply any kind of awareness unknown to the dreamer before the night of the dream, something more profound must be awaiting discovery. For women who are circling menopause or have already arrived there, this dream motif takes one of three forms, as described by one caller: "I'm either pregnant, have a new baby, or a handsome, young, viral, male is attracted to me. In each case there is a realization within the dream that I am way too old for each of these possibilities."

These three themes all reflect vital new possibilities. Symbolically, both pregnancy and infants represent newness, potential, the beginning of a yet unlived life. A new lover suggests integration with fresh ways of doing and thinking, new goals, or a different direction. The thrill, vitality, and passionate commitment of an energizing inner affair is needed to manifest any form of newness. After working with dozens of these dreams, I believe that the metaphor of being too old reflects an unfortunate cultural script that must be rewritten before it sabotages the dreamer's life. Most women have formed their ideas of postmenopausal life from the lives modeled by their grandmothers. Thus, a girl of ten may decide who she can and cannot become after mid-life. By the time the woman matures, her decision will be outdated by nearly a half-century. When this recurring theme plays out in dreams, it is likely that a script-based decision was, and still is, rudely and inaccurately limiting the dreamer, robbing her of years of personal joy and service to those around her.

A retired professional dancer, age fifty-six, had a series of dreams about being seduced by a variety of vital, young choreographers and performers. In successive dreams she refused to engage with the enticing masculine characters because she was "past her prime," "too old to dance," and "not attractive enough to be on stage." She was unable to get below her literal judgments and feelings until the last dream in the series, in which she replied to the advances of the young man with this statement: "I'm old enough to be your mother! What would my children think?" Since she had never given birth this idiosyncratic dream statement led her to realize that she had not allowed herself to engage with new possibilities in her life, fearing the judgments of others. The others, in this case, are identified as "her children," suggesting that she clearly fears her potential will not live up to what she has already produced. This is often the case when artists and performers doubt a second project will match the success of a first.

Georgina's recurring theme concerned very ripe pregnancies and/or the birth of extremely advanced infants who engaged her in deep conversations while suckling! In each dream Georgie stated unequivocally that she could not have given birth to such precocious progeny because she was already a great-grandmother. While joking with her daughter about these dreams, Georgie heard herself say, "Good Lord, it's hard enough to raise babies who cannot argue for a couple of years. Imagine having to deal with brand-new offspring who could tell you what you were doing wrong from the very beginning." This led Georgina to realize that she was fearful of committing to a pending partnership agreement in a craft store. She doubted her ability to deal with the demands and differences of opinions of her potential young partners and customers. Simply voicing the concerns led her to see the absurdity of the problem since, as her daughter pointed out, "No one has overwhelmed you in a disagreement since you were old enough to speak!" However, Georgie realized that she believed that "older people cannot hold their own" when confronted by the demands of those younger and "more savvy." Identifying this limitation allowed Georgie to proceed with the negotiations for her new business, a very demanding but equally exciting, stimulating, and rewarding "baby."

An Approaching Tidal Wave

Before the modern dream movement provided extensive examples of dreams from around the world, some psychiatrists thought the tidal wave dream motif warned of extreme emotional distress. For someone suffering from severe mental illness, that may be the case. However, by studying the material of a broader population of people who consistently work with their dreams, we now have a different view of this dream theme. As always, let's look at the images, define some terms, and identify some dream specifics:

- Define *wave.*
- What is a tidal wave? How is it different from a normal wave?
- Have you ever seen a tidal wave?
- How do you feel in the dream before the tidal wave becomes an issue?
- What are you feeling and how are you reacting to the wave?
- In the dream, do you actually see the wave or have you heard about it or do you just "know" about it?
- Are you with others you know? What do they do? Do the others agree with your response to the wave?

This dream theme is often simplified as an indication of being overwhelmed. Certainly a tidal wave is overwhelming, but not all dreams show that the dreamer is fearful. Therefore, I have learned to examine this type of dream for the process that it exposes—the ways in which the dreamer is coping with some feeling or circumstance that cannot be controlled by human will or intervention. Those with whom I work report fearlessness when approaching dream tidal waves nearly as often as the expected response of terror. Clearly the willingness to meet the challenge suggests a very different coping ability than fleeing.

Twenty-five years ago, when I was just beginning my inner journey, I dreamed repeatedly of joining others running from a tidal wave. In the first six dreams I felt and joined the collective terror, but in the seventh dream I decided to wait and see what the wave brought. That wait-and-see dynamic heralded a profound change, for in the following five tidal wave dreams I moved continuously closer to the ocean, anticipating the thrill of seeing the wave as others ran, screaming in terror, in the opposite direction. In the last dream of this part of the series, I saw the spectacular wave and walked confidently into the surf to greet it. I awoke feeling a profound peace. As I worked with the dreams, I felt that they accurately portrayed my emotional transformation as I embraced my own dreams. (The ocean is often thought to represent the unknown, unfathomable, the source of life, and the great collective unconscious, which includes the personal unconscious.)

This interpretation was supported by a second series of dreams in which I lived in a variety of "homes" in the ocean. Some of the structures were stationary, others floated, and all were made of glass, affording thrilling views of my exciting "neighborhood" in the depths. From this series I learned that there was nothing to fear by delving into my dreams. I learned that, when embraced, my dreams could not harm me. I discovered that my dreams would reveal what I needed to address to heal my past. Finally I realized that, by walking fearlessly into the depths, I would be led to a fulfilling future that I could live authentically, free of the oppression of former scripts. And, in a sense, these dreams were precognitive, since I now spend a majority of my professional time living in the depths of metaphoric oceans, swimming with the dreams of others.

Examine your tidal wave dreams for the following information:

- When this dream appears, are you aware of strong reactions to world news? Tidal wave dreams often reflect feelings about collective situations.
- Does the dream suggest helpful action on your part?
- Does the dream show a process that would be helpful to you? The following three dreams were called into my radio show. All three suggested possibilities helpful to the callers (and the listeners).

One caller believed that his tidal wave, which hit three times in one dream, predicted three courses of chemotherapy he would need to combat cancer, not yet diagnosed at the time of the dream. After each wave hit, the man was told to say his name and to call upon Allah. Feeling that his dream action connected him with the divine helped him cope well with the diagnosis and treatment of lymphoma. Before and during each treatment, the dreamer actively recalled the dream and relied on it for courage and peace.

Another caller reported the rather common dream experience of discovering he was able to breathe underwater after a tidal wave overcame him. This reassured him that, regardless of what was coming his way, he could adapt to the situation and survive it.

A woman caller dreamed of standing with her aging parents on a huge expanse of beach. She felt deep peace and a sense of being unlimited as she awaited the tidal wave she knew was approaching. This dream, like so many of this variety, provided her with profound calm despite the inevitable, though not yet imminent, death of her parents.

These dreams, collected from my radio audience and clients, do not reflect the universal themes of the general public. *Content analysis research* (studying dreams to determine which elements most frequently appear in the dreams of males and females of specified ages, cultures, or socio-economic groups) show that chase and flying dreams are the most common type of recurring theme. In the general population, the "exam dream" theme includes difficulties in finding the test building, arriving late to the testing place, seeing that the test is written in a foreign language, discovering that writing implements are nonexistent or broken, and realizing that time runs out before the test is completed. Natural disaster dreams include tornadoes, hurricanes, earthquakes, and collision with other planets. In the dream, possibilities are endless. Therefore, searching for understanding rests in the ability to ask the questions that will activate your own knowing.

The questions presented in this chapter provide models for pursuing common dream themes. Like the more personal and less common recurring symbols found in part 2, recurring universal themes—when recorded and examined—can lead you to freedom beyond cultural and familial scripts that no longer serve you. With patience and persistence, you can become as comfortable in your own depths as are the whales off California's coast. Like the participants in the studies for this book, you will find that recurring symbols lead below the surface of everyday life to the brilliance and beauty of your personal ocean, a place of profound healing and guidance.

BIBLIOGRAPHY

Barasch, Marc Ian. *Healing Dreams*. New York: Riverhead Books, 2000.

Barrett, Deirdre, ed. *Trauma and Dreams*. Cambridge, Mass.: Harvard University Press, 1996.

Berne, Eric. *A Layman's Guide to Psychiatry and Psychoanalysis*. New York: Simon and Schuster, 1968.

—————. *Transactional Analysis in Psychotherapy*. Secaucus, N.J.: Castle Books, 1961.

Berne, Patricia H., and Louis M. Savary, *Dream Symbol Work*. New York/Mahwah, N.J.: Paulist Press, 1991.

Bly, Robert. *The Little Book on the Human Shadow*. San Francisco: Harper & Row, Publishers. 1988.

Bosnak, Robert. *A Little Course in Dreams*. Boston: Shambhala, 1988.

Bulkeley, Kelly. *Transforming Dreams*. New York/Toronto: John Wiley and Sons, Inc., 2000.

Campbell, Joseph, ed. *The Portable Jung*. New York. Viking Press, 1971.

Cartwright, Rosalind. *Crisis Dreaming*. New York: Harper Collins Publishing, 1992.

Clift, Jean Dalby, and Wallace B. Clift. *The Hero Journey in Dreams*. New York: Crossroad Publishing Co., 1991.

—————. *Symbols of Transformation in Dreams*. New York: Crossroad Publishing Co., 1993.

Corriere, Richard, and Joseph Hart. *The Dream Makers.* New York: Funk and Wagnalls, 1977.

Delaney, Gayle. *Living Your Dreams.* San Francisco: Harper and Row, 1979.

Faraday, Ann. *The Dream Game.* New York: Harper and Row, 1974.

————. *Dream Power.* New York: Berkeley Books, 1972.

Feinstein, David, and Stanley Krippner. *Personal Mythology.* Los Angeles: Jeremy P. Tarcher, Inc., 1988.

Fontana, David. *The Secret Language of Dreams.* San Francisco: Chronicle Books, 1994.

Garfield, Patricia. *Creative Dreaming.* New York: Ballantine Books, 1974.

————. *The Healing Power of Dreams.* New York: Simon and Schuster, 1991.

————. *Pathway to Ecstasy.* New York: Prentice Hall, 1979.

Gendlin, Eugene T. *Let Your Body Interpret Your Dreams.* Wilmette, Ill.: Chiron Publications, 1986.

Hall, C. S., and V. J. Nordby. *The Individual and His Dreams.* New York: The American Library, 1972.

Hall, James. *Jungian Dream Interpretation.* Toronto: Inner City Books, 1983.

————. *Patterns of Dreaming.* Boston: Shambhala, 1991.

Hannah, Barbara. *Jung.* New York: G. P. Putnam's Sons, 1976.

Harris, Thomas A. *I'm OK. You're OK.* New York: Harper and Row, 1967.

Hill, Clara E. *Working with Dreams in Psychotherapy.* New York: The Guilford Press, 1996.

Hillman, James. *The Dream and the Underworld.* New York: Harper & Row, 1979.

————. *The Soul's Code.* New York: Random House, Inc., 1996.

Houston, Jean. *A Mythic Life.* San Francisco: Harper Collins Publishing, 1996.

Hull, R. F. C., trans. *Dreams/C. G. Jung.* Princeton, N.J.: Princeton University Press, 1974.

Johnson, Robert. *Inner Work.* San Francisco: Harper and Row, 1986.

Jung, C. G. *The Collected Works.* Edited by H. Read, M. Fordham, and G. Adler. Princeton, N.J.: Princeton University Press, 1953–60.

———. *Memories, Dreams and Reflections.* New York: Random House, 1965.

Kaplan-Williams, Strephon. *Dreamworking.* San Francisco: Journey Press, 1991.

Kelzer, Kenneth. *The Sun and the Shadow.* Virginia Beach, Va.: A.R.E. Press, 1987.

Krippner, Stanley. ed. *Dreamtime and Dreamwork.* Los Angeles: Jeremy P. Tarcher, 1990.

Mahoney, Maria F. *The Meaning in Dreams and Dreaming.* Secaucus, N.J.: The Citadel Press, 1966.

Moore, Thomas. *Care of the Soul.* New York: Harper Collins Publishers, 1992.

O'Connor, Peter. *Dreams and the Search for Meaning.* New York/Mahwah, N.J.: Paulist Press, 1986.

Perls, Frederick. *Gestalt Therapy Verbatim.* Lafayette, Calif.: Real People Press, 1969.

———. *In and Out the Garbage Pail.* Lafayette, Calif.: Real People Press, 1969.

Perls, Frederick, Ralph F. Hefferline, and Paul Goodman. *Gestalt Therapy.* New York: Dell Publishing, 1951.

Quenk, Alex, and Naomi L. Quenk. *Dream Thinking.* Palo Alto, Calif.: Davis Black Publishing, 1995.

Robertson, Robin. *The Beginners Guide to Jungian Psychology.* York Beach, Mass.: Nicholas-Hays, Inc., 1992.

Sanford, John. *Dreams, God's Forgotten Language.* New York: Crossroad Publishing, 1984.

———. *Healing and Wholeness.* New York/Mahwah, N.J.: Paulist Press, 1977.

Siegel, Alan B. *Dreams That Can Change Your Life.* Los Angeles: Jeremy P. Tarcher, Inc., 1990.

Signell, Karen. *Wisdom of the Heart.* New York: Bantam, 1990.

Steiner, Claude. *Scripts People Live.* New York: Grove Press, 1974.

Stevens, Anthony. *Private Myths.* Cambridge, Mass.: Harvard University Press, 1995.

———. *The Two-Million-Year-Old Self.* College Station, Tex.: Texas A&M University Press, 1993.

Sullivan, Kathleen. *Recurring Dreams: A Journey to Wholeness.* Freedom, Calif.: The Crossing Press, 1998.

Taylor, Jeremy. *Dreamwork.* New York/Mahwah, N.J.: Paulist Press, 1983.

———. *The Living Labyrinth.* New York/Mahwah, N.J.: Paulist Press, 1998.

———. *Where People Fly and Water Runs Uphill.* New York: Warner Books, 1992.